NEW PERSPECTIVES ON THE SOUTH

Charles P. Roland, General Editor

The Life &
Death of the
SOLID
SOUTH
A POLITICAL HISTORY

DEWEY W. GRANTHAM

THE UNIVERSITY PRESS OF KENTUCKY

Copyright © 1988 by The University Press of Kentucky

Scholarly publisher for the Commonwealth,
serving Bellarmine College, Berea College, Centre
College of Kentucky, Eastern Kentucky University,
The Filson Club, Georgetown College, Kentucky
Historical Society, Kentucky State University,
Morehead State University, Murray State University,
Northern Kentucky University, Transylvania University,
University of Kentucky, University of Louisville,
and Western Kentucky University.

Editorial and Sales Offices: Lexington, Kentucky 40506-0336

Library of Congress Cataloging-in-Publication Data

Grantham, Dewey W.
    The life and death of the Solid South : a political history /
Dewey W. Grantham

    p. cm.—(New perspectives on the South)
    Bibliography: p.
    Includes index.
    ISBN 0-8131-0308-8; -0813-6
    1. Southern States—Politics and government—1865-1950.
2. Southern States—Politics and government—1951-   I. Title.
II. Series.
F215.G737   1988
320.975—dc19   88-50

Contents

Tables

Graphs

Maps

Illustrations

Editor's Preface

Southern politics in the twentieth century, as during the entire course of southern history, was both national and regional in its purposes and means. But so visible were its regional manifestations during the first half of the century, so thoroughly were they stamped upon its national political presence, that V.O. Key in 1949 would accuse the South of employing the Democratic party as an "instrument for the conduct of [its] 'foreign relations' with the rest of the nation." One might also have said that the South used the United States Congress, in large part, as an assembly for accomplishing its regional diplomatic goals. Southern politics operated to preserve traditional southern prejudices and interests; its fundamental party characteristics were Democratic solidarity and white exclusivity.

During the past three decades, immense changes have occurred in southern party politics, including the disappearance of Democratic solidarity and white exclusivity. The excellent study offered here by Dewey W. Grantham, the preeminent historian of recent southern politics, tells why and how these changes came about. The book's title comprises its theme: the life and death of the Solid South. Yet the author concludes that many of the Solid South's essential elements and much of the political culture in which it flourished are still significant determinants of southern politics; that, ironically, these very elements and this very culture played an important role in the death as well as the life of the Solid South.

This book is indispensable for inclusion in "New Perspectives on the South," a series designed to give a fresh and comprehensive view of the region's history. Each volume is expected to be a discrete essay representing both a synthesis of the best scholarship on its subject and an interpretive analysis drawn from the author's own research and reflections. Eight volumes are now in print; an additional twelve or more are anticipated to complete the set.

Charles P. Roland

To: Charles F. Delzell
J. Leiper Freeman
V. Jacque Voegeli

Preface

Southern politics, like racial segregation and one-crop agriculture, was one of those peculiar institutions that differentiated the South from other American regions. This southern system—long referred to as the Solid South—embodied a distinctive regional culture and was perpetuated through an undemocratic distribution of power and a structure based on disfranchisement, malapportioned legislatures, and one-party politics. It was the mechanism that determined who would govern in the states and localities, and it was the means through which the South's politicians defended their region's special interests and political autonomy in national politics. This was the *Democratic* South. In its broad outlines, the history of this remarkable institution can be traced in the gradual rise, long persistence, and ultimate decline of Democratic dominance in the land below the Potomac and the Ohio.

Interpreters have sometimes exaggerated the monolithic character of southern politics and its divergence from political currents in other parts of the country. But the South's political sectionalism was exceptional. There is nothing else quite comparable in the nation's political history. The strength and durability of the Solid South resulted in good part from three circumstances: the South's poverty, its depressed economy, and the influence of its plantation-oriented elites; the federal system and the changing shape of national politics; and the potency of the region's political culture. The one-party system had, in V.O. Key's words, "an odd dual personality." In state politics the Democratic party was no party at all but "a multiplicity of factions struggling for office." In national politics, on the other hand, the party was the Solid South, "the instrument for the conduct of the 'foreign relations' of the South with the rest of the nation."[1]

Three fairly distinct periods mark the evolution of the Solid South. The first, lasting roughly from Reconstruction to the turn of the nineteenth century, represented the formative stage in the development of a one-party system in the southern states. The second, comprising the first half of the twentieth century, witnessed the operation of the system in the full panoply of its dominance. This was the classic era of the Solid South, which is defined in this study to include the eleven ex-Confederate states plus Kentucky and Oklahoma. The third period, beginning with the Dixiecrat revolt of 1948, brought the disruption of the Solid South, the gradual decline of the one-party system, and the transformation of southern politics. It is now possible to speak with some confidence of "the two-party South."[2]

Southern Democrats succeeded for almost three-quarters of a century after Reconstruction in defending their peculiar sectional interests in national politics. The federal nature of political parties in the United States facilitated this endeavor, and the skillful use of congressional power provided a means of warding off threats from the outside while simultaneously enlarging financial assistance from Washington. According to one political scientist, the South "influenced American politics in ways not dissimilar to the influence of Quebec in Canada or of Ireland in the United Kingdom in the years from 1870 to 1922. The massive influence of that deviant subculture upon national party politics and policy outputs has scarcely run its course a century after Appomattox."[3] For all its sectional perversity, southern politics has been a national as well as a sectional phenomenon. Today the South's politics is subject to greater national influence than at any time since Reconstruction, and the region's political future obviously depends on what happens in the rest of the country as well as on such state and local considerations as the fortunes of the influential black-white Democratic coalitions. There is talk nowadays of the "Southernization of America" and of a new role for the South in American life—the "nation's second chance."[4]

This volume presents a brief history of the Solid South. It might be thought of as a kind of "natural history" of a powerful regional institution, an institution that played an influential role in the continuing drama of modern American politics. The book is both a synthesis of the extensive literature on politics in the recent South and an interpretation of the region's political history since the end of Reconstruction. I hope that the study will interest students, general readers, and scholars and that it will serve both as an introduction to and an interpretation of a fascinating subject.

I am grateful to Charles P. Roland for inviting me to contribute to the New Perspectives on the South Series and for his critical and helpful evaluation of my manuscript. I am also indebted to two other friends, Numan V. Bartley and Jacque Voegeli, for taking time to read the manuscript and giving me the benefit of their keen understanding of southern history and politics. Dean Voegeli wrote a comprehensive critique of the manuscript that contributed substantially to whatever merit the published work possesses. I have profited as well from an authoritative evaluation by a specialist selected by the University Press of Kentucky. Finally, I am in the debt of a host of scholars for analyzing and illuminating so many aspects of southern politics in the twentieth century. Having mentioned these obligations, I am constrained to add that I alone am responsible for whatever errors and limitations this book may have.

Much of the preliminary work on this project was done at the National Humanities Center. I shall always treasure my stay at the Center, where I was a fellow during the academic year 1982–83, and I am indebted to its directors for financial support and for the stimulating intellectual environment they provided under the tall pines and blue sky of the North Carolina Piedmont. I want to thank the Department of History and the College of Arts and Science, Vanderbilt University, for enabling me to be on sabbatical leave in 1982–83 and 1986–87, and I am happy to acknowledge my indebtedness to the Holland N. McTyeire professorship at Vanderbilt for essential research assistance.

This book is, in some respects, the distillation of many years of research and reflection on regional politics and the role of the South in twentieth-century America. During this period I have had the good fortune to work in a large number of manuscript depositories and other research institutions, and I am grateful to the many archivists and librarians who aided my research during those visits. I am especially obligated to Alan Tuttle and Rebecca Sutton of the National Humanities Center, to Carolyn A. Wallace and her colleagues at the Southern Historical Collection, University of North Carolina, and to the staff members of the Vanderbilt University Library, the Division of Manuscripts of the Library of Congress, the Harvard University Library, the University of Virginia Library, the Clemson University Library, the Emory University Library, the Robert W. Woodruff Library of the Atlanta University Center, the University of Georgia Library, the University of Tennessee Library, the Tennessee State Library and Archives, the Alabama Department of Archives and History, the Louisiana State University Library, and the University of Texas Library.

It is a pleasure to acknowledge the research assistance given me by Henry M. McKiven, Jr., and Robert Tracy McKenzie. Mr. McKenzie deserves credit for most of the figures and tables in this volume. My work has also been facilitated by the word-processing skills of Julia Buzzell and Mary Frances Moore, whose help I much appreciate.

The publication of this book gives me an opportunity to express my admiration and affection for Charles Delzell, Leiper Freeman, and Jacque Voegeli, three longtime friends and colleagues who have helped me in many ways and who have improved by spirits over the years.

1 Forging the Solid South

The political solidarity of the twentieth-century South originated in the great sectional conflict of the nineteenth century. In the 1850s a virulent southern sectionalism destroyed the existing party system and created a powerful compulsion toward political consensus in the South. The Civil War itself heightened southern self-consciousness and increased the social solidarity of the region's white inhabitants, despite the divisions and enmities it brought to the surface. "Out of that ordeal by fire," wrote Wilbur J. Cash, "the masses had brought, not only a great body of memories in common with the master class, but a deep affection for these captains, a profound trust in them, a pride which was inextricably intertwined with the commoners' pride in themselves."[1] In the long run, the war did little to undermine the South's political autonomy. As the historian Roy F. Nichols once observed, "Did not the South by its war experience insure what it sought, an autonomy within the nation and a political power which enables it at times, as now, for all practical purposes to control national legislation?"[2]

As a matter of fact, southern white unity was more apparent after the war than it had been during that drawn-out conflict. The divisions over secession were a source of continuing irritation and bitterness among southerners, and during the war years islands of disaffection developed in various parts of the Confederacy. The new government was never able to institute effective political machinery within its jurisdiction. Appomattox had surrendered Robert E. Lee's armies but not the southern cause. As Robert Penn Warren declared long ago, the conflict of the 1860s "claimed the Confederate States for the Union, but at the same time, paradoxically, it made them more Southern." Or, to put the matter in political terms, "In defeat the Solid South was born—not only the witless automatism of fidelity to the Democratic Party but the mystique of prideful 'difference,' identity, and defensiveness."[3] The Confederate flag and "Dixie" became strong unifying symbols for most white southerners. Outside the South, of course, the war strengthened the bonds of loyalty to the Republican party. Not surprisingly, the war and its turbulent aftermath infused the nation's politics with sectional appeals and helped perpetuate the sectional alignment of party politics that had developed in the 1850s.

Reconstruction was no less important in the forging of the Solid South. Several developments of that era encouraged political competition in the southern states, and it is conceivable that the process of reconstruction could have contributed to a more rational and enduring political division among white southerners. With the collapse of the Confederacy, for example, many of the South's old Whigs assumed an important role in postwar politics. While this Whiggish element was usually identified with southern interests, it had little liking for Democrats, who had led the section into war. A much greater challenge to southern Democrats came with the organization of the Republican party throughout the South following the inauguration of Congressional Reconstruction in 1867. This brought the enfranchisement of perhaps a million freedmen, virtually all of whom became Republicans, and the formation of political coalitions in every southern state made up of blacks, "carpetbaggers," and "scalawags." Something like a fifth of the southern whites were included in these Republican coalitions.

Most white southerners feared and resented the basic features of Radical Reconstruction, which they viewed as the source of harsh and vindictive policies, of Republican abuse and corruption, and of black effrontery and southern privation. Southern Democrats set about uniting as many whites as possible in the party of opposition. They made use of economic pressure and social ostracism, chicanery and fraud, intimidation and violence, and a shrewd campaign of racial propaganda, as well as more traditional political appeals. These techniques soon proved effective. One reason was the continuing prestige of the old, experienced ruling class in the South. Another factor was the inability of the southern Whigs to retain their identity as a separate group. The Whigs differed among themselves as to policy, and their efforts to secure a moderate reconstruction program received curiously little support from conservative Republicans in the North. Many of them were ultimately driven by their frustration into the arms of the Democrats, whose policies they had so often condemned in earlier years. Radical Republican policies and the blandishments of the Democrats (who resorted to the term *conservative* in some states as a gesture of conciliation toward the Whigs) eventually destroyed the Whigs as a clearly recognizable entity in southern politics, while enhancing the reputation of the Democrats among white southerners generally. The economic plight of the postwar South—its wartime losses and its poverty, one-crop economy, and shortage of money—also played into the hands of the Democrats.

The overthrow of Radical Reconstruction governments in the ex-Confederate states was made easier by the intense Republican conflict within several southern states, by the division between the northern and southern wings of the party, and by the inconsistent Reconstruction policies of Pres. Ulysses S. Grant. Passage by Congress of a general amnesty act in 1872 restored the right to hold office to most former Confederates. The northern retreat from Radical Reconstruction was evident by this time, and in 1874 the Democrats won control of the national House of Representatives. Meanwhile, the "redemption" of the South from Republican control moved forward steadily. In most white districts, conservatives had held control of local governments from the outset. Tennessee and Virginia were reclaimed by the Democrats as early as 1870, and by 1876 only Florida, Louisiana, and South Carolina remained in Republican hands. They were "redeemed" in 1877, the last two as part of the Compromise of 1877. Southern leaders acquiesced in the election of the Republican Rutherford B. Hayes, satisfied with the promise of troop removal, home rule, and federal money for internal improvements in the South.

The political hegemony of the conservative Democrats who redeemed the South from Radical Reconstruction was formidable. Having restored all of the ex-Confederate states to home rule, southern Democrats moved to liquidate their Republican opposition in the region. The party of Lincoln, Grant, and Hayes steadily lost strength in the South. One of the party's members, Albion W. Tourgée, reported after the election of 1878 that "the Republican party of North Carolina is dead—dead beyond hope of resuscitation or resurrection!"[4] In the presidential election two years later, the Democrats carried every southern state. The Solid South had emerged in its pristine form, although it would not become a thoroughgoing one-party system for another two decades.

Politics in the southern states from the end of Reconstruction to the early 1890s was dominated by the Redeemers. The original architects of the Solid South, they made an enduring contribution to the character of southern politics in the late nineteenth and early twentieth centuries. The system they inaugurated, while elaborated and perfected by later Democratic leaders, provided the fundamental structure of political solidarity in the region for more than three-quarters of a century. The Redeemers (or Bourbon Democrats) regarded themselves as the "natural leaders" of the South. There was a good deal of truth in this view. The bulk of the section's traditional social and economic leaders, including most men of Whiggish persuasion, was identified with the Democratic party by the late 1870s. A Republican leader in Georgia warned as early as 1868 that recent elections "should teach us as Republicans that it is impossible to maintain the party in this State, or indeed in the South, without a division of the white vote." The Democrats, he conceded, "possess most of the intelligence and wealth of the State, which will always control tenants and laborers."[5]

One result of the Civil War, W.J. Cash suggested in 1941, was that "the habits of following and obedience" were more deeply engraved upon the common man than ever before. Cash also thought that the military leaders of the Confederacy were themselves profoundly influenced by their wartime service. "They were more set in the custom of command, much more perfectly schooled in the art of it, knew better how to handle the commoner, to steer expertly about his recalcitrance, to manipulate him without ever arousing his jealous independence."[6] These attitudes, one suspects, were reflected in southern politics during the Age of the Redeemers. Political candidates certainly found it advantageous to have served in the Confederate ranks. Indeed, Confederate veterans seem to have held a majority of the best offices at all levels of government during the period between Reconstruction and the 1890s. In Virginia, for example, James Lawson Kemper, a Confederate hero who had been wounded at Gettysburg, was elected governor in 1869. He became the first of a line of seven Confederate "brigadiers" to serve as governor of the Old Dominion. One study of 585 former Confederate leaders revealed that no fewer than 418 of them held elective or appointive offices after the war. It was, from the standpoint of the most prestigious political offices, the era of the Confederate brigadier. During the Forty-fifth Congress (1877–79), 77 of 107 members in the House of Representatives from the South had fought in the Confederate armies.

The Redeemers, of course, made good use of the romantic cult of the Lost Cause. They made the most of what David M. Potter has described as a "deeply felt southern nationalism" growing out of "the shared sacrifices, the shared efforts, and the shared defeat" of the war.[7] They helped establish an explicit linkage between Confederate images and religious values, joining with other southerners in making "a religion out of their history."[8] The Redeemers' version of Reconstruction provided another support for political conformity among white southerners. They told a grim story of human suffering and of the southern battle for civilization during Radical Reconstruction. "The slaughter and the sacrifices during our great civil war were terrible indeed," declared Rep. Hilary A. Herbert of Alabama in 1890, "but those dark days were lighted by the shining valor of the patriot soldier; the storm clouds were gilded with glory." In Reconstruction, on the other hand, Herbert could find "nothing but wretchedness and humiliation, and shame, and crime begetting crime. There was no single redeeming feature, except the heroic determination of the better classes in the several states to restore good government."[9] Conservatism, as one scholar has written of postbellum Virginia, "was not only a political party, it was also a social code and a state of mind."[10]

As might have been expected, the Redeemers represented the South's most influential social and economic elements. The bulwark of their political control was the black belt that stretched across the lower South, and planters constituted a major factor in the politics of the various states in the region, though not always the dominant one. There were patrician leaders among the Redeemers such as Francis T. Nicholls of Louisiana and Wade Hampton of South Carolina, who appealed to the traditions of the Old South, and a large number of conservative Democrats retained close ties with the land and with agriculture. Many if not most politicians in the new era lived in small towns and depended upon farmer constituencies. In short, as James Tice Moore writes, there is much evidence to support "the concept of a continuing and potent agricultural influence" in the politics of the Redeemer period.[11]

But if the planter exerted a controlling influence in the politics of the post-Reconstruction South, he was forced to share political power with a rising group of business-oriented politicians. "In the main," C. Vann Woodward asserts in his familiar characterization of the Redeemers, "they were of middle-class, industrial, capitalistic outlook, with little but a nominal connection with the old planter regime."[12] Although Woodward may have exaggerated the discontinuity in the political leadership of the Old South and that of the New, there was a powerful Whig-industrial faction in every southern state after 1877, particularly in the upper South. Railroad and bondholding interests were closely identified with the Redeemer governments, and the New South emphasis on industrialization, economic diversification, and northern investments was warmly endorsed by the dominant political leaders in most southern states. Georgia's leading Democrats "glorified the past, particularly the heroism of the Civil War; yet they emphasized youth, progress, and enterprise."[13] The state's famous triumvirate of Joseph E. Brown, Alfred H. Colquitt, and John B. Gordon, who dominated Georgia politics in the post-Reconstruction period, had all been prominent Confederate leaders. Yet in the new era they became businessmen and New South advocates. That the character of Redeemer leadership was somewhat more diverse than is often maintained is revealed in the Louisiana experience. In that state three major political power centers emerged: the landowner class; the so-called Lottery-Ring combination, an alliance between the Louisiana State Lottery and the Democratic organization in New Orleans; and an avaricious clique of legislators and other officials who profited from such policies as the state's convict lease system.

Having redeemed their individual states, Democratic leaders worked hard to maintain white unity and to perpetuate their control. While their tactics varied from state to state, their leadership tended to be oligarchical and conservative. In every southern state, a relatively small number of popular leaders dominated the Democratic party, determined the acceptable candidates for key offices, and decided upon the issues and candidates. The oligarchies moved quickly to secure control of the party organization in their respective states and to make sure that their lieutenants and friends were in charge of the election machinery. The concentration of authority in the hands of governors and legislators enabled these state leaders to appoint important local officials in every county. One of the steps taken by North Carolina Redeemers was to pass a law in 1876 designed to assure white Democratic supremacy throughout the state. It provided that the principal officers in each county would be appointed by justices of the peace, who were themselves to be named by the legislature. Conservative control depended on the popularity of Democratic leaders with white voters, but it also rested upon working alliances between state and local leaders. The latter were often part of what some contemporaries unflatteringly called courthouse "cliques" or "rings." These influential local politicians looked after the interests of the party hierarchy in their towns and counties, particularly the operation of the election system and the selection of local officeholders, including members of the state legislature.

Redeemer dominance was reinforced by an assortment of clever techniques and sharp practices: gerrymandering legislative districts, discriminatory apportionment of seats in party conventions, intricate registration and election laws, and use of fraud and intimidation at the polls. In some cases these New Departure Democrats made use of a kind of "captive black vote" against their opponents, even as they characterized themselves as defenders of white supremacy. Indeed, their use of the race question assumed the quality of a fine art. As one historian says of the situation in Mississippi, conservative Democrats used the black man "unsparingly to crush all incipient revolts against their authority."[14]

Lack of unity among the mass of small farmers and workers also aided the Redeemers. White yeomen in southern Appalachia generally supported the Republican party, as did most blacks throughout the South who continued to vote. The region's exploitative social structure—increasing farm tenancy, the pervasive furnishing system, and the growth of textile mill villages and mining towns—debilitated the political role of more and more small farmers and laborers. Agricultural and industrial workers were the victims of a regional labor market that was shaped by high population growth and isolation from national labor norms and pressures. This condition facilitated the structuring of the work force along the lines desired by the planter-merchant-industrialist interests.

Critics referred to the Redeemers and their successors as "Bourbons," likening them to the reactionary European monarchs who had "learned nothing and forgotten nothing." The term is misleading, however, for the southern Bourbons were less inflexible and more innovative than the epithet suggests. "Generally speaking," one historian concludes, "they were innovators in economic matters, moderates in race policy once white supremacy was assured, extremists in politics when their own supremacy was threatened, and profoundly conservative in most matters of social policy."[15] Their control reflected corporate and financial interests, especially those involved in railroad promotion, merchandising, and banking. The state governments under their leadership reduced taxes, starved public service agencies and eleemosynary institutions, and made economy in government a major priority. Yet many of them also advocated railroad subsidies and tax exemptions for new industries.

While proclaiming themselves the guardians of fiscal integrity and of a political climate favorable for economic developers, the Redeemers repudiated much of the Reconstruction debt in the southern states, took part in efforts to regulate railroads and other corporations, and supported appropriations for some state services, particularly to benefit farmers. If the new state constitutions whose drafting and adoption they spearheaded emphasized retrenchment in spending and low ceilings on taxation, they also included restrictions on state aid to private enterprises. Nor were the Bourbon Democrats as honest and fiscally responsible as they pictured themselves. They, too, were guilty in many instances of governmental corruption, financial peculation, and public scandals. Nevertheless, they left a lasting imprint on southern politics and society. Perhaps their greatest contribution was their influence in the cultural sphere—in their efforts to create a united southern people with a distinct cultural identity. Taking advantage of their reputation as natural leaders, they stressed the organic character of white society and appealed to the spirit of *"Herrenvolk* democracy"—a democratic society for whites only. They succeeded in large part because they were regarded as representing the "interests" of a majority of white southerners, who in the early post-Reconstruction years held conventional views on most economic questions and on the proper role of government, who considered race an important aspect of politics, and who were responsive to the pleas for southern white unity.

Although every southern state supported the Democratic presidential ticket in 1880, Republican strength in the South did not decline drastically during the last two decades of the century. Those southerners who belonged to the Grand Old Party in the post-Reconstruction years were largely of two very different and often mutually antagonistic types: the freedmen, who for the most part lived in the low country, and the white inhabitants of the mountainous areas. This Republican coalition of blacks and whites was a powerful political force in the late nineteenth-century South, particularly in Virginia, North Carolina, Kentucky, and Tennessee. But the place of blacks in the party was a divisive issue in southern Republicanism and one that GOP leaders were never able to resolve satisfactorily. "The Republican strategy," one authority observes, "became one of offering their black following just enough to ensure their continued support while emphasizing issues that would attract greater numbers of white voters."[16]

The four states of the upper South east of the Mississippi River remained a political battleground between the two major parties until the end of the century. The Republican percentage of the presidential vote in Virginia during the period 1876–1900 was never less than 39 percent, and in 1884 and 1888, it was 49 percent. During the same years, North Carolina Republicans dropped below 46 percent only once—with 36 percent of the total vote in 1892 (the Populist ticket obtained 16 percent). In Tennessee, meanwhile, the Republicans received at least 44 percent of the presidential votes in every election except those of 1876 and 1892, when their proportion of the popular vote dropped just below 40 percent. Kentucky Republicans were equally competitive, averaging well above 40 percent of the popular vote and carrying their state for William McKinley in 1896. Kentucky, Tennessee, and North Carolina elected Republican governors during this period, and each of the four states sent Republican congressmen to Washington, sometimes five or six at once. In the meantime, the Republican party dominated local elections in southwestern Virginia, western North Carolina, East Tennessee, and eastern Kentucky.

In another group of southern states—Alabama, Arkansas, Georgia, and Texas—Republican presidential strength was greater during the period 1876–1900 than is usually recognized, hovering around one-third of the total vote. As late as 1900, the Republican proportion of the vote was 35 percent in Alabama and Arkansas, 31 percent in Texas, and 28 percent in Georgia. In Florida the GOP percentage was

Table 1. Turnout and Proportion of Adult Males Voting for Each Party in the South in Presidential Elections, 1872–1908

Election	Democrat	Republican	Other	Turnout
1872	23.35	26.87	0	50.24
1876	38.73	26.70	0	64.94
1880	36.88	23.76	2.90	63.55
1884	37.20	25.70	0.34	62.84
1888	37.94	23.08	1.47	62.49
1892	33.87	14.58	9.71	58.16
1896	33.33	19.83	3.00	56.16
1900	26.54	15.35	1.22	43.10
1904	18.95	8.31	1.35	28.62
1908	19.44	9.58	1.15	30.18

SOURCE: Adapted from J. Morgan Kousser, *The Shaping of Southern Politics: Suffrage Restriction and the Establishment of the One-Party South, 1880–1910* (New Haven: Yale University Press, 1974), p. 12.

NOTE: These statistics refer to the eleven ex-Confederate states only.

40 or more in every election through 1888, after which it dropped to a steady level of about 20 percent. The decline in Louisiana began four years earlier, dropping from 42 percent in 1884 to 27 percent in 1888 and gradually sinking to 20 percent in 1900. Mississippi Republicanism showed the same pattern, declining from 36 percent of the total votes cast in 1884 to 25 percent in 1888 and reaching 10 percent in 1900. The South Carolina percentage declined steadily throughout this era, from 34 percent in 1880 to 9 percent in 1900. Thus, Republicanism in national elections did not become insignificant in most southern states until after the 1890s.

The persistence of southern Republicanism after 1876 can be attributed in part to GOP efforts at the national level to win support in the region. In an age of extraordinarily close elections, Republican leaders, frequently of Whiggish background and usually conservative in their views, turned naturally enough to their counterparts in the South—to what one Republican politician referred to as "the same class of men in the South as are Republicans in the North"[17]—in seeking to head off radical policies and maintain their control of the national government. Despite the return of home rule and Democratic control, there seemed to be some chance that interparty competition would continue in the South. In the presidential election of 1880, a majority of the black adult males in nine of the eleven ex-Confederate states cast their ballots. The percentage of adult males voting in presidential elections in the South between 1876 and 1896 was as high as 65 percent and never lower than 56 percent.

Seeing the cleavages that divided southern Democrats and recognizing the bankruptcy of their own Reconstruction policies, Republican leaders approached the "southern question" in a growing mood of experimentation. President Hayes, dreaming of a strong Republican party in the South, sought to attract southern conservatives with a generous patronage policy and favorable legislation. As it became more evident that southerners of Whiggish ancestry were finding a comfortable home in the Bourbon Democracy, James A. Garfield and Chester A. Arthur began to encourage independent movements that developed in one southern state after another. Benjamin Harrison attempted to use federal intervention, through the "force bill," to protect the voting rights of blacks and whites in the South. And in the agrarian upheaval of the 1890s, Republican leaders tried to work out successful coalitions with Populists and dissident Democrats.

But success was limited. The most spectacular Republican efforts to perfect coalition politics—in Virginia in the early 1880s and in North Carolina in the 1890s—provoked bitter conflict and recrimination and in the long run diminished the party's strength in the region. Those episodes also revealed the immensity of the obstacles confronting the Republicans. Their party lacked leaders, newspapers, and money in the southern states, and its ranks were torn by recurrent factionalism involving personal rivalry and strife between "black and tan" and "lily-white" groups. "From nearly every Republican county convention," a Tennessee newspaper reported in 1900, "comes the same story: Two conventions, a split and contesting delegations to the state convention."[18] Furthermore, southern whites found the Reconstruction image of Republicanism almost irresistible, and despite the willingness of many GOP leaders to abandon their reliance upon black support, a great many southerners continued to associate the Republican party with fears of Negro domination. Outside the mountainous areas, southern whites were inclined to be contemptuous of Republicans. In Florida, one authority has noted, a white man who voted Republican was likely to be called "white trash," while a black man who attemped to vote Democratic was apt to have his ballot torn from his hand.[19] John S. Wise, a prominent Virginia Republican, later lamented that the average southerner was incapable of doing justice to the region's Republicans, that he imputed to every one of them "sordid motives or distorted political ideas," and that the most liberal estimate the Republican could expect in the South was that "he is a crank."[20]

Republicans also encountered fraud and intimidation, as well as discriminatory election officials and harshly punitive election laws. Five southern states enacted new poll tax, registration, secret ballot, and other restrictive voting laws between 1889 and 1893. These measures took a heavy toll of black and white voters. Under the circumstances, it was virtually impossible for Republicans to formulate a policy on the national level that would appeal to the enemies of the conservative Democrats in the South and at the same time satisfy powerful GOP interests outside the region. Thus, the overtures President Arthur made to southern independents of a radical stripe proved disquieting to orthodox Republicans. The change of sentiment in the North, reflecting the drift away from Reconstruction idealism as well as the strong influence of business elements in the Republican party, doomed President Harrison's attempt to secure passage of the "force bill." And to complicate matters still further, the very threat of such legislation became an effective weapon in the hands of those who championed white supremacy and the Solid South.

Had the Bourbon Democrats been confronted only with the Republican challenge, they might have retained a greater degree of equanimity. Actually, the Republican presence probably contributed to Democratic unity and discipline in the post-Reconstruction period. On the other hand, the Democratic regimes in the various southern states were not monolithic; Redeemer control in one state was not a carbon copy of that in other commonwealths. The Democrats in every southern state were divided by internal squabbles, geographic differences, and factional groupings. In Tennessee, for instance, the Democrats were split into a Whig-industrialist wing and a state-rights-secessionist-planter wing. Still, there was a Redeemer-Bourbon type that was generally dominant in the region's politics and that was responsible for a pervasive political orthodoxy throughout the South. Leaders of this stripe also constituted an oligarchy that could not always conceal arrogant expectations in the exercise of power, personal prerogatives, and deferential treatment. Some southerners resented this state of affairs, and there was also widespread revulsion against the political chicanery and dictatorial methods of the entrenched Democrats. Here and there, moreover, aspiring politicians chafed at a leadership that denied many of them a larger role in Democratic politics.

Bourbon leaders were faced, almost from the beginning of their dominance, with intraparty dissension and protest movements that held out the dread possibility of a merger with the Republicans and a transfer of political authority. One of the earliest of these independent movements—and the most significant before the Populist uprising—was the Readjuster campaign in Virginia. This movement was organized in the late 1870s when the state's politics was reshaped on the basis of a struggle between those who insisted upon funding Virginia's large debt and those who demanded its "readjustment." The times were ripe for a political upheaval. The Republican party had been repudiated and was badly disorganized, while the triumphant Redeemers were faced with the problem of guiding an unwieldy party and providing answers to a number of perplexing questions, including the handling of the state debt. Economic conditions were poor, people complained about inequitable taxes, and the schools suffered from inadequate support. Criticism of the conservative Democratic leadership increased, farmers began to see political implications in the Granger movement, and some Virginians were attracted to the inflationary schemes of the Greenbackers. A remarkable political messiah then appeared on the scene to lead the revolt. His name was William Mahone, ex-Confederate general, railroad builder, erstwhile conservative, and political organizer extraordinaire.

The movement that Mahone led reflected the geographic and social composition of Virginia. Realizing the potential influence of an expanded electorate, Mahone appealed directly to the people. The general sought the support of the small white farmers and poorer classes, especially in the western part of the state, and he succeeded in combining those groups with a substantial number of blacks, most of whom lived in the eastern lowlands. The Readjuster leaders were, characteristically, middle-class men on the make who found few opportunities for political distinction in the conservative regime of the Redeemers. The Conservatives, as the Democrats were wont to call themselves, had about them an aura of aristocracy and the Lost Cause, but their fiscal orthodoxy and laissez-faire preachments brought them powerful allies from industrial and urban elements.

Readjuster control lasted only a few years, but it had a pronounced effect on Virginia politics. Capturing the state legislature in 1879, the Readjusters soon dominated every branch of the Virginia government, and at one time they also controlled the two U.S. Senate seats and six seats in the national House of Representatives. They readjusted the state debt, revised the system of taxation, repealed the poll tax, abolished the whipping post, provided liberal appropriations for education, and enacted legislation favorable to labor. At the same time, Mahone created a patronage machine and attempted to combine with the Republicans. The Conservatives, meanwhile, took advantage of Readjuster mistakes and warned loudly of Republican control and black domination. By the mid-1880s, they had redeemed the state from "Mahoneism." But in the process they borrowed some democratic features from the Readjuster program and, like many southern Democrats in the 1890s, sought to broaden their appeal to the white masses.

Although Virginia was the only southern state in which independents wrested control from the Redeemers in the 1880s, almost all of the former Confederate states experienced some degree of independent revolt in the decade following Reconstruction. One measure of this political dissidence is provided by the combined opposition (anti-Democratic) vote in the following gubernatorial elections: North Carolina, 48.7 percent and Georgia, 35.1 percent in 1880; Virginia, 52.8 percent and Mississippi, 40.2 percent in 1881; Texas, 40.5 percent, Alabama, 31.6 percent, and South Carolina, 21 percent in 1882; Tennessee, 48.7 percent, Florida, 46.5 percent, and Louisiana, 32.9 percent in 1884; and Arkansas, 45.9 percent in 1888.[21] Some of this political independence represented conflict over state debts and fiscal policies similar to the controversy in Virginia, although the repudiation or readjustment of Reconstruction debts was generally popular in the South and inextricably connected with the overthrow of Radical rule in most southern states. Opposition to Democratic conservatives frequently developed over such local issues as the unequal division of educational funds, inequitable tax rates, high interest rates, fence laws, business favoritism, the operation of the convict lease system, and local-option elections; but there were widespread charges of machine politics, "ring" rule, and manipulated elections. Dissatisfaction also grew out of the malapportionment of state legislatures and the black belts' use of Negro votes to strengthen their position. The convention system of making nominations and choosing party leaders, moreover, was often linked to the system of representation, which meant that black counties were given delegates far out of proportion to their voting strength. In South Carolina, to take an example given by C. Vann Woodward, "the upland plebeians found they had redeemed the state from the Carpetbaggers only to lose it to the lowland bosses."[22] Yet, as another scholar has written of the situation in North Carolina, "The impulse toward democracy struggled to take form and achieve self-conscious direction; the defense of undemocratic privilege adopted more extreme measures in the face of internal pressure and external shocks."[23]

Independent movements were a real force in the South of the late 1870s and early 1880s. In Georgia an independent campaign elected William H. Felton and Emory L. Speer to Congress but failed in an effort to overturn Bourbon control of the state. In 1878 William M. Lowe was elected to Congress as an independent from a north Alabama district, and in the same year, a Greenback-Labor candidate won a congressional seat in Texas. The Greenbackers made a strong showing in gubernatorial contests in Kentucky, Alabama, and Arkansas during the next two years, and in the early 1880s Democratic politicians reflecting the monetary proposals and economic radicalism of Greenbackism challenged the conservative political control in South Carolina, Texas, and other states. While the Greenback movement failed to obtain a substantial number of votes in most southern states, it mirrored, as did other independent movements of the period, strong dissatisfaction with Redeemer authority as well as the socioeconomic cleavages in southern society that belied the claim of a Solid South.

Yet by the mid-1880s the edge of political insurgency in the South had been blunted. All the old techniques of social and economic pressure perfected in the battles against the Reconstruction Radicals had been employed in ruthless campaigns against party independents. The same methods would be applied even more savagely against Populists in the 1890s. At the same time, the southern economy improved as farm commodity prices increased and as the nation entered into an era of unprecedented railroad construction and industrial expansion. There was a feeling of general satisfaction in the South, moreover, with Grover Cleveland's victory in 1884 and the return of the Democrats to national power early the next year. But the relatively placid years of the mid-1880s were not to last long, and the late 1880s and much of the 1890s witnessed growing agrarian distress, industrial crisis, and political conflict all over the country.

The agrarian revolt marked a decisive stage in the evolution of modern southern politics. While gathering strength from the independent movements and farmer organizations of the 1870s and 1880s, the revolt was fundamentally a protest and a countermovement against the encroachment of modern industrialism upon rural society and rural values. It was a social as well as a political movement. There was, to be sure, a solid basis for the agrarian unrest. Farmers in the South and West for two decades after 1870 had suffered from steadily declining agricultural prices, inequitable taxes, inadequate facilities and high interest charges, a contracting currency, a high tariff on the products they bought, and monopolistic power in business, whether exercised by the middlemen they dealt with firsthand or the railroads and industrial "trusts" somewhat further removed. Nor was that all. During those years farmers frequently experienced a social stagnation and loss of personal dignity and community status that produced widespread despair, resentment, and defiance in the agricultural regions. In the South the situation facing the farmer, especially the millions of small operators and tenants, was even worse since it reflected the postwar revolution that introduced peculiar and regressive arrangements in labor, land tenure, and credit.

Of the numerous agricultural organizations that sprang up in the 1880s, the most important was the National Farmers' Alliance and Industrial Union. Originating in Texas, the Farmers' Alliance spread rapidly through the South in the late 1880s, pulling other farm groups and thousands of unaffiliated farmers into its ranks. By 1890 over a million southerners were members of the Alliance. Among these recruits were farm leaders and substantial landowners as well as small operators. The major source of the organization's popularity was its promise of direct economic relief, particularly through its cooperative program, and the sense of community fostered by its local chapters and activities. It was the Southern Alliance, as it was called, that formulated the economic and political ideas that were soon identified with the People's party and populism. Prominent among these were reform measures looking to currency inflation, government-based credit, land reform, railroad and trust regulation, and democratization of the political process.

In the beginning the agrarian reformers tried to capture the Democratic party in the South, and in the elections of 1890 they won victories for the Alliance standard in several states. They could point to successes in more than half the legislative seats in eight states, to six Alliance governors, and to more than fifty congressmen bearing the organization's stamp of approval. The established Democratic leadership, under mounting criticism in recent years, was alarmed and fearful. But the Southern Alliance soon discovered that it was more difficult to secure legislative reforms than to obtain campaign endorsements from Democratic politicians. The scene changed rapidly in 1891, and by early 1892 the formation of the Populist party on a national basis had injected the "third-party" issue into southern politics. The Alliance's decision to "move into politics" in 1892 and the "radicalization" of its leadership reflected a major crisis in the society's cooperative program resulting from the pressure of falling cotton prices.

The result was incomparably bitter and confusing. The intensity of the campaign of 1892 divided communities, churches, and even families. It destroyed the Farmers' Alliance as a viable institution. Many southern farmers took the plunge and became members of the new party, while others who subscribed to Populist principles tried to avoid the pain of breaking old party loyalties by calling themselves "Jeffersonian Democrats" and the like. Nevertheless, most southerners remained faithful to the Democratic party, responding to the campaign on behalf of Grover Cleveland, as well as the wild talk about the "force bill" and the approval of Alliance demands by some Democratic leaders. Still, the People's party showed surprising strength in the South. When the Cleveland administration floundered amid the national currents of depression and economic uncertainty, while demonstrating its conservative orthodoxy and lack of understanding of agrarian unrest, southern Populists looked to greater things. The election of 1894 gave them a good deal of encouragement, for the third party made gains in several southern states. It did especially well in North Carolina, Alabama, and Georgia, receiving almost 45 percent of the votes in the last state. In North Carolina the Democrats lost the general assembly to the Populists and Republicans, who then prepared the ground for an ill-fated fusion regime that captured control of the entire state in 1896. Meanwhile, the new party attempted to fuse with the Republicans on the state and local levels in a number of other states. North Carolina's "fusionist" legislature of 1895 enacted sweeping reforms, including an election law that enabled more blacks to register, a measure that prohibited interest rates over 6 percent, and the return of self-government to the counties. Following the election of 1896, the new Republican governor, Daniel L. Russell, set out to build an alliance of reformers from all parties.

By 1896 southern opponents of President Cleveland's policies, prodded by his heavy-handed use of patronage and his adamant position on the currency question, had captured control of the Democratic party in virtually every state in the region. To the consternation of People's party leaders, these anti-Cleveland Democrats had taken over a large part of the Populist platform, including the iridescent free silver symbol. Southern Democrats then helped place William Jennings Bryan at the head of their party's national ticket. The ever-present danger that the third party would join forces with the Republicans in the South, as it did so spectacularly in North Carolina, gave impetus to this liberalization of the southern Democracy. It was also a factor in persuading some Democrats to remain within the party fold. The agrarian radicals represented a coalition of rural interest groups that were by no means monolithic in politics. As one scholar has pointed out, "When southern Alliancemen had to choose between participating in traditional friends-and-neighbors politics and supporting specific, controversial proposals, the order's internal conflicts burst into the open."[24] In addition, the strength of the agrarian movement varied from one part of the South to another. The revolt in Tennessee, for example, was limited and halfhearted, a consequence, no doubt, of the state's relatively diversified and self-sufficient agricultural economy, reasonably low interest rates, and large percentage of owner-operated farms. The Populists, especially those in the South, faced a cruel and baffling dilemma in 1896. There was, in fact, no way out for the People's party. It could not resist the pressure to endorse Bryan, and the fusion—and confusion—that followed the Nebraskan's valiant campaign soon brought an end to the third party everywhere.

Southern farmers, like various other economic and social elements in the United States during the era, tried with some success to consolidate their forces to deal with powerful interests and competing groups generated by the new industrialism. Their coalescence under the banner of the Farmers' Alliance made them a potent interest group, and their resort to politics challenged the established Democratic leadership in every southern state. Much of the radicalism associated with populism was indigenous to the South, and the movement probably had its greatest strength in that region. It is true that populism was freighted with a decided provincialism and negativism. One historian has characterized the Southern Alliance as "pro-agricultural, anti-urban, anti-merchant, anti-banker, anti-foreign," while Sen. John Sharp Williams in later years described the basic motivation in the Populist movement as "a revolt against all manner of superiorities."[25] Yet the Populists not only stressed the centrality of tangible production as a social good; they also called for a revival of democratic principles in politics and appealed to the ideal of an orderly community and a harmony of interests in society. They attacked the capitalist system but retained faith in the benefits of private property and the market economy. Their espousal of positive governmental action, business control, and political democracy made a lasting impression on southern politics, even though southern Populists suffered humiliating defeat. Their emphasis on monetary inflation and credit needs, marketing reforms, minimum prices and acreage controls, and better farming methods was destined to have a great effect on twentieth-century politics and policies.

The program of the Farmers' Alliance and the proposals of the People's party threatened to overturn the whole structure of Redeemer politics and to halt the creation of a more thoroughgoing one-party system. For a moment in the early 1890s, the South seemed to stand on the threshold of a political revolution in which a coalition of up-country dwellers, black and white farmers, and industrial workers might overcome the powerful black belt planters and their business allies and reverse the political and economic trends of recent years. Suddenly, there were contests for state and local positions that had real meaning—with party choices and clear-cut issues. The Populists challenged the "New South" system frontally, challenged its conservative policies and political oligarchies, challenged the southern mythology that helped sustain it. Populism looked to a combination of dispossessed farmers and blacks along economic and social lines, and it brought into sharp relief longtime cleavages that the Redeemers had never been able to suppress completely.

While populism grew out of genuine grass-roots protest, it was a complex movement that represented a number of different social elements. Numan V. Bartley suggests that in Georgia the movement embodied at least two separate strains of social protest: a group of disaffected planters led by Thomas E. Watson and centered in "the worn and declining old cotton belt" and a large number of small farmers whose concerns were essentially local.[26] Populism's greatest appeal was probably to the region's small farmers. Populists in Alabama, one historian has concluded, "were only tenuously connected to society by economic function, by personal relationships, by stable community membership, by political participation, or by psychological identification with the South's distinctive myths. Recruited heavily from among the downwardly mobile and geographically transient, they were vulnerable to feelings of powerlessness. They were largely superfluous farmers or ineffectively organized workers who were not linked to influential Alabamians by kinship or close association. They tended to come from isolated areas, from areas experiencing extraordinary influxes of population, and from areas with increasingly large concentrations of tenant farmers."[27] For southerners such as these, the economic and political trends of the late nineteenth century were disastrous. The expansion of cotton culture outside the antebellum plantation areas, the long agricultural depression, and the declining self-sufficiency in food production led to deteriorating material conditions for millions of landless blacks and white yeomen, whose economic prospects and independence were increasingly jeopardized by crop liens, sharecropping, merchant monopoly, and coercive labor controls.

These marginal elements in southern society made their last political stand in the agrarian upheaval of the 1890s. They were revolting not only against conditions that shackled them to an exploitative economy but also against a politics that denied them an effective voice in public affairs. They disliked the political domination of the black belts and the alliances between plantation leaders and city politicians that controlled state and local government. It was, as the saying went, a struggle of the "wool-hat boys" against the "silk-hat bosses." There may have been a few "silk-hatted" Populists—certainly there were some well-to-do farmers in the movement—and one should not make the mistake of interpreting populism exclusively in terms of class. Yet, in the South at least, social and economic divisions were clearly revealed during the controversies over populism, and they rested on far more than the demands for agricultural parity in the national economy. Fundamentally, it was a matter of power and privilege. Commenting on the situation in North Carolina, one historian has written that "the self-annointed 'better half,' including planters, merchants, professionals, and most of the state's industrialists, remained satisfied with a version of the New South that enhanced their position while inhibiting social and economic progress for others."[28]

Although the Populist assault shook the Democratic hierarchy to its foundations, leaving a habit of radicalism in some quarters,[29] the

revolt was quelled, and political solidarity was made even more complete during the years that followed. Democratic leaders hurriedly
invoked the race issue, rang the changes on the dangers of bolting
the party, and fell back on skillful election maneuvers and fraud to
win endangered districts. Populist candidates for state offices were
almost certainly counted out in Alabama and Louisiana. "Any Democrat might just as well go straight into the Republican party as into
the ranks of its active ally, the People's party," warned a prominent
Democratic newspaper in Tennessee.[30] In Texas the prospect of a
Populist-Republican coalition in state politics threatened Democratic
control and brought the charge of "Negro domination." Conservatives never tired of pointing to the fusionist government of North
Carolina and pleading for escape from the horrors of a second Reconstruction. Southern Populists, observes Vann Woodward, "daily
faced the implacable dogmas of racism, white solidarity, white supremacy, and the bloody shirt."[31] Small wonder that southern whites
should learn, as a perceptive contemporary put it, to set men above
principles and "good government" above freedom of thought. Some
southerners, of course, were influenced by the constitutional and
state-rights arguments of the conservatives; they were suspicious of
the centralizing effect of Populist remedies or fearful of new competition and injurious regulation of local business interests.

Still other factors worked to the advantage of the Democrats in
the crisis of the 1890s. For one thing, they retained a monopoly of
the region's customary leadership. It was difficult for political rebels
to unify the southern masses, given the insistent pull of party tradition
and the barriers of race and rural-urban differences. The Populists
had little success, except for modest achievements in Alabama and
Texas, in uniting farmers and industrial workers. The restrictive suffrage laws enacted by several southern states in the late 1880s and
early 1890s also handicapped Populists and Republicans, and the
Democrats, as their critics charged, were not averse to the use of
"fraud, forgery, falsehood, and fiction" in the conduct of elections.[32]
Southern Democrats, moreover, endeavored to counter the Populist
appeal by endorsing some of the reform demands of the agrarian
radicals. This was more than a matter of political calculation. It also
represented the changing nature of the Democratic party in the South,
the emergence of new leaders, and the influence of reform ideas
among confirmed Democrats. In Texas and a few other southern
states, politicians such as James S. Hogg eschewed third-party politics
but waged a battle for reform within the Democratic party. They became enthusiastic champions of William Jennings Bryan. Many of
these "halfway Populists" attempted to make their party organizations more responsive to the interests of varied groups and areas.

Democratic leaders in the South moved quickly following the political upheaval of the 1890s to prevent a recurrence of the Populist revolt and to strengthen southern solidarity. They approached the problem on two fronts. One of these was the regional campaign to secure the legal disfranchisement of blacks. Democrats in several states had begun, even before the climactic events of the mid-1890s, to press for the adoption of literacy tests, poll taxes, and other voting requirements. This movement was accelerated during the next few years. Disfranchisement advocates, sensing an issue that would rally white southerners and, some supporters argued, even undermine conservative party bosses, moved energetically and with mounting confidence to complete the task. At the same time, the rising tide of Jim Crow legislation reinforced the political proscription of black southerners.

A campaign to call a constitutional convention in Mississippi was successful in 1890, and a new document was drafted to replace the Radical constitution of 1868. The constitution of 1890 included several franchise provisions: a literacy test, cumulative poll tax, long residence requirement, registration four months before an election, and disqualification for a list of crimes. An alternative to the literacy requirement was devised for illiterate white men—the ability to "understand" and give a "reasonable interpretation" of any section of the constitution. In 1895 South Carolina followed Mississippi's course in adopting disfranchisement features as part of its new constitution. Louisiana, which resorted to constitutional disfranchisement in 1898, invented the "grandfather clause" as a temporary alternative to its literacy requirement. This provision exempted from the literacy test those who were entitled to vote on January 1, 1867, together with their sons and grandsons. North Carolina, acutely conscious of the actions of Mississippi, South Carolina, and Louisiana, adopted wide-ranging disfranchisement provisions in the form of a constitutional amendment in 1900. Alabama took a similar step by approving a new constitution in 1901, and Virginia followed suit the next year. Georgia added a comprehensive suffrage amendment to its constitution in 1908. Oklahoma, in 1910, was the last state to enact constitutional disfranchisement.

Though the other southern states refrained from amending their constitutions to disfranchise black voters, all of them except Kentucky approved restrictive measures in one form or another. Tennessee took action in 1889 and 1890 by adopting a harsh registration act, a poll tax requirement, and a secret ballot law. By 1904 every southern state except Kentucky and Oklahoma had made the poll tax a prerequisite for voting. In some cases disingenuous registration and voting acts paved the way for formal constitutional disfranchisement by restricting the electorate, particularly blacks and poor whites. The white primary was also an effective disfranchising weapon. In the early years of the twentieth century, most of the Democratic state committees or conventions introduced statewide primaries that excluded blacks.

The intense struggle within the party of Redemption during the 1890s soon weakened the position of blacks in southern politics and made them a natural scapegoat in the aftermath of the agrarian revolt. As might have been expected, the regular Democrats, particularly in the black belts, assumed an instrumental role in disfranchisement, which they saw as a means of striking at the Republican party as well as discouraging third-party ventures in the future. Some Democratic leaders may have supported suffrage restriction because it promised to deprive illiterate white men of the ballot and thus of any part in party politics. In a number of states, such as Virginia, Democratic opponents of entrenched party organizations apparently hoped that disfranchisement would undermine the power of the ruling political factions. Some agrarian reformers and ex-Populists such as Tom Watson in Georgia became champions of Negro disfranchisement. Men like Watson, dispirited, often disillusioned, and sometimes embittered over the failure of their Populist dreams, turned on blacks with a vengeance. But in general Republicans and Populists proved to be the most forthright supporters of universal manhood suffrage and fair election laws. Many poor whites, especially those in the mountain and hill regions, looked with suspicion on disfranchisement schemes that might be turned in their own direction. Some white southerners undoubtedly believed that removing blacks from politics would end the political corruption of the 1890s and enable whites to deal constructively with substantive issues. Indeed, contemporary white southerners were inclined to view the suffrage restrictions as a necessary step, even a reform, but the "race question" could not be so easily exorcised. It continued to supply politicians with an issue that aroused the average white man even more powerfully than economic and class exhortations.

In the end the restrictionists carried the day, though not without a fight. It was, in a sense, the denouement of the agrarian revolt and one of the last major steps in the creation of the Solid South. The significance of disfranchisement is suggested in J. Morgan Kousser's assertion that the post-Reconstruction period of transition, uncertainty, and fluctuation ended "only with the restriction of the suffrage and the consequent stifling of anti-Democratic political parties." Kousser also observes that the new political structure ensured "the absolute control of predominantly black counties by upper-class whites, the elimination in most areas of parties as a means of organized com-

petition between politicians, and, in general, the nonrepresentation
of lower-class interests in political decision-making."[33] The new suffrage laws drastically reduced the size of the southern electorate,
decimating the remaining black vote and depriving a multitude of
lower-class whites of the ballot. With the shrunken electorate and the
end of interparty competition came sharply falling turnouts in state
and national elections.

The second front on which southern Democrats acted was, paradoxically, the movement to liberalize party rules, particularly the
introduction of statewide primary elections and such democratic innovations as the direct election of U.S. senators. This movement was
in part a legacy of populism, and it was related to the Bryanization
of the Democratic party in the South and to the persisting demand
in the region for social reform. While the exclusion of blacks from
participation in southern primaries was itself a key disfranchising
tactic, the adoption of the primary was also related to the widespread
distrust of the old convention system and to efforts by party leaders
to persuade white Populists and independents to join Democratic
ranks. The primary provided a vehicle for intraparty competition, and
it helped abolish the minority party's last remaining resource, its monopoly of opposition. Public regulation of primaries, along with progressive measures such as the Australian ballot, registration laws,
corrupt practices legislation, and nonpartisan municipal elections,
was no doubt meant to "purify" the electorate, do away with electoral
corruption, and limit the influence of political bosses and vested interests. But the result was further to restrict the political involvement
of the southern masses and to create a politics that was primarily
responsive to organized groups representing businessmen, planters,
and the growing middle and professional classes.

By the turn of the nineteenth century, the one-party system
loomed in bold relief over the political landscape of the South. If its
creation seemed, in some respects, to have been predetermined, the
process that culminated in its clear-cut emergence was by no means
smooth or free from controversy and struggle. Indeed, the period
between Reconstruction and the end of the century was one of great
turbulence, disagreement, and division in southern politics. It was a
transitional period dominated by an interplay of issues that reflected
economic, political, and racial concerns. Not until the end of the century were the region's political leaders able to deal with questions of
class, party, and race in a way that would minimize the divisions
within the South and safeguard its political solidarity.

The power and resilience of the Redeemers contributed to this
political outcome. Enjoying the advantage of wealth, established leadership, and influence, they were able to dominate the region's political

life for a long time, while charting a conservative course and serving their own class interests. When forced on the defensive by Democratic independents or agrarian radicals, they appealed for party regularity and were usually flexible enough to make judicious concessions to their opponents. Despite their privileged position and the recurrent challenge to their control, one should not exaggerate the internal struggle and class conflict during their regimes. The Redeemers identified themselves with the larger white community in terms of cherished southern myths and cultural values, and except for times of acute economic distress, they were perceived as representing the "interests" of most white southerners. In confronting the race question, they could act the role of paternalist in seeking black support and also resort to white-supremacy alarmism when it suited their purposes. Still, their political control was never secure; it was threatened by Republicans, Populists, and the possibility of a fusion of the two groups.

Although the Republicans were a minority party in every southern state during the late nineteenth century, they remained active and constituted a powerful presence in several states. The party was sustained by the continued involvement of a substantial number of black men and the loyalty of mountain residents in the upper South. National GOP leaders in the 1880s kept alive their hope of strengthening the party's southern ranks. There was a class as well as a racial dimension to this Republicanism, since it depended on the black masses and on many disadvantaged inhabitants of the mountains. That may explain why southern Republicans displayed a greater willingness than did the Democrats to support education, to oppose the use of convict labor, and to seek certain kinds of government aid. They were also more solicitous of blacks, despite the divisions that frequently developed among them over candidates, patronage, and the prerogatives of each race. But the region's Republicans were never able to overcome the barriers of race and party. *Republicanism*, because of its Reconstruction connotations and its black support, was an epithet to many white southerners, and that provocative identity, along with restrictive voter legislation and the political harassment of Afro-Americans, was a constant problem for Republicans in the southern states. Nevertheless, the political upheaval of the 1890s brought the party new opportunities in the South. It also brought the Democrats the most serious crisis they had confronted since Reconstruction.

Populists, like the Republicans, soon discovered the sanctity of traditional party allegiance. Southern Alliance leaders first tried to take control of the Democratic party, but they were unable to transform the party. When the more radical insurgents organized a third party, they were bitterly attacked for disrupting the unity of white society in the South. Although the new party no doubt attracted some men because it gave them a chance to move up in politics, a far greater number of sympathetically minded Democrats could not bear the thought of leaving the party of southern orthodoxy. Populism reflected and endeavored to capitalize on class divisions in southern society—on the differentiation between the bourgeois world of landlords, merchants, and bankers and that of workers, particularly of tenants, sharecroppers, and small landowners. Populism did appeal strongly to dispossessed elements in the South, but its leaders found it impossible to mobilize a majority of these working-class southerners, many of whom were too depressed and isolated to take much part in politics. Economic incentives were frequently outweighed by considerations of race and party. Even at the height of the dramatic struggle of the 1890s, class was scarcely the most compelling issue in southern politics, and in the climactic campaign of 1896 the conflict between class and party was eased when the People's party endorsed the Democratic Bryan. Finally, there was the question of race. The Populists sought the votes of blacks and tried to promote their economic and political advancement. Yet there were limits to the racial tolerance of white Populists, and their appeals for interracial cooperation made them vulnerable to the charge of dividing the white community and opening the door to "black domination" of southern politics. In the aftermath of the agrarian revolt, many Populists resigned themselves to Negro disfranchisement and even made the black man the scapegoat for the failure of their movement.

Thus, the contours of the new political system in the South were profoundly influenced by party, race, and class. By the late 1890s, the Republican and People's parties were discredited. The triumph of the one-party system was related to the loss of economic independence and the growing political isolation of a large number of white southerners, whether as landless farmers or unorganized industrial workers. Black southerners also slid further into the abyss, largely abandoned by the Republican party and the federal government and increasingly subjected to economic and political discrimination within the South. Most blacks and many whites were disfranchised. The power of planters and businessmen had increased. And in the future class and racial issues would be considered only within the confines of the Democratic party.

Meanwhile, in the larger context of national parties and policies, the South was moving into a new position. The political upheaval of the 1890s, the Cleveland administration's inability to deal effectively with the debilitating economic crisis, and the critical presidential election of 1896 produced a great realignment of the political system. The realignment transformed the Republicans into the nation's majority party. It also had important repercussions in the South. It ended the Republican party's serious interest in the region's politics, removed the last institutional obstacle to the Solid South, and made the southern Democrats a majority faction in a minority party.

2 The One-Party System

With the completion of disfranchisement, the politics of the southern states had been restructured. The suffrage was drastically limited, the political influence of black belt planters and urban business and professional elements was enhanced, and the new system was safeguarded by a formidable array of registration and voting laws. Literacy tests, the poll tax requirement, and the administration of stringent registration statutes prevented millions of southerners from taking any part in politics. A great majority of those who could vote identified themselves as Democrats, and except for isolated areas, the Republican party had declined to insignificant proportions. Although Populist issues and ideas still appealed to many southerners, their influence was largely confined to factional differences within the Democratic party. Indeed, government in all its aspects was dominated by a single party.

One might conclude, given the place of factional groupings in early twentieth-century southern politics, that the South really had no party system. Nevertheless, each of the region's states had an institution called the "Democratic party," which performed important functions. As V.O. Key later noted, the "party" had an organization, it was the mechanism for making nominations, and it had a hand in the conduct of elections. The nature of the party organizations in the South varied. One or two states such as Virginia were controlled by tight-knit and durable factional organizations. But the Democratic organization in most southern states was amorphous and transitory, depending on the ascendancy of particular leaders and factions at any given moment.

The supreme governing authority of the party in each state was the Democratic convention and the Democratic executive committee. The state convention, which normally met every two years, certified the winners of statewide primary elections, adopted a platform, selected all or part of the state executive committee, and during presidential years chose delegates to the party's national convention, selected a slate of presidential electors, and debated resolutions on national issues. Party affairs between conventions were conducted by the Democratic state committee. There were also county and municipal committees and, in most southern states, an intermediate level of district committees. These were primarily concerned with the arrangements for and the conduct of local and congressional primaries, which also played a role in the election of delegates to the state convention and, in some cases, members of the state executive committee. Ward and precinct organizations were rare, except for the Choctaw Club of New Orleans and a few other city "machines." The Republican party in most southern states had no such elaborate organization.

No feature of the one-party system was more vital than the primary election, which superseded the state convention as a means of selecting nominees for statewide office during the early years of the twentieth century. Primaries were used in some localities as early as the 1870s, apparently as a way to secure the nomination of white candidates, and by the 1890s they were widely employed in nominating county officials. The political convulsion of the 1890s and the pressures that led to disfranchisement and the reinforcement of southern one-partyism hastened their adoption and elaboration. First adopted on a statewide basis by South Carolina in 1896, the primary system spread over the region during the next decade and by the end of the progressive era had been extended, by party regulation or state law, to encompass the nomination of candidates at all levels of government. In Virginia, for example, the state Democratic convention authorized a statewide primary in 1904, and the first such election was held in 1905 to nominate the party's candidates for governor and U.S. senator. A state primary law was enacted in 1912 and amended in 1914. It provided for a uniform primary day—the first Tuesday in August in election years—throughout Virginia. Local officials rather than party representatives were charged with the supervision of the ballot boxes and the printing of the ballots. While the state assumed the costs of conducting statewide primaries, each candidate was assessed a filing fee. The law did not provide for a run-off primary; the winning candidate in each contest needed only a plurality of the votes cast. Participation in statewide primaries was limited to persons who were qualified to vote in the general election. And in order to take part in a primary, a voter must have cast his ballot for the party's nominees in the last general election.

In many respects the primary became the capstone in the southern structure of suffrage restriction and political solidarity. "If we can get an effective suffrage *article* in the new Constitution," wrote a Virginia leader in 1901, "the *primaries* will or can be made to be the real elections."[1] Disfranchisement dealt a final blow to whatever lingering hopes the Republican party had in the South, and nomination in the Democratic primary soon came to be the equivalent of the "real election." Democratic leaders in some southern states established "closed primaries" based on certain tests of party loyalty. The closed primary was not designed to keep out the small number of Republicans but rather, in V.O. Key's words, "to assure the finality of the primary," that is, to keep voters loyal to the party nominees.[2] In a sense, moreover, the adoption of the direct primary was an inevitable consequence of the one-party system in the South since, with the dominance of a single party, "the logic of democracy" required a direct vote on nominees rather than selection by a convention.[3] A majority of the southern states soon introduced the second or "run-off" primary as a means of ensuring majority decisions.

The party primary in the South was represented as a democratic instrumentality, a means of enhancing the ordinary white man's influence and of enabling white voters to divide on issues other than those of race. There was some truth in this claim. The primary facilitated the reabsorption of Populists and other dissidents into Democratic ranks, and it fostered and legitimized greater competition within the party. It also undermined older, oligarchical arrangements, and its adoption was a demand of Democratic reform factions in virtually every southern state. The primary election law of 1902 in Mississippi, for example, weakened the delta's control of Democratic state conventions and party machinery, helped bring the "rednecks" to political power, and set the stage for an era of progressivism for white Mississippians. On the other hand, it is difficult to understand why the liberal proponents of the compulsory primary assumed, in view of the restricted electorate, that the new system would work against the conservative leaders who had long controlled the party. The so-called regular Democrats throughout the South accommodated themselves to the primary. At the same time, the primary system did encourage southern progressives and further their objectives.

Meanwhile, party rules prevented blacks from taking part in Democratic primaries. These elections became *white* primaries. In South Carolina, for instance, every Negro "applying for membership in a Democratic club, or offering to vote in a Democratic primary election, must produce a written statement of ten reputable white men who shall swear that they know of their own knowledge that the applicant or voter cast his ballot for General [Wade] Hampton in 1876 and has voted the Democratic ticket continuously ever since."[4] In Georgia the state Democratic executive committee welcomed "all white voters without regard to party political affiliations who desire to align themselves with the Democratic party and who will, if their right to participate in said primary be challenged, judge themselves to support the nominee of the Democratic party."[5] It was paradoxical that the white primary should serve as the ultimate disfranchising device in the southern states and at the same time provide a new avenue for demagogic appeals to racial passions, particularly in the deep South. This was true in part because the southern primary did a good deal to legitimate individual and factional competition within the party. In practice the primary contributed to a politics of personality and rhetorical excess. It helped create a stylistic division in the ranks of southern politicians, a cleavage between what one historian has described as "respectability and audacity."[6]

Primaries in the early twentieth-century South customarily attracted more attention than the general elections, which were often uncontested, and frequently more votes were cast in the former than in the latter. Yet voter turnout, even among whites, dropped sharply after the turn of the century, and the rate of voter participation in most southern primaries was much below that in the general elections of states having more competitive parties. In Texas the vote in the state Democratic primary during the first two decades of the century ranged from a high of over 40 percent to a low of about 20 percent of the potential electorate. White registration in Louisiana reached only 53 percent in 1904 and in Mississippi only 63 percent in 1908. No more than 35 percent of Alabama's white men voted in that state's hotly contested gubernatorial primary of 1906. J. Morgan Kousser estimates that participation in the primary with the highest turnout in each of the southern states between 1902 and 1910 averaged a mere 30 percent of the total adult population and only 48.8 percent of the white adults. During the years following 1920, about 30 percent of all southern adults generally voted for governor in Democratic primaries. Once elected, moreover, southern politicians could use their incumbency to great advantage. In studying 3,843 primary elections in the South during the first half of the twentieth century, the political scientist Cortez A.M. Ewing found that 41 percent of them were uncontested. "All in all," he concluded, "the data reveals that incumbency is the most important factor in the nomination results of Southern primaries."[7] Even so, the white primary was immensely important as a symbol—a symbol with both racial and democratic connotations.

One aspect of the movement to establish a system of primaries in the South was the use of such contests to secure the popular election of U.S. senators. A favorite Populist proposal and one strongly supported by most reform Democrats, the direct election of senators was endorsed by many southern legislatures around the turn of the century. Long before the ratification of the Seventeenth Amendment in 1913, most southern states had secured the popular election of sena-

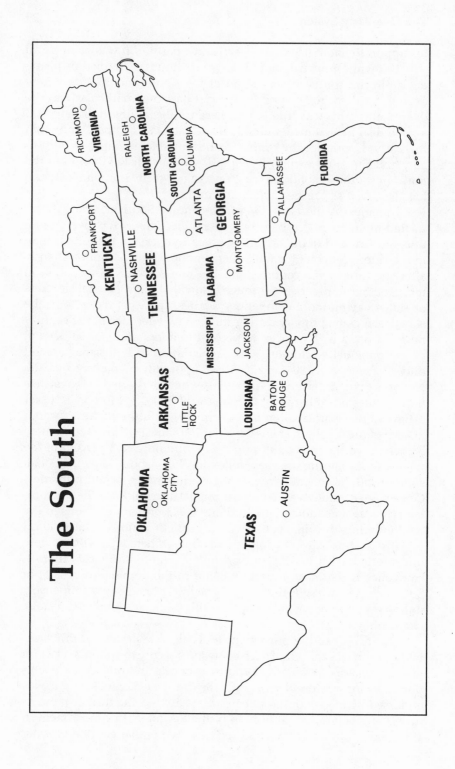

The South

tors through Democratic party rules that bound party members in the legislatures to vote for the top man in special preferential primaries. Proposals for the introduction of the initiative, referendum, and other forms of direct democracy made relatively little progress in the southern states, although such innovations were popular in the Southwest, and Oklahoma and Arkansas adopted the initiative and referendum on a statewide basis.

The broadening sweep of public regulation, gradually bringing party primaries within its scope, eventually came to cover almost all aspects of the electoral process. The southern states enacted laws designed to limit and publicize the campaign expenses of candidates, to outlaw the issuance of free passes by railroads, and to restrict lobbying by corporations and other vested interests. Thus, an Alabama law of 1915 set limits to campaign expenditures and required every candidate to file an itemized statement of expenses as well as a list of contributors and contributions to his campaign. Another statute, also enacted in 1915 and amended in 1919, sought to prevent corporation involvement in Alabama elections and to regulate all forms of campaign advertising. Many of these laws, such as Louisiana's Corrupt-Practices Act of 1912, were not well enforced, testifying to the influence of powerful economic interests.

Although the one-party system soon became characteristic of every state in the South, the makeup of factional politics was different in each state, depending upon such variables as the nature of the economy, intrastate sectionalism, class and racial consciousness, distinctive traditions, and the extent of Republican competition. The quality of a state's political leadership was also important. In general, the early years of the twentieth century were characterized by an upsurge of intraparty conflict in the South, and in a rough way this competition reflected the historic divisions and evolving society of the individual states. There were, broadly speaking, three discernible groups of states in this period. The deep South, stretching from South Carolina to Mississippi, was dominated by a politics of race, disfranchisement, and rural poverty. The upper South, somewhat less concerned with racial issues, was more diversified economically and politically. The Republican party retained some strength in this subregion. The four states west of the Mississippi River constituted a third subregion with fairly distinctive political attributes, including a pronounced strain of agrarian radicalism and more active involvement by farm and labor organizations in political affairs.

The tendencies of the new age in southern politics were clearly revealed in Mississippi.[8] In no other state was preoccupation with the race question so complete, nor did any other part of the South offer more fertile ground for the cultivation of the mystique of the Lost

Cause and the myth of Reconstruction. Blacks were no longer able to vote, the Republican party had all but disappeared, and the dominance of the one-party system could scarcely have been more absolute. Yet the political divisions among white Mississippians during the first part of the century were sharp, and the fierce conflicts of those years possessed a degree of economic and social relevance. In fact, Mississippi experienced a political upheaval and a kind of democratic triumph during this period.

Geographical contracts provided the foundation for a powerful intrastate sectionalism in Mississippi. The most favored section was the delta, a rich and vibrant cotton empire extending two hundred miles from Memphis to Vicksburg. There were also a few plantation counties along the eastern part of the state, but in general the land beyond the delta was poor. Eastward from the Yazoo River lay a series of bluffs, rolling tablelands, and sand-clay hills. Much of the southern half of the state, except for the relatively small coastal terrace, was covered with timber, and the piney woods of the southeast were rapidly being felled by the great lumber companies. Antagonism between the hills and the delta had long manifested itself in the politics of the Magnolia State. As a rule, the planters of the delta and black counties, in alliance with commercial and industrial interests, arrayed themselves against the small farmers of the hills and piney woods.

A "redneck" revolt, encouraged by populism and the rise of a reform faction in the Democratic party, threatened to shift the locus of power in the state's politics at the turn of the century. One of the leaders in this movement was James Kimble Vardaman, the dominant figure in Mississippi politics during the first decade and a half of this century. Following the enactment of a state primary law in 1902, Vardaman began a long campaign that culminated in his nomination as the Democratic choice for governor. A magnificent actor, he projected a magnetic personality on the platform, and his swelling oratory lifted his audiences out of themselves. "The White Chief," as he was called, combined an attack on the trusts and special "interests" with an assault on the hapless black man. His campaigns divided white Mississippians into those who supported him and those who opposed him. Another champion of the rednecks was Theodore Gilmore Bilbo, who won the governorship in 1915. Bilbo, a young politician from the piney woods of the south, rose to prominence as an ardent Vardaman man, first as one of his lieutenants in the state senate and then as lieutenant governor. A diminutive dynamo, he was a skillful stump speaker, a master of invective and scurrility who delighted in the rough-and-tumble of Mississippi politics.

What Albert D. Kirwan described as a period of "almost incessant agrarian revolt" in the late nineteenth century finally engulfed the state. While the conflict between the hills and the delta and between insurgent and regular Democrats may not have been as clear-cut as Kirwan thought, the primary election law of 1902 and other changes revolutionized political campaigning, made possible the rise of new leaders, and created a new and more competitive factionalism in the state's Democratic party. The number of white voters remained relatively high, at least in primary elections, and such democratic procedures as mandatory primaries, direct election of U.S. senators, the initiative and referendum, and an elective judiciary were adopted by the state's lawmakers. These developments broke the domination of the black counties in statewide elections, though without greatly diminishing their influence in the legislature. In the altered political setting of the early 1900s, organized farmers, businessmen, teachers, and other groups brought new issues to the fore and in many instances obtained their objectives. A series of reform governors developed legislative programs and secured the enactment of noteworthy progressive measures. They also extended and institutionalized, through legal and quasi-legal means, an increasingly harsh system of racial segregation and discrimination against blacks. Their factional opponents, meanwhile, managed more often than not to defeat progressive legislation and to weaken the implementation of progressive statutes.

Alabama shared many of the economic, ethnic, and political qualities of Mississippi. One of the dynamics of its politics was a hardy and persistent sectionalism. Spread across the south central part of the state were about a dozen counties known as the black belt, an area of rich soil and a heavy concentration of Negroes. On the south the black belt sloped off to the sand hills and the coastal plain, while on the north it was absorbed by rising foothills and, in the northeast, mountains. The seat of Alabama's plantation system in the antebellum period, the black belt continued in the twentieth century to be the center of the state's social and political power. In addition to their wealth and prestige, black belt leaders enjoyed a significant advantage in the disproportionate representation given their section in the legislative apportionment of 1901. The piedmont and hill sections to the north, as well as the wiregrass country of the southeast, had long distrusted and opposed the black belt. Although northern Alabama was the fastest growing part of the state in the late nineteenth and early twentieth centuries, the black belt frequently allied itself with the industrialists and financiers of Birmingham—the "big mules"—in order to control state politics. Localism—a pattern of "friends and neighbors" support—was also an important aspect of one-party politics in Alabama.

Intense factionalism in the 1890s, reflecting the state's sectional divisions, was carried forward in attenuated form into the twentieth century. One wing of the Democratic party was identified with the regular, conservative leaders; the other was oriented toward agrarian reform and such causes as free silver, primary elections, and railroad regulation. But this Bourbon–agrarian reform bifactionalism was soon modified. Unlike certain county rings or "courthouse crowds," which sometimes stayed in power for decades, political factions at the state level depended upon the success of a particular candidate. Few state officials remained in office very long, since most of them, including the governor, were constitutionally ineligible to succeed themselves. Other factors also affected the older bifactionalism. The economy was becoming more diversified, and many Alabamians, perhaps a majority of them, were committed to the New South ideas of economic development and thus were reluctant to endorse radical agrarian schemes. The development of urban and middle-class groups, motivated by entrepreneurial and professional concerns and a growing interest in solving social problems, injected a new element into the crucible of political decision making. The emergence of railroad regulation as a compelling political issue and the rise of a new leader in connection with that issue were also important in the manifestation of a different factional pattern in the state's Democratic party.

Braxton Bragg Comer, a businessman and a political newcomer, gradually assumed leadership of the incipient movement to secure more effective regulation of railroads in Alabama. In 1904 Comer was elected president of the state railroad commission, and two years later he threw himself into a heated campaign to win the governorship. In railroad regulation, one historian has written, the political neophyte had found an issue that could bring together "the interests of Black Belt planters, substantial farmers, town merchants, small manufacturers, and the professional men who identified with these groups."[9] Comer won a smashing victory in the Democratic primary; his forces gained control of the party machinery and committed themselves to a broad program of reform. As governor, he moved vigorously and with a good deal of success to regulate railroad rates in Alabama. But well before the end of his four-year term, a new issue—statewide prohibition—replaced railroad regulation as the center of reform controversy. Comer became a champion of prohibition, and while there was a general correspondence between the supporters of that reform and those seeking stronger railroad controls, the question provoked great confusion and bitterness. It also brought setbacks to "Comerism," in 1909 in the defeat of a constitutional amendment providing for prohibition, in 1910 in the defeat of the prohibition candidate for governor, and in 1914 when Comer himself failed in an attempt to win a second term as governor. Nevertheless, Comer's leadership was a central issue in Alabama politics during the decade after 1904, and his policies were a potent factor in creating bifactional groupings in the state's dominant party.

Somewhat surprisingly, Alabama politics became more open and more competitive after 1901, notwithstanding disfranchisement and the restriction of the electorate. This was true, at least, for the property-owning, professional, and middle-class elements. Although a coalition of black belt and urban-industrial interests frequently exerted controlling influence in political affairs, the exercise of political power was not monolithic. The introduction of a state primary system, including the popular election of U.S. senators, paved the way for new political leaders and encouraged the consideration of diverse issues by the white electorate. Many business and urban groups, as well as black belt planters and organized farmers, now found it possible to advance their legislative concerns and to join in the pursuit of broader "reforms." The cement that held these elements together in loose and shifting combinations was their common commitment to organizational tactics and a measure of state intervention, as well as their growing acceptance of the idea that social institutions needed to be modernized and made more efficient. Still, the pluralistic nature of the state's interest-group politics should not be exaggerated. The most influential elements in the structure of political power in Alabama were planters and "big mules" and their urban allies, who were usually able to limit the scope of decision making in state government and more often than not to control the outcome of major elections and policy debates.

None of the states of the lower South displayed more vigorous factionalism in Democratic party politics than Georgia. The cleavage in the Georgia Democracy revolved around an aggressive and ambitious lawyer from Atlanta named Hoke Smith, who emerged as the leader of a popular antirailroad movement and who in 1906 was swept into the governorship on a reform platform that included Negro disfranchisement. The intense struggle that disrupted the party for a decade after 1905 was encouraged by the rivalry between the Atlanta *Journal*, which Smith had once owned and published, and the Atlanta *Constitution*, whose editor, Clark Howell, was a legislative leader, longtime member of the Democratic national committee, and gubernatorial aspirant. Smith's determined quest for power shattered the complacency of the state's established hierarchy, brought a surge of excitement and anticipation to the electorate, and forced most Georgians into two Democratic factions. Although Smith dealt Howell a humiliating defeat in the primary election of 1906, the anti-Smith faction won its share of victories. In fact, neither wing of the party seemed able to secure complete control of the state's politics.

One reason for this inconclusive struggle and for the blurring of Georgia's Democratic factionalism after 1914 was the role of Thomas E. Watson, the state's leading Populist in the 1890s. In 1903 Watson began to exert a decisive influence on the course of the state's politics, first by throwing his support to Hoke Smith and then by becoming Smith's implacable enemy. Thousands of former Populists remained loyal to Watson and returned with him to the Democratic party; in close elections like that of 1908, his voice was sometimes the deciding factor in the outcome. Watson and other Populists were also instrumental in popularizing reform issues such as railroad regulation, abolition of the convict lease system, and Negro disfranchisement. By 1912 Watson's authority in the Democratic party was so great that few statewide politicians dared oppose him. He made and unmade governors. The agrarian leader seized upon such events as the Leo Frank case[10] to demonstrate his appeal to the Georgia masses, and he further confused the state's politics by lashing out at the Wilson administration and depicting himself as a martyr in opposing the national government's wartime restraints.

There were also other ingredients in the volatile mixture of early twentieth-century Georgia politics. One of these was the tyranny of racism. Skillful use of racial issues by agitators like Tom Watson and Hoke Smith not only contributed to a terrible race riot in Atlanta in 1906 and to disfranchisement but also helped produce the average Georgian's deep-seated and distorted complex of racial fear and hypersensitivity. Sectional conflict, which found expression in occasional charges in the southern part of the state that the more industrialized and urbanized region to the north got more than its share of statewide offices, was not a major theme in Georgia politics. More important was a pronounced urban-rural conflict. Georgia's commercial and industrial growth after 1880 and the neglect of its large farm population sharpened the impact of the agrarian revolt in the state. But if Henry W. Grady's New South creed appeared to be gaining ascendancy over Tom Watson's agrarianism in later years, Georgia's county-unit system gave the state's many rural counties a disproportionate influence in primary elections.[11] When the Smith faction endeavored to scrap the county-unit arrangement and to replace it with a "direct popular vote," Watson stirred up the country people by predicting that Atlanta would soon dominate the state's political life. The issue was one that could be invoked repeatedly, even after the nominating scheme had been safeguarded by legislative act in 1917. The system itself enhanced the political power of Georgia's county-seat governing class, which incorporated the planters and the local elites in the state's hundreds of villages and small towns.

Politics and political reform in Georgia were strongly conditioned by the introduction of the primary system, the development of a fierce bifactionalism in the Democratic party, a substantial infusion of agrarian dissatisfaction, the anomalous role of Tom Watson, and the challenging leadership of Hoke Smith as a self-styled progressive. Although the power of the countryside and rural hamlet remained strong, urban pressures, particularly in Atlanta, and organizations like the Atlanta Freight Bureau were also important in state politics early in the new century. Indeed, the small town elite had much in common with the "uptown" leadership in the cities and larger towns, including a commitment to economic growth, social stability, and "modernizing" improvements. The result was a politics in which new issues arose and a variety of interests emerged. While party factions and interest groups were constantly shifting during this era, the demands on state and city government steadily increased, and the pressure for reform mounted.

South Carolina politics also embodied the main characteristics of the deep South pattern. Underlying the clash and clamor of politics in the Palmetto State were sharp sectional, class, and racial differences. Sectionalism was an old phenomenon, emerging in its earliest form in colonial times with the demand of the back country for self-government and equality with the dominant coastal region. In time a fairly clear-cut division developed between the coastal plain and the piedmont plateau, which stretched in a northwesterly direction from the fall line to the foothills of the Blue Ridge Mountains. This sectionalism reflected but did not altogether coincide with a hardy strain of class antagonism. During the late nineteenth century, this antipathy was perpetuated and in some respects intensified by the continuing influence of the old aristocracy, in combination with the rising financial and industrial interests, on the one hand, and the growing farm dependency and mushrooming factory working class, on the other. By 1900 three out of every five farmers in South Carolina were tenants, and by 1914 one-fourth of the state's population lived in textile mill villages. The political upheaval of the 1890s brought the rise of new and more vigorous politicians, but the agrarian revolt was complicated by the pervading sense of the black man's presence.

The most significant of these leaders was the redoubtable Benjamin Ryan Tillman, the principal architect of disfranchisement in South Carolina. A rude and one-eyed farmer from Edgefield in the upcountry, "Pitchfork Ben" Tillman, as he was called, was a leader of skill, audacity, and explosive energy. He led the embattled farmers to victory in 1890, aroused the upcountrymen against the Charleston aristocracy and government by "gentlemen," and provoked the bitter hostility of business and professional elements. His leadership was a powerful force in causing South Carolina Democrats to divide into

two clearly defined factions. Yet "Tillmanism" offered no radical solutions, avoided third-party politics, and busied itself with capturing
control of the Democratic party.

By 1910, when a flamboyant upcountry politician named Coleman
Livingston Blease was elected governor, Tillman was no longer the
predominant figure in the state's politics. Blease, a professed heir of
"Pitchfork Ben," was extraordinarily effective in winning the loyalty
of textile mill workers, a group Tillman had contemptuously called
that "damned factory class." Ambitious and opportunistic, a man of
forceful personality and a colorful oratorical style, "Cole" Blease appealed to the racial, religious, and class prejudices of the South Carolina masses. It should be noted that, in contrast to the practice of other
southern states, South Carolina did not require those who took part
in its primaries to meet the qualifications for the general election.
There were few obstacles to participation in the state's primary elections, and most white men voted in at least some of these contests.
Blease, in the words of a contemporary newspaperman, "articulated
the poor man's unexpressed emotions, ambitions and disgruntle-
ments, did it garishly, did it sentimentally, did it courageously."[12] A
recent interpreter concludes that the upcountry politician brought to
a focus "the sharpest class confrontation between white men" ever
to appear in South Carolina.[13] However negative his philosophy and
program may have been, he extended the meaning of white democracy and helped produce a dramatic increase in the voting participation of white South Carolinians. He was also a powerful factor in
the creation of a new dual factionalism in the state's politics.

Unlike several other southern states, South Carolina failed to produce a dynamic progressive governor in the first years of the twentieth
century. Tillman remained powerful for a time, but he demonstrated
little interest in social reform. Blease enlivened state politics and
aroused the interest of many ordinary South Carolinians, but he was
not an advocate of a reform program or of new public services. There
was still no effective reform coalition in the state: political leadership
was lacking, the rural and industrial elites were generally reactionary
and defensive, and the middle-class and professional elements in the
cities and towns were not yet well organized. A reform breakthrough
finally came with Richard Irvine Manning, an anti-Blease leader who
was elected governor in 1914. As governor, Manning became a crusader against lawlessness, something of a social reformer, and un-
questionably the state's most constructive governor during the two
decades after 1900. He succeeded in broadening support for change
and carried through a more positive program based on expanding
state services, greater administrative efficiency, and the modernization of social institutions.

The fifth deep South state in the early 1900s was Florida. Although the state's population was small—only slightly more than half a million in 1900—its geography did not facilitate speedy communication or easy assembly of people on a statewide basis. Innumerable lakes and marshes made travel difficult, and distances were very great. While it was only a subdued note in the clash of factional politics before 1920, a distinctive sectionalism was emerging in Florida. It was a north-south cleavage, in which the older section, bordering Georgia and Alabama, was opposed by the growing peninsular region. The newer and less developed areas to the south were more diversified in their economy than north Florida, less "southern" in population, less traditional in outlook, and more absorbed in the New South approach to development. Because of the state's obvious transportation needs and the spreading enthusiasm for the development of the central and southern parts of the peninsula, legislators and administrative officials were reluctant to apply stringent regulations to railroads and other corporations. Yet a current of agrarian radicalism carried over from the 1890s into the new century, and an anticorporation bias supplied a rallying ground for political reformers. Contemporaries referred to the conflict between "corporation" and "anticorporation" Democrats.

In the amorphous and kaleidoscopic milieu of southern politics, wrote V.O. Key in 1949, "only the most able—or spectacular—personality can function effectively in the organization of a stable following."[14] Such a personality was Florida's Napoleon Bonaparte Broward, who created the most enduring faction among the state's Democrats in this period. He became a hero of the common man, a champion of the "Crackers" against the railroad interests and "land pirates," and a forceful leader of the anticorporation faction. Broward was elected governor in 1904. His administration sponsored a number of reforms, including an audacious scheme to drain the Everglades. His opponents condemned him as a demagogic radical whose innovations would frighten away much-needed capital. Broward's influence continued after his death in 1910, both because of the impetus his leadership had given to a bifactional grouping of the voters and because of the way it had encouraged Florida progressivism. Park Trammell, one of Broward's lieutenants, was elected governor in 1912. But by the time Trammell left office in 1917, the Broward era was clearly drawing to a close, and the old factional lines were disappearing.

A new leader came to the fore about that time in the person of Sidney J. Catts. A Baptist minister, insurance salesman, and political unknown, Catts was elected governor as an independent in 1916. He capitalized on prohibition sentiment, fear of what he called the

"Catholic menace," opposition to the enforcement of the state fish and oyster conservation law, and the controversial Democratic primary that denied him the party nomination in 1916. The stormy Catts, disrespectful of the established political order and of social pretension, in the manner of Coleman L. Blease, plunged the state into four years of turmoil. Though identified with the support of penal reforms, public health programs, educational improvement, labor unions, and woman suffrage, he made full use of the spoils system and fought many battles with the legislature and the press. Catts suffered an overwhelming defeat in an attempt to win a Senate seat in 1920, and he was unable to perpetuate his influence in Florida politics. Politics in the Peninsula State thereafter became calmer but also more conservative.

Virginia was part of a subregion that differed markedly from the deep South. Except for tobacco, a major staple in the southern part of the state, the Old Dominion was not extensively involved in the South's cash crop agriculture. Tenancy was actually declining in the years after 1900, and such diversified activities as livestock production and truck farming were growing rapidly. While still largely rural, Virginia was undergoing notable industrial development and urban growth. At the same time, its characteristic social and political outlook was thoroughly traditional. Indeed, no other southern state was so dedicated to cavalier ideals—to the notions of personal honor, gentility, and paternalism. To the concepts of limited government, state rights, and white supremacy was added a conviction that government was the responsibility not of ordinary men but of the best families. Style was important in politics, and a measure of decorum was expected. In Virginia, the home of Robert E. Lee and the Confederate capital, there was a special veneration for the heroes of the Lost Cause, and this too blended into the nostalgia for the great days of the past.

Virginia politics incorporated a strong intrastate sectionalism. Moving from east to west, one encountered the familiar geographical divisions of the Southeast—tidewater, piedmont, and mountains. The plains of the Tidewater gave way, in the north, to rolling hills and, in the south, to the Southside, a crescent-shaped black belt whose base extended for a long distance along the North Carolina border. Farther west lay the Blue Ridge Mountains and beyond them the Allegheny highlands. In the southwest was a large upland area that reached into the very center of the Appalachians. This was Republican country. The minority party normally elected at least one congressman and polled a third or more of the votes in presidential elections. The Republican presence had a disciplinary effect on the state's Democrats.

The basis for a dual factionalism in the Democratic party was laid in the 1890s by Thomas Staples Martin, a little-known railroad lawyer who was elected to the U.S. Senate in 1893. Unpretentious and diffident, a conservative but above all else a political pragmatist, Martin was a skillful organizer and an able tactician. His leadership was strengthened by a cadre of shrewd and dedicated lieutenants such as Henry D. Flood and Claude A. Swanson. Martin's organization was a disciplined hierarchy whose sources of control included the legislature, Democratic party machinery, and strong outposts at the city and county levels. The legislature was a powerful institution in Virginia, not least because it appointed the members of the state's several courts. The county and city court judges in turn appointed a number of key local officials, including the electoral boards. The Martin organization worked closely with the important elective officials of the various counties, who looked to the machine's control of the legislature for protection against changes that might affect their authority or compensation, and these courthouse "cliques" were usually able to furnish votes to the machine. The Martin faction enjoyed great strength in rural areas, and with the small electorate after 1902, the local leaders were strategically placed to provide the margin of victory in most district and state elections. So small was the Virginia electorate that state employees and officeholders cast about one-third of the total vote in state elections between 1905 and 1948.

By the turn of the century, an increasing number of "independents" were challenging the regular Democrats led by Senator Martin. They demanded clean elections, a party primary system, and stricter regulation of railroads and industrial corporations. In 1901 an independent named Andrew Jackson Montague won the governorship. His administration proved to be moderately progressive and was identified with advances in public education, the adoption of primary elections, and support of the good roads movement. The "independent versus machine" struggle continued for a decade or more, but the regulars won almost all of the important statewide races. Despite the enmity between the two factions, they were not divided by sharp ideological differences. Furthermore, organization leaders gradually accepted the major reforms advocated by their opponents, and they were adept at neutralizing or absorbing their enemies. A bitter opponent of the machine named Westmoreland Davis managed to win the governorship in 1917, but he was unable to build an organization of his own and was decisively defeated in a bid for the Senate in 1922. Following Martin's death in 1919, the organization seemed momentarily to be adrift, but after a brief period it acquired a new pilot in Harry Flood Byrd.

Another of the upper South states was North Carolina. Less involved in the plantation economy than most southern states, its economic life was correspondingly more diversified. Although its inhabitants were less bound by regional traditions than Virginians or South Carolinians, their politics turned again and again to the explosive issue of race. The black man's part in the fusion movement of the 1890s and the white supremacy campaign that overthrew fusionism in 1898 and 1900 were too vivid in the minds of North Carolina Democrats to permit the abandonment of race as an issue. The uneven distribution of the black population was one of the aggravating factors in the political sectionalism of the Old North State. In antebellum times the plantation system was centered in the eastern section, and that area was far more ardent in support of secession than the western part of the state, where farms were small and slaves were few. Unionist sentiment and Republicanism became strong in the extreme western counties. The fastest growing section in the early 1900s was the Piedmont, which served as a transition between plains and mountains and, after disfranchisement, between Democrats and Republicans. While the Republican party no longer had any real chance of winning statewide elections, it usually attracted about a third of the state's votes and controlled local government in some of the western counties.

An inchoate bifactionalism characterized North Carolina Democrats in the 1890s, with a rough division being manifest on such issues as the regulation of corporations, free silver, and the leadership of William Jennings Bryan. Conservative Democrats were generally ascendant. The chairman of the Democratic state committee and the strategist who led the party to victory in the white supremacy campaigns of 1898 and 1900 was Furnifold M. Simmons. He headed a group of powerful politicians who directed the party's course during most of the quarter-century after 1900. Another source of support for the regular Democrats was their close relationship with financial and business leaders. The Simmons faction was also identified with a group of able young leaders who came to public attention in the party battles of the late 1890s. The most important of these new men was Charles Brantley Aycock, a politician of great eloquence and popularity who was elected governor in 1900. Aycock gained a reputation as North Carolina's "educational governor," and it was during his administration that a spirit of self-examination in public affairs began to bring significant changes to the state.

After 1905 the reform movement in North Carolina quickened, the "machine" was subjected to mounting criticism, and an array of progressive legislation was enacted. In 1908 William W. Kitchin, an antiorganization Democrat, won the governorship. The independents failed, however, to build a strong organization that could overcome the regulars. Simmons and his allies remained in control, although the familiar factionalism in the party seemed to be losing strength by 1917. Political affairs in North Carolina during the progressive era bore the heavy imprint of the race issue, disfranchisement, a restricted electorate, and a long-established Democratic hierarchy. The continued existence of a minority party, ineffective as it was, brought a degree of discipline and coherence to state politics. Important also was the diversified nature of the economy, which fostered the emergence of a variety of interest groups, including organized shippers, the Farmers' Union, and social welfare elements. A substantial body of social reforms was enacted. Ultimately, Tarheel progressivism was shaped by the support of shifting coalitions that changed with different issues and circumstances, by the rough consensus on popular reforms that developed among political leaders, and by the state's basic conservatism.

Perhaps the most diversified southern state was Tennessee, whose narrow territory reached more than five hundred miles from the mountain town of Bristol in the extreme northeast to the delta city of Memphis on the Mississippi River. The state was marked off into three grand divisions that were set apart from each other by distinctive geographical, cultural, and political characteristics. East Tennessee, a land of mountains, plateaus, and valleys, had not been suitable for slavery. An area of small farms and increasing industrialization in the late nineteenth century, it had opposed secession, supported the Union, and become Republican in its politics. The western division, lying between the Tennessee River and the Mississippi, was the center of the state's cotton production and had the heaviest concentration of blacks. Although it contained the largest city in the state, West Tennessee was the most rural of the three divisions. It had been ardent in its support of secession and war and was strongly attached to the Democratic party. Middle Tennessee was comprised of the highland rim and the central basin, a region that extended from the Cumberland Plateau in the east to the Tennessee River in the west. It was dominated by Nashville and the fertile bluegrass basin in which the capital city was located. Middle Tennessee's economy was more varied than that of West Tennessee, but it had supported the Confederacy and was stoutly Democratic in its politics.

The Republican party was an institution of greater consequence in Tennessee than in any of the other ex-Confederate states. It controlled a majority of the county governments and usually won two congressional districts in the eastern division, as well as a few counties along the highland rim of West Tennessee. Nevertheless, in state government and statewide elections, one-partyism had become the rule in Tennessee. Republicans still suffered from their identification with Reconstruction and black participation in politics, and they were sometimes weakened by vexatious internal strife. The operation of the poll tax, the registration laws, and the Democratically controlled election system also hurt the Republicans and diminished voter participation in general. Among the state's Democrats in the late nineteenth century, an industrial New South element frequently clashed with the party's Bourbon leadership, which disdained the New South creed and remained loyal to a Jeffersonian philosophy and to Old South traditions. On the other hand, agrarian radicalism was relatively weak in the Volunteer State. Nor did "liberal" and "conservative" factions of the sort that developed in Virginia and some other states emerge distinctly in Tennessee during the early years of the new century.

This situation began to change in 1905 and 1906 with a burst of factional maneuvering among Democrats and hard-fought contests for a U.S. Senate seat and the governorship. In 1908 Gov. Malcolm R. Patterson and Edward Ward Carmack, a former U.S. senator, engaged in a fierce struggle for the Democratic gubernatorial nomination. Carmack was defeated and a few months later was killed on the streets of Nashville by one of Governor Patterson's friends. Since Patterson and his followers controlled the governorship and the party machinery, many of the Carmack partisans, calling themselves independent Democrats, refused to participate in regular party affairs and endorsed Ben W. Hooper, the Republican candidate for governor in 1910. Hooper was elected and managed to win reelection two years later with the support of the independent Democrats. By 1914 this period of schism in the majority party was about over, and in that year a reunited and chastened Democratic party came back into control of the state government.

Independent and regular Democrats sometimes disagreed over such matters as "machine rule," the need for a primary election law, and the nomination of Woodrow Wilson for president in 1912. But the most telling issue in separating independents and regulars and the one that served as a catalytic agent in creating the factional alignment for a decade after 1905 was the struggle over statewide prohibition of alcoholic beverages. Although prohibition was adopted by the legislature in 1909, the whole problem continued to dominate Tennessee politics until the election of 1914. Governor Hooper, a reformer and a vigorous opponent of the "whiskey evil," led a movement that possessed some of the aspects of a religious crusade. Yet he found it difficult to enforce the state law, particularly in the larger cities. The problem was further complicated by the role of Mayor Edward H. Crump of Memphis, whose organization made him a formidable protagonist in Democratic politics and state government. The intense controversy surrounding the prohibition issue and the disruption of the Democratic party in Tennessee make it hard to relate the social reformism of this period to political and factional divisions in the state. There was, in fact, increasing support for "reform" from both parties and from various segments of the Democratic party after 1905. While lacking a militant antirailroad campaign like that of Alabama and North Carolina, Tennesseans were nonetheless quite responsive to "the rhetoric of reform."

Kentucky, one writer has observed, "waited until the war was over to secede from the Union."[15] There was considerable truth in this hyperbole. The Democrats swept the elections of 1866, and for a generation Kentucky was virtually a one-party state. Though more southern than northern, it was a border state. Its subdivisions were similar to those of Tennessee: the mountains in the east, the Bluegrass region in the middle, and the generally flat farming area of the west. After the Civil War, many of the former Whig slaveholders, who were mostly located in the Bluegrass country, moved into the Democratic party, where they joined with the small farmers of western Kentucky to give their party predominance in state politics. The conservative leadership of the Democratic party also reflected the political leverage of Kentucky's rapidly growing industrialists.

The severity of the depression of the 1890s, the appeal of the nativist and anti-Catholic American Protective Association, and the increasing disunity within the Democratic party enabled the Republicans to elect a governor in 1895 and to carry the state for William McKinley in 1896. Always ready to take advantage of the majority party's factionalism, they had become a serious competitor of the Democrats. Kentucky Republicanism was strongest in the east, where the Whig party and Unionist sympathies had centered. The state's blacks, who made up about 13 percent of the population in 1900, were also staunch Republicans, and in Kentucky they were not disfranchised. Although unable to gain control of the legislature, the Republicans won the governorship in 1899, 1907, and 1919. There were usually one or two representatives and occasionally a senator from Kentucky in Congress during this period.

If the regular Democrats were challenged by the Republicans in the 1890s, they were also opposed by a coalescing group of dissident Democrats. The struggle that ensued was both ideological and organizational. It was a conflict between the conservative planters of the Bluegrass counties and their corporate allies in the cities, on the one hand, and the populistic western farmers and urban workers, on the other. The issues involved the money question, the regulation of corporations, and new election laws, but the immediate stake was control of the party. The first phase of this internecine strife culminated in 1900 with the assassination of William Goebel, a leader of the reform Democrats. In the tumultuous aftermath of that spectacular incident, Goebel became a martyr in the eyes of many Kentuckians, and a stringent law to regulate the state's railroads was quickly enacted. But the bifactional groupings that emerged after 1900 were less distinct than they were at the height of Goebel's leadership. John C.W. Beckham, a Democrat who served as governor for almost eight years, made his peace with the Bluegrass conservatives and the business interests.

James B. McCreary, a more reform-minded Democrat than Beckham, won the governorship in 1911. He established a progressive record as chief executive. Yet his reforms and the anticorporation campaigns of agrarian leaders like Augustus O. Stanley did not mean that the industrial and commercial interests were curbed in the Bluegrass State. In general, the conservative Democrats of the middle section and the Republicans in the eastern part of the state dominated Kentucky politics after 1900, just as the Bluegrass and western regions had combined to control public affairs before the end of the 1890s. Still, there were progressive tendencies in Kentucky, particularly among social reform leaders and organizations, and the state legislature did approve a direct primary system, greater controls over corporations, modest labor and prison reforms, increased support for schools and highways, and a modicum of tax reform. At the same time, however, the diverse character of the state's economy, the great power exerted by railroads and other business interests, and the shifting nature of Democratic factionalism seem to have limited progressivism.

The other states of the early twentieth-century South lay west of the Mississippi River. Arkansas was perhaps the least characteristic of the four-state group. At the turn of the century, it was an overwhelmingly rural and agricultural state. Its largest city, Little Rock, contained only 65,000 people as late as 1920. Arkansas had already begun to acquire an image of poverty, of slow economic development, of what one of its historians later referred to as "recalcitrant backwardness and resistance to change."[16] It was divided, geographically and to some extent culturally, into two major sections. A line drawn diagonally from the northeast to the southwest, passing through Little Rock in the middle of the state, would separate the northern and western highlands from the southern and eastern plains. One part of the state consisted of hills, mountains, and valleys, while the other was made up of delta, prairie, and flatlands. One was the habitat of small farmers and mountaineers, the other of cotton planters, black tenants, and rice growers. Despite the division between the highlanders and the residents of lowland areas, political sectionalism in Arkansas was less pronounced than in several other southern states.

The principal basis for political division in early twentieth-century Arkansas was the cultural split between town and country.

Arkansas politics after the Civil War mirrored the familiar sequence of Reconstruction, Redemption, and Redeemer control. Although the Republican party was strong in several northwestern counties, it offered no serious challenge to the majority party in the post-Reconstruction period. But by the mid-1890s, the established Democrats were beginning to lose their hold on the state's politics. The opposition came largely from within their own party and was stimulated by the force of agrarian protest. Then, at the end of the century, a new and spectacular leader arose to articulate the state's agrarianism and to shape its politics for more than a decade. He was Jeff Davis, a boyish looking lawyer who was elected state attorney general in 1898. Davis identified himself with the growing enthusiasm for a system of primary elections, and he created a sensation by launching a host of antimonopoly suits against insurance companies and other corporations. His antitrust campaign catapulted him into the governorship in 1900; he was twice reelected and went to the U.S. Senate in 1907. Thoroughly at home with the white dispossessed, Davis was, in the words of a contemporary writer, "surcharged with personal magnetism. He makes the people think he is persecuted for their sake, and stands between them and oppression."[17] No politician had ever aroused the Arkansas proletariat like this "Karl Marx for Hill Billies," for he "evoked a hierarchy of angels and demons in which there were no neuters."[18] He set the "rednecks" of the backwoods against the "high-collared crowd" of the city. He was firmly rooted in the agrarian folk culture of the South.

Although Jeff Davis and his friends controlled the party machinery during the early years of the century, they were unable to perpetuate their hold on state politics. The electorate tended for a time to divide itself into two camps on the basis of Davis's dramatic politics, but it soon lapsed into an amorphous and shifting factionalism with little coherence or continuity. Nevertheless, Davis broke the custom of organizing state campaigns around courthouse cliques and took his electioneering to the voters at the grass roots. Furthermore, as one scholar has argued, the Arkansas leader "pushed the ideological center of the [Democratic] party well to the left. And he politicized a generation of Arkansas farmers whose faith in political action had been flagging, stroking their egos and giving them a renewed sense of dignity and hope."[19] Near the end of the progressive era, a new face came to the fore. It was that of Charles H. Brough, a professor of economics and sociology at the University of Arkansas who was elected governor in 1916. Brough was a reformer, and he directed a major fiscal reorganization and a notable extension of state activities.

But his leadership failed to alter the basic pattern of the state's politics. While there was a strain of agrarian radicalism in Arkansas politics in the first part of the twentieth century, it was offset by a drastically restricted electorate, by the entrenched position of local elites, and by the conservatism of executive and legislative leaders in Little Rock.

Louisiana was another of the southwestern states. It produced two great cash crops, contained a large French and Catholic population, and had a powerful urban machine. Much of the state was made up of river bottomlands, lakes, and swamps. Flowing south, the Mississippi and Red rivers eventually joined to form a Y-shaped drainage basin. Most of the northern part of the state, except for the alluvial river bottoms, was comprised of hilly lands whose inferior soils were cultivated by poor white farmers and tenants. North Louisiana was cotton country, the most productive of which was the counterpart of Mississippi's delta—a land of rich soil and many blacks. Another staple was produced in south Louisiana, in the flood plain between the Red River and the Gulf; this was sugar country, the scene of a capitalist and large-scale planting economy. Late in the nineteenth century still another staple crop—rice—was successfully introduced to the prairies of southwestern Louisiana. Commercial lumbering was important in many parts of the Pelican State, and the production of petroleum became significant in the second decade of the new century.

The pattern of the state's politics revealed three geographical components: north Louisiana, south Louisiana (more precisely the triangular-shaped area from Lake Charles in the southwest to New Orleans in the east to Alexandria in the north), and Orleans Parish (with the city of New Orleans). There was a rural-urban conflict in Louisiana, and the rural elements, particularly in the northern section, feared and distrusted the economic and political power of New Orleans. A religious and cultural contrast—between the Creole-Catholic south and the Anglo-Protestant north—cut across economic and social lines.

Although the conservative Democrats who ruled Louisiana during the generation following Reconstruction were plagued by sharp factional divisions, they carried out the wishes of the planters, the commercial and financial interests centered in New Orleans, and the railroad and lumber companies. Resentment at this state of affairs fanned the fires of agrarian radicalism in the 1890s and helped precipitate a crisis for the established Democrats. The People's party was strong in the hill parishes of north Louisiana, and in the state elections of 1894 and 1896, it undertook a fusion campaign with the Republicans, themselves a renewed threat to the majority party following a decade of steady decline. The regular Democrats managed to win both the state and national elections in 1896, and they then moved to prevent a recurrence of the Populist-Republican challenge. They accepted some of the reform proposals put forward by their critics and carried out a process of disfranchisement. The disfranchisement of blacks and the introduction of statewide primaries altered the relative voting strength of the state in favor of New Orleans and the white upland parishes, at the expense of the planters, who were no longer able to dominate party nominations. Yet, unlike its immediate neighbors to the north and east, Louisiana failed to produce a charismatic champion of the poor whites and rednecks in the manner of Jeff Davis and James K. Vardaman.

One reason for this failure was the important role of New Orleans in the state's politics. The city had a population of almost 300,000 people in 1900, and Orleans Parish normally accounted for nearly one-fourth of the electorate and representation in the general assembly. Politics in the Crescent City was dominated by the Choctaw Club or "Old Regulars," an organization led by Mayor Martin Behrman for almost two decades after 1904. Behrman and his assistants ran a disciplined machine and one that mobilized the immigrant and lower-class voters, worked closely with financial and corporate interests, and assumed a "let live" attitude toward gambling, drinking, and prostitution. While the Choctaws became a consistent obstacle to labor legislation and the effective regulation of business, they were willing to accept some reform legislation. The New Orleans machine was probably the single most powerful voice in state politics, and, in combination with upriver cotton planters, it exerted decisive influence in Louisiana politics. The Choctaws pulled Democratic factionalism in the direction of bifactional groupings and gave a measure of coherence and stability to the state's politics.

Despite the sectional, class, and cultural divisions that set Louisianans apart from each other, conservative Democrats managed to retain the allegiance of most voters. A flare-up of radicalism among some of the old Populists and lumber workers in the hill region led to a Socialist vote of over 5,000 in the election of 1912, but this rustic rebellion soon subsided. In the same year, John M. Parker, a prominent planter and New Orleans cotton factor, launched a more significant assault on the Democrats by organizing the Progressive party in Louisiana as a part of Theodore Roosevelt's new third party. The regular Democrats controlled the governorship, except for the years 1912–16, when Luther E. Hall, an advocate of "good government," held the office. Parker ran for governor on the Progressive ticket in 1916, polling 37 percent of the total vote, and in 1920 he won the governorship on the Democratic ticket. In earlier years Parker and other urban reformers had sought to bring about a civic transformation in New Orleans and to defeat the Behrman machine. Their success was limited, but they were instrumental in securing a commission form of government for the city. At the state level, a surprising amount of progressive legislation was enacted during the first two decades of the century. There was an urban flavor to much of this legislation, deriving from the influence of New Orleans reform organizations and professional groups as well as the machine that controlled the city's politics.

Texas had been a Confederate state, was dominated by the Democratic party, and had a substantial black population (about 20 percent in 1900). It was clearly a part of the South, but the Lone Star State was also characterized by a western outlook that set it apart from its neighbors to the east. Although it was still overwhelmingly agricultural and cotton remained its most valuable product, Texas had a more diversified economy than most other southern states, and the pace of industrialization was noticeably quickening. The spectacular oil discovery at Spindletop in 1901 opened the petroleum era in the Southwest and broadened the base of the state's economy still further. Despite the considerable concentration of blacks in East Texas, the race question did not as a rule assume great importance in state politics. The population, moreover, was somewhat more heterogeneous than that of the average southern state. In ten or twelve counties south of Austin, nineteenth-century German immigrants gave a distinct cast to one part of Texas. Farther south, along the Rio Grande, a large number of Mexican-Americans provided another ethnic variation. Ethnic-religious voting blocs were formed by persons of German Lutheran and Catholic ancestry and of Mexican Catholic background. The state's remarkable growth in the late nineteenth century and its vision of further economic development inevitably influenced its politics. Yet visitors were struck by the force of tradition among Texans. From their conversation one might think that "the massacre of the Alamo happened last month, that the Mexican War occurred last week, and that the Civil War was a tragedy of yesterday."[20]

Populism had a marked effect upon Texas politics. The ferment of the 1890s also produced James Stephen Hogg, a popular campaigner with a strong anticorporation bias. Hogg, who was elected governor in 1890, managed to steer a middle course between the Populists and the regular Democrats who preceded him as party leaders. A "reform Democrat," he built up a sturdy political organization and momentarily compelled most Texans to divide into Hogg and anti-Hogg factions. Conservative elements dominated the Democratic party as the new century began, but the legacy of James S. Hogg's politics was an important element in the eventual revival of political and social reform in Texas. A burgeoning array of interest groups began to press for more vigorous governmental action in the new century. Among these organizations were the Farmers' Union, the State Federation of Labor, the Federation of Commercial Clubs, the Texas Federation of Women's Clubs, and the Texas Local Option Association.

How to handle corporate wealth and how to restrain the power of the railroads, lumber companies, and oil corporations became the central public issue in Texas during the first decade of the twentieth century. In 1905 an impressive number of reformers appeared in the state legislature, and a new attorney general launched a vigorous antitrust attack. The following year brought the election of Thomas M. Campbell, who became the state's outstanding progressive governor. What one historian has referred to as a coalition of "small businessmen, young professional politicians, and organized farmers" paved the way for Campbell's success.[21] A series of legislative reforms was enacted during Campbell's four years as governor. The tide of progressivism weakened in 1910, when Oscar B. Colquitt, a more conservative leader, won the governorship. Texas progressives demonstrated their greatest strength in rallying to the cause of Woodrow Wilson in 1911 and 1912. They dominated the state convention in the latter year and sent a solid Wilson delegation to the Democratic national convention. During the decade after 1906, the pattern of Democratic politics in Texas revealed a distinct bifactional configuration. Though the division shifted from one issue to another, the "progressive" faction tended to support stricter regulation of corporations, to oppose Sen. Joseph W. Bailey, to champion prohibition, and to be identified with the presidential campaign to nominate Wilson.

After 1911 the "liquor question" became the most divisive issue among Texas Democrats. The relentless controversy over prohibition dominated the state's politics for several years, generally aligning drys and progressives on the same side. Then, in the gubernatorial primary of 1914, a new actor appeared on the political stage. He was James E. Ferguson, a farmer, lawyer, and small-town banker who had never before run for public office. A colorful campaigner, "Farmer Jim," who was elected in 1914, made a strong appeal to the state's poor farmers. His first important legislative accomplishment was an act to put a ceiling on farm tenancy rentals. Ferguson was easily reelected in 1916. But he ran into trouble during his second term and in 1917 was impeached and removed from office for misapplying public funds and interfering arbitrarily in the affairs of the state university. "Fergusonism" now became an issue in itself, and Ferguson's personal following was destined to make him an important factor in Texas politics for almost two decades. Fergusonism and the events of World War I disrupted the pattern of the state's politics, and, as in other southern states, the old dual factionalism rapidly disintegrated. Yet, for all of their internal conflict, the Democrats' flexible party organization, understanding of the state's varied economic and cultural interests, and willingness to provide at least a measure of state and federal involvement helped them retain the loyalty of a majority of the Texas voters.

Of the thirteen states that seem to warrant inclusion in the early twentieth-century South, the least "southern" was Oklahoma. The frontier was everywhere in evidence in this unfinished state, which did not enter the Union until 1907, and in many ways it was as much western as southern in its attitudes and behavior. The white population was diverse in origin, there was a large Indian minority, and blacks made up only a little over 8 percent of the inhabitants in 1910. Although the economy was predominantly agricultural, it was based in part on the growth of wheat, on mining, ranching, and lumbering, and on oil, of which it produced one-fourth of the national output by 1913. Nevertheless, Oklahoma felt the pull of strong centripetal forces that bound it to the South. Many of its inhabitants were natives of other southern states, and southerners, whose influence was pronounced in the eastern and southern sections, dominated the early years of statehood. Southern attitudes on race were much in evidence, and state leaders quickly devised a means of disfranchising black voters. Oklahoma also shared the cotton culture of the eastern South, and the staple spread during this period from the southeastern section to the central and southwestern areas.

A latent radicalism—manifesting itself as twentieth-century populism—burst into bloom by the time Oklahoma became a state. Nowhere in the United States was agrarian protest more conspicuous. The Farmers' Union and organized labor exerted great influence in the new state's politics. William Jennings Bryan was the idol of the Oklahoma masses. The hazards of farming in the Sooner State, the increasing percentage of farm tenancy (over half by 1920), and the role of large corporations in exploiting the state's resources fostered a populist spirit among the people. This radicalism was reflected in the Democratic party, but it was expressed more dramatically in the Socialist party of America. The Oklahoma party had more paid-up members than any other state by 1910, and in 1914 its state ticket received more than 52,000 votes. Before the war decimated their members, the Socialists had become an alarming specter to the Democrats and tangible evidence of the desperate conditions surrounding many Oklahomans. Populism, "Bryanism," and rural socialism helped shape progressivism in Oklahoma, along with farm organizations, organized labor, and various social reform groups. The emergence of an interest-group politics was a key factor not only in the enactment of progressive legislation but in the general conduct of political affairs in the state.

Oklahoma became a strong Democratic state and a part of the Solid South. Democratic leaders, who were responsible for the constitution of 1907, got the new government off to a good start. Taking advantage of the spreading enthusiasm for progressive action, the Democrats eagerly embraced "reform" and worked closely with a progressive coalition made up of the Farmers' Union, the Twin Territorial Federation of Labor, and independent social justice advocates. In addition to their attack on the Republicans for opposing ratification of the constitution, Democratic leaders derisively identified the opposition party with "the Carpetbagger, the Corporation, and the Coon." The Republicans, moreover, made the mistake of ignoring reform issues in favor of traditional GOP policies, and they were hurt by the disfranchisement of blacks in 1910. Yet the party was a substantial threat to the dominant Democrats. Strongest in the northern third of the state and generally in the western section, its gubernatorial nominees obtained over 40 percent of the votes in the elections before 1920. Every legislature during this period contained a strong and active Republican contingent. The GOP congressional nominees usually won two or three House seats and in 1910 captured a majority of them.

Meanwhile, the triumphant Democrats were unable to maintain party harmony very long. Differences between Democrats from Indian Territory and Democrats from Oklahoma Territory did not completely disappear after statehood. More important was the rivalry that soon developed between leaders such as Charles N. Haskell, the state's first governor, and William "Alfalfa Bill" Murray, who served as president of the constitutional convention of 1906–7. For several years factional alignments based on the personal followings of the founding fathers provided the most discernible structure of the state's Democratic party. This factionalism soon declined, however, and another organizing principle did not immediately take its place. Confronted by the Socialists on the left and the Republicans on the right, the Democrats tended increasingly to find leaders who represented business and professional interests rather than the reform coalition of earlier years. The bitter rivalries within their party weakened the Democrats, as did the Socialist upsurge before the war and a vigorous Republican challenge during the postwar reaction against "Wilsonism." In 1920 Oklahoma Republicans carried the state for Warren G. Harding, elected their first U.S. senator, and won five of the state's eight congressional seats.

The pattern of state politics in the early twentieth-century South had a good deal of uniformity, despite the individuality of the various state designs. The Democratic party dominated every state in the region. Most of the southern states enacted election "reforms" around the turn of the century that included some form of Negro disfranchisement, the poll tax as a voting prerequisite, and tough election laws. These so-called reforms, whatever their effect in preventing fraud, created a new and greatly restricted electorate in most of the states. At the same time, the introduction of state systems of primary elections brought an increase in the number of political candidates and encouraged bifactional groupings among Democrats. Two competing factions emerged in almost all of the states below the Potomac and the Ohio, giving an appearance of well-defined and ongoing political divisions analogous to a two-party system. The primaries also provided an arena for interest groups and reform causes. Intraparty competition, along with interest-group politics, contributed to the rise of a group of colorful and influential reform governors, the most successful of whom served as focal points for progressive coalitions and assumed a new role as legislative leaders. In the meantime, the legislatures were becoming more important, with the development of numerous progressive campaigns and the increasing demand for state regulation and public services.

On the surface the new structure of politics in the southern states was paradoxical. Disfranchisement and elaborate voting requirements denied a substantial portion of the potential electorate any part in politics. On the other hand, primary elections were in some respects more open and competitive than the old convention system, and they facilitated the political role of new organizations and interest groups. Political power was still centered in the planters and the black belts, in the rising industrialists, and in the county-seat governing class. Yet it was redistributed to some degree after the turn of the century. The beneficiaries of this shift in power were the emerging middle-class and professional elements in the growing cities and towns, people who filled the ranks of numerous civic, commercial, and professional organizations. These groups were instrumental in efforts to expand the functions of state and municipal governments and to use them for novel purposes.

Southern politics clearly possessed a rural and provincial cast during this period. This was evident in the controlling position of the local elites in hundreds of small towns and rural hamlets, whose power was magnified by overrepresentation in state legislatures and party conventions, and in the fact that a majority of the successful politicians and officeholders were products of the countryside and small towns. But even so, the political leverage of "uptown" residents increased as the years passed. Basically, southern politics reflected the realities of a system that was undemocratic, conservative, and rural-oriented, and one in which enormous power was concentrated in the hands of established and influential groups. The system was not altogether closed, however, for it sometimes fostered change, innovation, and even "reform." An important reason for the system's response to the demands for "progress" was that the dominant political and social elements were themselves willing to accept and occasionally to promote change for the sake of order and stability, efficiency, and "modernization."

Despite the limited electorate, southern politicians were not unresponsive to the attitudes and desires of the white masses. Given the prevailing assumptions about the proper role of government, the strong tradition of individualism in a largely rural society, and the pervasive longing for economic development, political leaders were reasonably faithful mirrors of their white constituents. Southern politics also responded in some measure to the pressure of groups that were normally outside the political process—to Republicans in some areas, to Socialists in the Southwest, to women throughout the South, and to blacks, particularly in the cities. James R. Green describes "a new kind of class struggle in the Southwest," one that "united the rural producers—indebted yeomen and the landless tenants—against the 'parasites' in the towns and cities" but was also attached firmly to the "principles of Marxian socialism."[22] The creative response of southern women to the plight of the poor and disadvantaged was notable in the South's uplift campaigns, and by the end of the progressive era a genuine woman suffrage movement had taken shape in the region. Blacks never ceased struggling to protect their interests. Their civic organizations, boards of trade, public welfare leagues, and community betterment groups labored to extract worthwhile concessions in education and other public services from the white system, to secure more adequate correctional facilities for black juveniles, to improve housing and sanitation in black areas, and to promote moral conduct, social order, and efficiency in the Negro community.

The ambiguities of the political system can be seen in the complex of reform movements that comprised southern progressivism. A number of tendencies—quickening social change, an emergent ideology of southern progress, a broadening humanitarianism, and the transformation of politics around the turn of the century—converged to provide a favorable setting for southern progressivism. Politics, of course, constituted an essential medium for the waging of these campaigns. State and local governments were the primary agencies for the resolution of conflicts in the community and for the regulation of business practices and social behavior, as well as the source of public services. The South's economic growth and diversification increased the demands on state and local governments for franchises, services, and regulations. The expanding cities and towns were confronted with especially troublesome problems, which often required action by state legislatures. With the enhanced role of government came a dramatic enlargement in the part played by economic and professional organizations in the formulation and enactment of public policy. Chambers of commerce, freight bureaus, farmers' organizations, labor unions, professional associations, and scores of other groups were soon participating in local and state politics throughout the region. Reform Democrats, influenced by populism and the leadership of William Jennings Bryan, were particularly responsive to the political demands of these groups.

A series of progressive movements unfolded in the South as hundreds of politicians, newspaper editors, educators, and members of the professions cast themselves in the role of reformers, launching scores of campaigns for public education, railroad regulation, more efficient agricultural methods, a more adequate welfare system, and so on. One group of reform efforts was primarily concerned with governmental regulation and the imposition of social controls in troublesome areas such as race relations and corporate enterprise. A second significant category of progressive campaigns in the South was dominated by the theme of social justice, by efforts to outlaw child labor, to establish juvenile courts, and the like. Social efficiency, especially as it related to economic development, was another focus of the reform movements. The campaigns for efficiency in agriculture, municipal government, and industrial labor led to greater emphasis on scientific knowledge, expertise, and effective administration in the public arena. Similar pressures emanated from other reform campaigns, such as the movements for public education, public health, and good roads. The incentives that underlay the reform movements were varied and overlapping; issues like compulsory education and restrictions on child labor reflected an interest in social control as well as humanitarian concern. Virtually all of these progressive campaigns had assumed a regionwide character by 1910, and they were almost always promoted as "southern" reforms. But for all their talk of democracy, morality, and social uplift, southern progressives were cautious reformers, led by middle-class and professional men and women who were generally amenable both to the limits imposed by the centers of power in their states and to the restraints of regional values and traditions. Unlike the third-party radicals of the 1890s, the progressives contributed to the white consensus on the race question and did not make the mistake of bolting the Democratic party.

By the time Woodrow Wilson assumed the presidency in March 1913, the reform movements in the South, as in other sections, were increasingly influenced by national organizations, standards, and solutions. This nationalization of reform was apparent in two of the southern progressives' most vigorous regulatory movements: the campaign to control railroads and the crusade to prohibit the sale and consumption of alcoholic beverages. It was manifested as well in the reform legislation enacted by the Wilson administration. World War I also had a nationalizing effect on the South. It contributed to the region's prosperity, brought an expansion in the functions of government, encouraged civic cooperation, enhanced the role of voluntary groups, and opened new avenues of social control, efficiency, and social justice.

Southern progressivism could claim some impressive achievements, notwithstanding the region's inherently undemocratic political system. It was a major factor in shaping the South's politics and social thought for the next half-century. The progressives created a synthesis of the antithetical approaches of the Redeemers and the Populists. They were to function both as agents of modernization and as guardians of southern tradition. They attracted support from diverse social elements, including the region's civic-commercial elites and upwardly mobile urban groups. Progressivism also drew on the swirling protest of the 1890s, and agrarian radicalism influenced the politics of the new century, helping to account for the anticorporation sentiment, intraparty competition, and morality-oriented campaigns. The progressives promoted the reform of southern institutions, the development of more efficient government, and the expansion of public services. They sought to integrate the South more fully into the political life of the nation and were eager for southerners to play a more constructive role in national affairs.

Well before the United States entered World War I, the Solid South had become a southern—and an American—institution. Although the Republicans controlled some local areas in the upper South and the Socialists in Oklahoma were a threat for a few years, there was no serious challenge to Democratic hegemony in the region. Political competition, which was often intense, was restricted to the Democratic primaries. While politics was of central importance to the well-being of most southerners, it was most responsive to the property-owning and professional elements. The one-party system revolved around a severely limited electorate, factional competition *within* the white primary, a pronounced rural and small-town orientation, and a process of decision making that was ultimately determined by a relatively few well-organized and powerful interests. Having become established, the system continued year after year, decade after decade. It became an accepted feature of southern life. Meanwhile, the region's role in national politics was also contributing to the image of the Solid South.

3 In the National Arena

The American political universe that took shape in the realignment of the 1890s reflected what one political scientist calls "the most enduringly sectional political alignment in American history."[1] So paramount were the Republicans in this party system that much of the North and West was scarcely less subject to one-party politics than was the South. Except for the special case of 1912, 84.5 percent of the total electoral vote for Democratic presidential candidates between 1896 and 1928 came from the southern and border states. In gubernatorial elections between 1894 and 1931, Republicans won 83.1 percent of the contests in the Northeast and 67.2 percent of those in the Midwest and West. On the other hand, one scholar has estimated that between 1876 and 1945 Democratic candidates were victorious in almost 95 percent of all political contests in the eleven ex-Confederate states. Genuine competition was limited to a relatively few states such as New York, New Jersey, Maryland, West Virginia, Ohio, Indiana, and Missouri. "The Republican party's domination of national partisan politics," one historian has written, "reflected the concentration of people and economic power in the northeastern-midwestern states, and it consolidated the transfer of political power to northern financial-industrial elites that had begun in the 1850s."[2]

Few observers suspected at the beginning of the twentieth century that the South would soon play a larger role in national politics. Writing in 1910, one commentator called attention to the region's continuing obsession with the race issue, lack of free thought as compared with other parts of the country, and longtime political isolation within the nation. Save for the ill-fated Andrew Johnson, no southerner had occupied the White House since the Civil War, nor had any southern leader been nominated for president or vice-president in that period. The South had seldom been represented in the cabinet or on the Supreme Court, and relatively few from the region had served in the diplomatic and consular services during those years. As for Congress, one contemporary wrote, "If for fifty years there has been a single

great general law or policy initiated by Southerners or by a Southerner, or which goes or should go by any Southerner's name, the fact
has escaped me."[3] The southern political leader, observed *World's
Work* in 1902, "has a nationality inside of a nationality. He is suspicious. He seems to belong to a special cult. He does not take up
national problems as if they were his problems, but rather as if they
were somebody else's whose work it was his duty to criticize."[4] Although William Jennings Bryan, the foremost Democratic leader in
national politics between 1896 and 1912, had a large following in the
southern states, most of the party organizations in the South were
racked by continuing struggles between the Bryanites and more conservative factions.

Nevertheless, in one respect the South's role in national politics
after the 1890s was greater than it had been in the late nineteenth
century. It had a strong voice in the decisions of the national Democratic party and to some extent in the policies of the national government. This was true in part because the region normally made up the
largest and most dependable component of the Democratic party in
national elections. Southern Democrats usually constituted a majority
of their party's members in Congress. The Fifty-seventh Congress
(1901–3), for example, contained ninety-five Democratic representatives and twenty-two Democratic senators from southern states, as
against fifty-six Democratic representatives and nine Democratic senators from other regions. The average Democratic congressman from
the South enjoyed a longer tenure than his counterpart from other
areas. Incumbency was a decided advantage in most primary elections
for congressional seats, while the lack of Republican opposition in
general elections was also a significant factor in the seniority acquired
by many southern congressmen. There was an element of deference
in the attitude of the southern electorate toward their established
representatives in Washington, a disposition to view them as natural
leaders and as patriarchal statesmen.

Their long service, seniority, and ranking positions on standing
committees enabled southern congressmen to master the organizational and procedural structure of the U.S. Senate and House of Representatives. They made adroit use of the committee system, usually
dominated their party's congressional caucuses, and began to discover the possibilities of unlimited debate in the Senate. Elaborating
these political devices, they were able to maintain a position of power
in the national government and in principle to apply John C. Calhoun's concept of the concurrent majority. The constructive contributions of these southern congressmen were greater than might be
thought. They provided sturdy support for railroad regulation, tariff
and tax revision, and a variety of agrarian reforms during the ad-

ministrations of Theodore Roosevelt and William Howard Taft. Yet they struck many observers as being peculiarly undisciplined, quixotic, and anachronistic.

One reason for this impression was that racial considerations seemed to color every political issue in the South. As one southern senator pointed out, in explaining the reaction of his fellow southerners to the presidential appointment of a black man to federal office, "Of course, there are some senators . . . who will be more loud-mouthed and exclamatory in opposition to the Negro's confirmation than anybody else but who really are at heart perhaps glad that you sent the name in; it gives them an opportunity to roar through the press and otherwise for home consumption. It is grist come to their mill, while for conservative men who have been and want to remain friends of the administration it is most embarrassing, in fact, either hurtful to them or suicidal to them at home, depending upon what course they take."[5] Another factor was the vigorous factional struggles that developed at the state level throughout the region and the rise of a new group of colorful and demagogic politicians whose personalities and rhetoric appealed strongly to the white masses and who were regarded with contempt in the North. Some conservatives bewailed the new "radicalism" of southern politics. In 1906, for instance, the editor of the Charleston News and Courier deplored "the political proletairism [sic] which has controlled the South." He expressed the opinion that, in time, "the conservative spirit of our people would undoubtedly have prevailed in the politics of the nation, but [that] in no other part of the country have the Socialistic tendencies of the times so largely affected the political activities of the people as in the Southern States."[6]

The complex of reforms identified with William Jennings Bryan did introduce an issue with a certain ideological coherence into the factional conflicts among southern Democrats. This division was reflected in Bryan's presidential nomination in 1900 and 1908, as well as in the nomination of the conservative Alton B. Parker in 1904. Although Bryan was resented and opposed by numerous politicians, newpaper editors, and businessmen in the South, he had a telling effect on southern political attitudes. As a leading historian has written, the southern states became "the most thoroughly Bryanized region in the country."[7] "If we can't win with you," an Alabama congressman wrote Bryan early in 1908, "it seems to me that we can't win with anybody. We don't want another Judge Parker or anybody else that had a violent pain in the conscience in 1896 on account of free coinage. . . . [The money power opposes you] because it knows that you stand and will continue to stand for the control and regulation of the great corporations, including the railroads, and that you favor an income tax."[8] In the opinion of the Chicago *Chronicle*, a Republican newspaper, the southern Democratic leadership during this period was just as "wrong-headed and fanatical on economic questions and as strong in its socialistic tendencies as the Bryan and Hearst Democracy in the northern states."[9] Bryan's appeal in the South was related to the revival of Jeffersonian principles, especially the agrarian side of Jefferson, but it was centered even more solidly in the Nebraskan's advocacy of currency and banking reform, railroad regulation, democratic innovations, and the like.

A minor but persistent refrain in the political discourse of the early twentieth-century South was the call for a more independent and nationally oriented politics. One source of this dissatisfaction was the growing capitalist sentiment in the southern region, which encouraged a certain restlessness among businessmen and expressions of discontent with the Democratic party's position on such issues as the tariff, ship subsidies, and foreign policy. There were also complaints from a group of latter-day "mugwumps," whose views were a manifestation of the new social criticism in the South and who in a broad sense were a product of the emerging professions and growing middle class in the cities. These critics contrasted the economic advances and bright industrial prospects of their region with its political intolerance, lack of influence in national affairs, and loss of "the old time southern force and character." They longed for an end to the Solid South, for the expulsion of its "narrow and sectional spirit," for greater independence of thought, and for discussion of national issues. The Solid South had turned out to be a misfortune, the young historian Ulrich B. Phillips wrote in 1904. "It has prevented her having due influence upon national legislation and administration, and what is worse it has proved perhaps a greater check to freedom of thought than slavery was."[10] "We have been told for years," complained Walter Hines Page in 1900, "that if the negro vote were eliminated, the Southern white vote would be divided on National questions." Yet there was little indication of such political competition in the aftermath of disfranchisement. The trouble with southern politics, Page wrote a few years later, could be summed up in five words: "small men in public life." The region desperately needed new political leaders. This leadership must "leave the [Civil] war alone—and the Negro question," must not be afraid of "Mr. Bryan, nor of the backward Southern press," must speak the language of Grover Cleveland, and must be "national" in thought.[11]

Some of the independents hoped that the South's political emancipation would be accomplished through presidential leadership. They spoke kindly of William McKinley, were alternately encouraged and disappointed by Theodore Roosevelt, and for a brief time placed their confidence in William Howard Taft. "Roosevelt," a North Carolinian predicted in October 1901, "is going to break the back bone of the old moss back democratic ring rule in the South, as sure as fate."[12] Such wistful expectations were never realized, of course, and the twenty-sixth president's racial mishaps and controversial appointments provoked an outpouring of scorn and condemnation in the southern states. Still, southerners could not entirely resist the effervescent Roosevelt, even though few of them were ever willing to vote for him. Professor Edwin Mims of Trinity College noted in 1905 that many southerners were drawn to Roosevelt because of his "intense Americanism" and "disinterested public service." Mims also thought that the president, who boasted that his ancestry was half southern, acted like a southerner in displaying "a certain quality of enthusiasm, demonstrativeness, and cordiality." Alexander J. McKelway, a prominent child labor reformer, declared that the New Yorker's advocacy of progressive measures like pure food, meat inspection, and railroad regulation had made him many friends in the South. During the Roosevelt years, McKelway remarked, southerners began for the first time since the Civil War to consider the federal government as possibly a "beneficent agency."[13] On the other hand, Roosevelt failed to reform the Republican party in the South, despite his bold pronouncements. While the president relied upon the black educator Booker T. Washington as a southern adviser, he gave tacit encouragement to the developing lily-white movement in states like North Carolina and Louisiana. Republican leaders in the South continued to devote their energies to the politics of selecting delegates to the national convention, to federal patronage, and to the control of the party machinery in their respective states.

In 1908 William Howard Taft increased the Republican percentage of votes in most of the southern states, and after his election he attracted attention in the region with several sympathetic speeches and felicitous statements designed to appeal to the sensibilities of white southerners. Perhaps the new president could revitalize the Grand Old Party in the South, transform it into a respectable alternative to the Democratic party, and end the region's isolation in national politics. That was the wish of men like Walter Hines Page, who persuaded Taft to address a meeting of the North Carolina Society of New York in December 1908. Page described the affair as "a bugle call to all progressive Southerners."[14] When the new president appointed the Tennessean Jacob McGavock Dickinson to his cabinet, many conservative southerners began to show greater interest in national politics. "The time has come," a small businessman in Mississippi asserted, "for our Southern States to take the position to which they are entitled. We must cut loose from 'Bryanism,' 'Vardamanism,' and all other 'Isms' that have kept our country back for the past 25 or 30 years, and look to the development and up-building of our Southern country."[15] Whatever hopes southerners may have had for Taft's southern policies were soon obliterated by the disruption of the Republican party and the controversy surrounding the Taft administration. But as the fortunes of the Taft presidency declined, prospects for the Democratic party rose. Confirmation of these possibilities first came in the midterm congressional elections of 1910, when the Democrats won control of the House of Representatives. Southern congressional leaders began to come to the fore in 1911, most conspicuously in the person of Oscar W. Underwood of Alabama, chairman of the Ways and Means Committee and majority leader in the lower house. This southern leadership in Washington aroused pride and anticipation among southerners, many of whom were showing heightened interest in national legislation such as tariff reduction, railroad regulation, aid to agriculture, and constitutional amendments providing for an income tax and direct election of U.S. senators.

Southern interest in national politics rose to new heights with the nomination and election of Woodrow Wilson as the nation's twenty-eighth president. The presidential election of 1912 was the first such contest in almost forty years in which the South played a central part. Southerners were quick to claim Wilson, who had been born and reared in the South, as one of their own, and his spectacular rise as a reform governor of New Jersey was followed with keen interest by newspaper editors, educators, and public leaders all over the region. Richard Evelyn Byrd, speaker of the Virginia house of delegates, wrote Wilson after the latter's election as governor in 1910: "I regard you as the best & most available candidate for the Presidency on the democratic ticket of 1912."[16] There were numerous messages of this kind, and Wilson's campaign of 1911 and 1912 for his party's presidential nomination evoked an enthusiastic response throughout the South. Even so, he was forced to divide the southern delegations to the national Democratic convention with two other popular candidates: Representative Underwood and Rep. Champ Clark of Missouri. Underwood was a formidable contestant in the deep South, while Clark was very strong in Kentucky and the Southwest. Wilson won Texas and South Carolina, three-fourths of the North Carolina delegates, and a portion of those from Louisiana, Virginia, and Tennessee.

The spirited preconvention contest for southern support in the Democratic convention was itself a factor in stimulating regional thinking about national issues. The fact that two native southerners— Wilson and Underwood—were genuine candidates for the presidential nomination heightened southern interest. "It is good to be a Democrat in this year of our Lord," exclaimed the president of the

University of Virginia, who went on to assert: "The leaders of the party that bears the great name in the Federal Congress are going about the tasks imposed upon them by the nation with a sobriety and an intelligence, a self-sacrifice and a calmness, very disappointing and surprising to their enemies and very heartening to their friends."[17] Although Wilson's campaign for the nomination in the South did not invariably lead to a progressive-conservative cleavage, it was generally the case that his strongest support came from the so-called reform factions, from the old Bryan elements, from anticorporation and antiboss Democrats. He faced powerful opposition from old-style Democratic leaders, who were suspicious of him as a party outsider. Of course, southerners of different ideological persuasions were no doubt attracted to the New Jersey governor because, in Arthur S. Link's words, they "saw in him the South's great hope for presidential preferment."[18] Meanwhile, Theodore Roosevelt's strenuous campaign as the Progressive party's nominee for president added to the excitement in the South. While the split in the Republican party that led to Roosevelt's candidacy assured Wilson's election, southerners were very conscious of the fact that the Democratic nominee had received his strongest electoral support in the South and the border states.

Woodrow Wilson's election to the nation's highest office seemed to mark the beginning of a new era in southern politics. Millions of southerners experienced an unaccustomed excitement—a thrill of pride and exhilaration—in the knowledge that one of their own had at last ascended to the presidency. "Long ago," a North Carolinian wrote, "I had despaired of ever seeing a man of Southern birth President." But a dramatic change had taken place. "Wilson's elevation to the Presidency marks an era in our national life. With it we have the ascendency of men of Southern birth and residence to the seats of power and responsibility such as has never been seen in our day. There is a change in personnel and policies. The world is looking on to witness the result. I have comforting hopes, and shall indulge them until driven to disappointment which I pray may not come."[19] Southern editors and public speakers never tired of reminding their audiences that Wilson was a man of southern birth, upbringing, and culture, a man who understood and exemplified the region's finest traditions. He was, his more enthusiastic supporters contended, a man of destiny who would end the South's long political isolation and respond generously to its political and economic needs. Southern representation in the new president's cabinet, in Congress, and in the Democratic party strengthened the South's expectations. Five of Wilson's cabinet members in 1913 had been born in the South, and Edward M. House, who became his chief adviser and confidant, was a Texan. Southerners made up half of the Democratic majority in the

Patterns of Turnout in U.S. Presidential Elections, 1860–1964, by Region

Reprinted with permission from Walter Dean Burnham, "The Changing Shape of the American Political Universe," *American Political Science Review* 59 (March 1965): 11.

Senate and more than two-fifths of the party's majority in the House of Representatives. A southern atmosphere unmistakably surrounded the new administration, and a number of journalists suggested that after a long absence the South was once again "in the saddle." The implication was that the southern states would now dominate the national government as well as the Democratic party.

Wilson's election led many of his southern adherents to anticipate presidential assistance in their continuing struggles with opposing Democratic factions for state and local control. A Texas progressive warned the president-elect soon after the election, however, that "the Democratic Party is now in a most perilous situation. The danger lies largely in the Southern States and arises out of the fact that a large element of the Party in those states are not Democrats in reality, but stand-pat Republicans, sailing under the colors of Democracy, and others who, having no political convictions, are machine gangsters."[20] Indeed, the hopes of many reform-minded southerners were soon dashed by what Arthur Link describes as "the realities and necessities of practical politics."[21] Wilson, determined to enact his New Freedom agenda and to make his party a disciplined instrument for that purpose, was confronted with a situation in which conservative Democrats, particularly from the South, held powerful positions in Congress and were established solidly in their constituencies. The president soon capitulated, deferring to the recommendations of Postmaster General Albert S. Burleson and other conservatives and permitting much of the federal patronage to go to old-line Democrats in the South. In one southern state after another—Virginia, Kentucky, Alabama, and so on—the result was to disappoint and weaken the reform factions.

In Virginia, Wilson's campaign was paralleled by a struggle between the dominant faction led by Sen. Thomas S. Martin and antiorganization Democrats, who supported the New Jersey governor. Wilson's decision to work with the Martin regulars marked what one scholar has described as "the final demise of the anti-organization faction in Virginia politics."[22] The independents fought on for a time. In 1914 they organized the Virginia Progressive League, with a renewed attack on the state "machine" and an effort to popularize a broad reform program. But the results were disappointing, and the factional division based on the Wilson movement of 1911–12, never clear-cut, became steadily less distinct in the face of the president's wide appeal in the state and region. Meanwhile, North Carolina progressives, inspired by Wilson's New Freedom and disheartened by the conservative character of the state legislature, set about the formulation and adoption of an ambitious program of social reform, including a statewide primary, revision of the state tax system, more stringent regulation of business, new child labor legislation, a minimum school term of six months, and a series of constitutional amendments. They arranged a progressive convention in 1914 and publicized their demands widely through the state, only to have their proposals repudiated by the next state Democratic convention. Progressives in Virginia and North Carolina—and in other southern states—achieved a number of their legislative objectives over the course of the next few years, but these successes were not the result of presidential intervention in the South's factional politics.

Southern congressmen were quite favorable in their response to Wilson's leadership. Few of these men had ever enjoyed the kind of power and patronage that came to them during the Wilson era. Their seniority and the Democratic majorities enabled them to dominate the committee structure in both houses of Congress. Twelve of the thirteen principal committee chairmen in the House and twelve of fourteen in the Senate were southerners. Most of the southern congressmen were in general agreement with Wilson's reform proposals in 1913 and 1914, and they provided strong support for the major legislative features of the New Freedom. Indeed, experienced southern leaders such as Underwood of Alabama and Furnifold M. Simmons of North Carolina skillfully guided the administration's tariff, banking, and business regulation measures through Congress. The prototypical southern congressman in this period was middle-aged, well educated, and a lawyer by training. An experienced officeholder, he had been born in a rural place and resided in a small southern town. A majority of the southern lawmakers were steeped in local politics and in the traditions and tactics of Congress. They were experts, moreover, in the substantive details of their committees.

Despite their state-rights tradition and instinctive distrust of federal activism, southern congressmen during the Wilson period were forceful advocates of national assistance, especially in the field of agriculture. The South's support of New Freedom legislation was more than a matter of party loyalty and regional pride in Woodrow Wilson. It also resulted from the fact that a great many of the Wilson reforms were widely popular among southerners: tariff reform, a new banking and currency system, antitrust legislation, a national rural credit program, federal aid to agricultural and vocational education, government support of shipping, and federal assistance for highway construction. Southern senators and representatives provided large majorities for long-term rural credits, a federal warehouse statute, an agricultural extension program, vocational education, and more effective regulation of commodity exchanges. The Democratic congressmen, most of whom were southerners and westerners, were unusually cohesive in supporting these reform measures.

Congressional Democrats from below the Potomac shared a commitment to white supremacy, a proud and sensitive attachment to the idea of the South, and an inclination to believe that their region had long been exploited by powerful economic and political interests in the Northeast and Midwest. Yet they frequently disagreed among themselves. During the Wilson presidency, they seemed to be divided into two discernible categories. One group was an administration faction typified by Representative Underwood; its members were generally conservative but reliable supporters of the party and the president. The second group included agrarian liberals like Claude Kitchin of North Carolina, who succeeded Underwood as majority leader in the House of Representatives in 1915. Other southern congressmen were not readily identifiable with either group. The agrarian reformers, who were well represented in the House, expressed a kind of neopopulism and Bryanism that looked to Washington for both antitrust action and federal assistance to farmers and small businessmen. Their ranks included, in addition to Kitchin, Robert Lee Henry and

Rufus Hardy of Texas, Otis T. Wingo of Arkansas, and J. Willard Ragsdale of South Carolina. These southern agrarians helped secure progressive changes in the Glass Banking and Currency Bill, pushed for more vigorous antitrust legislation, worked for more democratic tax schedules in such measures as the Revenue Bill of 1916, and championed a system of rural credits and other agricultural aid. Southern backers of new federal programs also contributed to the metamorphosis of the Wilsonian program into a series of broader and more vigorous federal policies in 1915 and 1916.

Nevertheless, southern congressmen objected to several of the more advanced progressive proposals considered during Wilson's first term. They were especially apprehensive about issues that involved race relations and state rights. There was marked southern opposition to the Alaskan Railroad Bill, the La Follette Seamen's Bill, workmen's compensation for federal employees, the Keating-Owen Child Labor Bill, and a constitutional amendment to enfranchise women. Southern lawmakers were often suspicious of legislative proposals with a pronounced labor or urban orientation. Southerners were more inclined to support certain measures of social control. They took the lead in the passage of a bill to restrict foreign immigration in 1914 and 1915 and in the successful repassage of a literacy requirement for immigrants early in 1917. Southern leaders were even more ardent in their advocacy of Negro proscription in Washington and the federal service. Indeed, southern pressure, in and out of Congress, was the most important influence in the Wilson administration's thoroughgoing segregation of government workers and denial of federal appointments to blacks, as well as the flood of Jim Crow bills introduced in the Sixty-third Congress (1913–15). "Between 1913 and 1917," one historian has concluded, "the direct impact of race consciousness upon national politics stemmed largely from the reinvigorated influence of southern Democrats in Washington."[23]

Two of the most controversial issues of the early Wilson years were national prohibition and federal legislation to outlaw child labor. The South was divided in its reaction to federal intervention in these two areas. Yet the limitations of state action, in the South as elsewhere, persuaded more and more southerners to join the movement for reform at the national level. The accelerating movement for national prohibition was accompanied by a new prohibition surge in the South. This antiliquor wave was first manifested in Virginia, where favorable action in 1914 climaxed a long and complex struggle. The next year brought Alabama, Arkansas, and South Carolina into the dry ranks. In Congress, meanwhile, the movement for national prohibition steadily grew stronger. A prohibition amendment to the federal Constitution, sponsored by the American Anti-Saloon League, was introduced in the House of Representatives by Richmond Pearson Hobson of Alabama and in the Senate by Morris Sheppard of Texas. When the amendment was approved by Congress in 1917, southern members voted overwhelmingly in its favor.

They were much less enthusiastic about federal child labor legislation. The most important measure of this kind was a bill introduced in 1914 by Rep. A. Mitchell Palmer of Pennsylvania and Sen. Robert L. Owen of Oklahoma. It provoked resolute opposition in the southern textile states. The bill passed the House in 1915, with most of the negative votes coming from six southern states, but the Senate failed to act on the measure. A new child labor proposal, the Keating-Owen Bill, was passed by both houses in 1916, however, and again the principal opposition came from the southern textile states. Even so, outside the four southern textile states, a majority of the region's congressmen voted for the bill.

Although southerners found much to applaud in the New Freedom, there were two periods of strain and criticism in the South's reaction to the Wilson administration between 1913 and 1917: the crisis that enveloped the cotton market in the autumn of 1914 and the first part of 1915 and the struggle over neutrality and preparedness in 1915 and early 1916. While the gloom in the cotton areas gradually disappeared, as Allied purchases and an economic upturn at home caused staple prices to go up, some southern congressmen continued to attack the British blockade and to criticize the administration's neutrality policies. "The town is beginning to fill up with men of the restless, meddling sort," President Wilson wrote a friend in August 1915. "Some of them are southern congressmen with wild schemes, preposterous and impossible schemes to valorize cotton and help the cotton planter out of the Reserve Banks or out of the national Treasury—out of anything, if only they can make themselves solid with their constituents and seem to be 'on the job.' "[24] Wilson's decision in late 1915 to launch a preparedness program brought a good deal of opposition from the South, much of it reflecting Byranite sentiment against involvement in European wars and a latent suspicion of the role of corporations and cartels in the great conflagration. The region harbored what one authority has described as "a widely prevalent rural-progressive opposition to war and militarism."[25] But most southerners were predisposed to take the side of the Allies, and their congressmen provided impressive support for the president's diplomatic and defense policies.

The South's involvement in national affairs was stimulated still further by World War I. The war spirit intensified the patriotism of most southerners and made them more self-conscious about their Americanism. The war led to an expansion of government, particularly in Washington, and fostered civic cooperation and community programs. There was some resistance to the draft in the Appalachian South and among isolated elements such as the radicalized share-croppers of Oklahoma, and there were virulent anti-Wilson attacks by a few influential southern spokesmen like Thomas E. Watson and Coleman L. Blease. Despite some quibbling and uneasiness over fed-eral controls and the determined opposition of a handful of southern congressmen such as James K. Vardaman of Mississippi and Thomas P. Gore of Oklahoma, most of the region's congressmen stood with Wilson on all of the major war measures. They did so even though the war legislation increased the functions and powers of the federal government and thus tended to undermine state-rights principles. Those who persisted in opposing the administration's war policies found themselves denounced in the southern press and confronted with grass-roots petitions demanding that they either work with the administration or resign. Several of Wilson's congressional critics were defeated in the Democratic primaries of 1918. On one issue, a constitutional amendment to enfranchise women, a majority of the congressmen from southern states stubbornly resisted approval, even when urged to do so by the president. Paradoxically, many southern members stood firmly on the principle of state rights when it came to woman suffrage but overlooked that principle in supporting na-tional prohibition. Some of the southern lawmakers favored the Eigh-teenth Amendment because they assumed that it would have a good effect on black men but opposed the Nineteenth Amendment because they feared that it would raise the question of black women's right to vote.

In general, southern congressional leaders, entrenched in pow-erful committee positions, gave constructive and indispensable leg-islative assistance to the enactment of Wilson's wartime program. Most southern congressmen remained fervently loyal to Wilson dur-ing the bitter controversy over the Treaty of Versailles and the League of Nations. Richard L. Watson concluded, in studying the wartime record of these Dixie congressmen, that "they had responsibilities to constituents, to party, and to principle, and they looked upon these as responsibilities, not roles to play, because in their view party loyalty and loyalty to constituents were in themselves principles. . . . each congressman weighed constituents, party, and principle and deter-mined the final balance in different ways."[26]

A sweeping Republican victory in the election of 1920 ended the Democratic interlude of national control and completed the breakup of the political coalition that had made Woodrow Wilson's reelection possible in 1916. In the 1920s the Democrats were returned to their familiar position as the nation's minority party. While southern au-

thority in Washington was diminished somewhat, the region's influence in the Democratic party was, if anything, greater than ever.
Southerners continued to dominate the Democratic party in Congress.
They were still the mainstay of the party in national elections, although as time passed their influence was increasingly resented and
challenged by an emergent element from the Northeast.

Republican successes in the 1920s included modest gains in the
South itself. In the election of 1920, GOP percentages went up in
every southern state, and the Republicans carried Tennessee and
Oklahoma. They won ten congressional districts in those two states,
as well as a governorship in Tennessee and a U.S. Senate seat and
control of the state house of representatives in Oklahoma. For the
most part, however, southerners who might have turned to the Republicans in the new era were satisfied with the business-oriented
and forward-looking governments in states like Virginia, North Carolina, Tennessee, and Alabama, and with the passing of Bryan and
Wilson they had less reason to be alarmed because of upsetting economic policies or liberal ideas emanating from the national leaders of
the Democratic party. There were, no doubt, many Democrats in the
same boat with the Arkansas lawyer who wrote, soon after the election of 1920, "I am one of the numerous Southern Democrats who
voted for [James M.] Cox and rejoiced in the election of Harding."[27]
Yet it was becoming easier to think of Republican affiliation in a region
so strongly committed to the gospel of business expansion and economic diversification. Republican leaders were aware of this prospect,
and during the late 1920s there was renewed talk of a revitalized
minority party in the South, encouraged perhaps by the threatened
disruption of the southern Democracy. Efforts to make Republicanism
more respectable in the southern states by transforming it into a "lily-
white" party, a movement that had been under way for a generation
or more, received new impetus. Near the end of the decade, Herbert
Hoover attempted "to build up a Republican party in the South such
as would commend itself to the citizens of those states."[28]

Meanwhile, the southern presence in Congress was a distinct
reality. Southerners made up a majority of the Democratic members
in each of the two houses, and southern senators and representatives
held the major party posts and the ranking minority positions on most
of the important committees. In the House of Representatives, for
example, as the 1920s began, Finis J. Garrett of Tennessee was minority leader, John Nance Garner of Texas was the ranking member
of the Ways and Means Committee, and William Oldfield of Arkansas
was serving as party whip. In the upper chamber, such veteran legislators as Furnifold M. Simmons, Duncan U. Fletcher, Joseph T. Robinson, Carter Glass, and Oscar W. Underwood were established in

powerful positions. The southern senators demonstrated their negative strength in 1922, when they were primarily responsible for the defeat of an antilynching bill. After passing the House by a large margin, the measure was killed by a southern-inspired filibuster in the Senate.

Southern leadership in Congress during the 1920s was generally cautious and conservative, especially after 1924. Congressmen from the South did contribute to the farm bloc that pushed through agricultural credit, business regulation, and cooperative legislation early in the decade, and many of them supported a liberal alternative to Secretary of the Treasury Andrew Mellon's tax-cut proposals. While differing over the various efforts to dispose of government facilities at Muscle Shoals, Alabama, on the Tennessee River, the southern lawmakers were enthusiastic supporters of regional development. This explains their backing of numerous federal aid programs in such areas as agriculture, highway construction, flood control, and public health.

Politics in the southern states was strongly influenced by the economic and social conditions of the 1920s. The pace of industrial and urban growth picked up at the same time most farmers encountered severe economic problems and the countryside lost population and vitality. Hundreds of thousands of southerners were uprooted from their rural and village life, moving to the cities and larger towns in quest of new economic and cultural opportunities. But industrial progress and urban growth led many southerners to assume that the economic transformation of the region would steadily alleviate social problems. The quality of life itself changed as a result of technological marvels like the automobile, radio, and a host of appliances for the home. These developments were pleasurable and exciting as well as useful, but they were also threatening. "The 1920s," Numan V. Bartley writes of Georgia, "brought the first serious crisis for the old order and intensified the defense of traditional values."[29] The same was true of the other southern states.

Challenges to established habits and values seemed to come both from within the South and from the outside. It was the outside, however, that most alarmed and frightened southern traditionalists. The greatest threat apparently came from the Northeast and, to a lesser extent, the Midwest, with their huge polyglot cities, Roman Catholic and Jewish religions, and foreign cultures. While much more than a sectional division, a conflict over cultural values raged throughout the 1920s, pitting the urban-Catholic-immigrant North against the rural-Protestant-Anglo-Saxon South. The Democratic party became a major focal point of this sectional clash, and such issues as prohibition, the Ku Klux Klan, and religious fundamentalism quickly emerged as divisive themes in the debate. All of these themes were closely associated with the South. The conflict was, in a sense, the culmination of a struggle between an "old" and a "new" America.

Sectional animosity in the United States was rooted, of course, in the momentous political struggles of the nineteenth century. Faint echoes of that sectionalism could be heard in recurrent twentieth-century episodes involving the South's treatment of blacks, and during the Wilson years, outbursts of northern antipathy were directed at Claude Kitchin and other agrarian radicals in Congress. Such views were, to some extent, a reflection of the struggle for power in Congress. Thus, Representative Kitchin wrote a southern colleague in November 1915, "I have had many letters from Northern Members saying that some complaints are made in their section that the South is getting all the Chairmanships, and some insisting that several of the vacancies should be given to Northern Democrats."[30] In 1918 the New York *World*, a Democratic newspaper, predicted that there would never again be a Democratic Congress until "the Northern States have some reasonable assurance that such bodies will not be controlled by vengeful and parochial politicians from the South."[31]

The sectional division within the Democratic party was evident as early as the election of 1916, when western Democrats played a key role in Wilson's narrow reelection. They resented the proprietary attitude of party leaders in the East and South toward the president, and many of them felt that their hard work and personal sacrifices during the campaign had been taken for granted. They also disliked the sectional pattern of the Wilson administration's patronage policies. These feelings were revived early in 1917 when Thomas S. Martin of Virginia was chosen over Thomas J. Walsh of Montana as the new Democratic majority leader in the Senate. Meanwhile, certain legislative proposals tended to divide Democrats along sectional lines. National prohibition was an issue that came to be identified with southern congressmen. Opposition to woman suffrage—a somewhat less divisive party issue—was also associated with southern lawmakers. To northern Democrats from cities, prohibition symbolized the domination of the congressional hierarchy by southerners. One Boston Democrat was quoted as saying in 1917, "I am unalterably opposed to the Southern Democrats remaining in the saddle throughout the coming Congress."[32] Sectional ill will was a significant factor in the midterm elections of 1918, when many farmers in the western grain states deserted the Democrats. They complained about the low minimum wheat prices established by the government, while cotton prices were never regulated.

Democratic sectionalism assumed a more ominous character in the 1920s. The extent of this sectional cleavage was revealed in the presidential politics of 1924. A fierce struggle for the party's presidential nomination developed between William Gibbs McAdoo and Alfred E. Smith. McAdoo, a native southerner who had recently moved from New York to California, had served as secretary of the treasury in Woodrow Wilson's cabinet and had married Wilson's daughter. A progressive of sorts, he was a strong prohibitionist and had the support of a large number of Ku Klux Klan members. Governor Smith of New York, son of Irish immigrants and a product of Tammany Hall, was a critic of prohibition, an opponent of the Klan, and a champion of the urban masses. He was also a member of the Catholic Church. Another candidate was Sen. Oscar W. Underwood of Alabama, but he proved to be no match for McAdoo, who won a large majority of the southern delegates to the Democratic national convention in New York.

The convention, which lasted for seventeen days, was described by one newspaperman as a "snarling, cursing, tedious, tenuous, suicidal, homicidal rough-house."[33] A proposal to censure the Ku Klux Klan by name, opposed by most southern delegates, came within one vote of passing. The sectional division within the party was vividly illustrated in the lengthy balloting for a presidential nominee, in which McAdoo and Smith were the leading contestants. Neither could get the necessary two-thirds majority, however, and on the 103d ballot the exhausted delegates finally selected John W. Davis of West Virginia as a compromise candidate. The southerners, staunch supporters of McAdoo, had given Smith virtually no votes in the long balloting process. In the November election, all of the southern states except Kentucky dutifully cast their votes for the Democratic presidential ticket.

Sectionalism in the Democratic party reached its apogee in the presidential election of 1928. William G. McAdoo withdrew in September 1927 as a candidate for the party nomination, leaving Alfred E. Smith as a strong favorite for the honor. Although there was widespread opposition to Smith throughout the South, as there had been in 1924, he was nominated on the first ballot at the Democratic national convention. The New York governor remained critical of national prohibition, but he sought in some ways to mollify the South. The national convention was held in Houston, Texas, and Joseph T. Robinson of Arkansas, the Senate minority leader, was selected as Smith's running mate. Nevertheless, concerted opposition to the Democratic nominee developed rapidly in various parts of the region. His religion, while infrequently invoked directly, and his stand on prohibition made him vulnerable. As David Burner observes, "Al Smith's stand against prohibition ended an alliance between the drys and the Democrats that had prevailed in the region for decades."[34] Protestant leaders such as Bishop James Cannon, Jr., of the Methodist Episcopal Church, South, organized to defeat Smith. "By rumor, speech, and broadside," one historian has written, "the Roman menace was flaunted across the South."[35] While most Democratic politicians supported their party's ticket, in many cases reluctantly, a number of prominent party leaders refused to vote for Al Smith. Among these Democrats were Furnifold M. Simmons of North Carolina, J. Thomas Heflin of Alabama, Robert L. Owen of Oklahoma, Thomas B. Love of Texas, and Sidney J. Catts of Florida. The Republican party campaign in several southern states was merely a formality, while the real campaign was carried on by the so-called Hoover-Democrat organization. The result was an unaccustomed division among southerners in a presidential campaign. Nicholas Murray Butler, the president of Columbia University, remarked, "It is certainly a relief to find the South divided on almost everything, even if it be bigotry."[36]

The outcome of the presidential election shocked many southerners. Herbert Hoover, the Republican nominee, carried seven of the southern states, and he came close to winning Alabama. His winning percentages in the South ranged from 51.8 in Texas to 63.8 in Oklahoma. Analyzing the election in 1949, V.O. Key demonstrated that the most steadfast Democrats in the South were the white residents of the black belts, while the areas that showed the greatest shift to the Republicans were the counties with fewest Negroes.[37] Thus, Democratic defections were least in Mississippi and South Carolina, the two states with the highest proportions of blacks. Key also identified other significant factors in the election results, including party loyalty, which aided the Democrats, and organization, which generally worked to the advantage of the Republicans. Hoover made his best showing in the peripheral South, and he won such growth-minded cities as Dallas, Houston, Birmingham, Atlanta, and Richmond. The most loyal Democratic areas were characterized by a complex of factors—ruralism, cotton growing, plantation organization, intense Reconstruction memories—as well as racial fears and a strong Democratic tradition. Both parties tried to exploit racial fears in the South, but the major sources of Hoover's appeal to white southerners were a combination of Smith's religion, his opposition to national prohibition, and his New Yorkism, which to southerners symbolized a disquietingly different Democratic party.

If the election of 1928 illustrated the deep North-South cleavage that had developed in the Democratic party, it also provided dramatic evidence of a divided South. The Solid South had cracked. The dissenters in 1928, unlike those in the 1890s, made no attempt at third-party politics; instead, they tried to capture control of the Democratic

Democratic Percentage of the Presidential Vote, 1900–1944

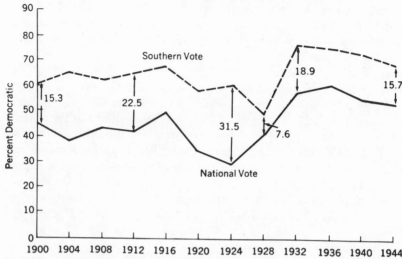

Reprinted with permission from Everett Carll Ladd, Jr., with Charles
D. Hadley, *Transformations of the American Party System: Political Coalitions
from the New Deal to the 1970s*, 2d ed. (New York: W.W. Norton, 1978),
p. 43.

party machinery at the state and local levels and to swing their states
to the Republicans in the presidential contest. Thomas Watts Gregory,
a Texan who had served in Wilson's cabinet, expressed the opinion
of many Democratic loyalists when he asserted that "you might as
well talk about a white negro or a green blackbird as to speak of a
man as a 'Hoover Democrat.' "[38] Yet the differences among southerners were so great, at least for the moment, that such a course
seemed to be the best alternative to party regularity. In some respects,
the political conflict in a number of southern states had been going
on for years. One student of Texas politics concluded that the presidential campaign of 1928 in that state was "just another prohibition
contest." He found that in almost every county there was "a return
match staged between the old time dry and wet leaders as had been
the case in several former prohibition elections."[39] This no doubt
oversimplifies the situation, but it appears that in several southern
states the personalities and issues of 1928 offered an opportunity and
a pretext for one group of politicians to challenge the control of the
party by another. This seems to have occurred in Texas, where a group
of young, self-styled Democrats challenged the control exercised by
Thomas B. Love and the "old guard," who struck the insurgents as
being fanatics in their support of prohibition. In addition, the divisive

campaign elicited among some journalists and in certain other quarters a new brand of southern liberalism, one that was suspicious of sectional shibboleths, more concerned with individual liberties, and even willing to accept an Irish Catholic from New York as the Democratic presidential nominee.

It remained to be seen, of course, whether the events of 1928 would mark the end of the political era that began in the late 1890s. The intervening years constituted a period in which, except for the border states, every southern state was so wedded to the Democratic party that any break in its solidarity on the state and national levels was almost unthinkable. It was a period, moreover, in which the southern handling of the race question encountered little interference from Congress or the president, met few challenges in the federal courts, and received the general approbation of public opinion in the country at large. Even a liberal Democratic administration in Washington had served, ironically, to increase the region's attachment to the Democratic party. Nor was that all. The South was the bulwark of the Democratic party, and the powerful influence of its congressional delegations safeguarded its peculiar interests and obtained their share of federal benefits. But in the 1920s conditions were changing, and a more vigorous Democratic party began to emerge in other parts of the country. In 1928 the South found it impossible to veto the nomination of a candidate it strongly opposed. At that point thoughtful southerners could see that continued Democratic growth outside the South would almost certainly reduce their region's influence in the party.

4 The Classic Period of Southern Politics

For three decades following World War I, the distinguishing features of the South's one-party politics survived with little change. The Democratic party remained dominant in every state in the region. Planters, industrialists, and other representatives of vested interests, along with the far-flung county-seat governing class, continued to exercise a controlling influence in politics even as they slowly made room for new business and professional groups. Poll taxes, literacy tests, and low voter turnouts were typical characteristics of southern politics at the state level. In the 1920s, after the enfranchisement of women, scarcely more than a fifth of adult southerners voted in either Democratic primaries or general elections. The only meaningful elections were the primaries, which were closed to most blacks until the 1940s. Most political campaigns revolved around the personalities and qualifications of the candidates instead of more significant issues. Nevertheless, the region's politics did change in some respects. New issues and new leaders emerged, and the functions of state government were greatly expanded in the postwar period. The configuration of factional politics in the various states also underwent alteration, gradually assuming their characteristic form in the modern era. With the coming of the Great Depression and the New Deal, moreover, the South faced new and disconcerting challenges to the autonomy of its established politics.

"Any serious effort to understand Southern politics in the 1920s," George B. Tindall has written, "must begin with a recognition that the progressive urge did not disappear but was transformed through greater emphasis upon certain of its tendencies and the distortion of others."[1] While the impulse for "good government" and public services remained strong, the propensity toward reform was largely absorbed by a drive for moral righteousness and conformity, a somewhat muted theme in earlier progressivism. One of the strains of this reformism expressed itself in the zealous campaign to enforce prohibition, which remained a divisive issue in state politics during the

1920s. Alarmed by the growing secularization of their society, southern fundamentalists became more involved in the support of prohibition, the antievolution movement, and the conservative Protestant opposition to Roman Catholicism. The conflict over Darwinian evolution became a hot political question. William Jennings Bryan, now a resident of Florida, traveled over the South condemning the doctrine of evolution, while fiery evangelists like J. Frank Norris of Fort Worth, Texas, spoke in defense of traditional religion. By 1921 a movement for the passage of laws to prevent the teaching of evolution in the public schools was under way, and during the next few years the issue was considered in most of the state legislatures in the southern states. Tennessee and Arkansas enacted such laws, while several other states took administrative actions in an effort to accomplish the same purpose. This fundamentalist crusade contributed to the image of a benighted South held by many Americans in other sections—a South that was viewed as socially backward, intolerant, and prejudiced.

Another reason for such ideas was the Ku Klux Klan. Organized in Georgia in 1915, the secret order spread rapidly through the southern states during the early 1920s. Though the Klan became a national phenomenon, its growth was most notable in the southern states. Its membership and power were especially great in Georgia, Alabama, Arkansas, and Texas, as well as in cities such as Atlanta, Birmingham, Houston, Dallas, Little Rock, and Tulsa. In the South KKK members seemed to be motivated by religious and ethnic prejudices but also by fears of social change and a desire to coerce conformity through morality campaigns and political action. The organization's entry into politics was inevitable, and it enjoyed some political successes in state and local campaigns. It elected or had a hand in electing several governors and U.S. senators in Texas, Georgia, Oklahoma, and Alabama. The Klan declined during the late 1920s but for several years it was a powerful influence as well as an incendiary issue in the Democratic politics of the southern states. In Oklahoma it was an issue in every major political contest during the 1920s.

The prohibition movement and other antivice efforts were expressions of a widespread southern concern over immoral behavior, as well as an aspect of the reformers' commitment to the solution of social problems. The zeal that many southerners had earlier displayed for attacks on trusts and campaigns to overthrow political "machines" drew upon the spring of this morality. It was closely identified with evangelical Protestantism, with rural and small-town life, with agrarian reformism, and with the politics of William Jennings Bryan. Wartime dislocations and rapid social change in the postwar years heightened the social apprehensions of southern moralists and strengthened their resolve to defend the traditional culture. The work of the Ku Klux Klan, for all its prejudice and violence, was in part an expression of that resolve. Community morals were an overriding concern of the organization's members, whose activities represented, among other things, a general quest for moral and social conformity. A similar insistence upon moral conformity was embodied in the anti-evolution crusade and especially in the efforts of Protestant fundamentalists to stamp out "the specter of infidelity." The region's defensive temper in the 1920s was intensified by what its moral custodians interpreted as challenges to southern orthodoxies. One result was a kind of "political fundamentalism," in which defenders of traditional morality sought to deny divisions in southern society by appealing to regional loyalties and coercing a sense of unity. This fundamentalism contained an element of popular democracy, since it reflected the belief of many southerners that their society was being reshaped by a diverse but powerful economic group that seemed to disregard long-established traditions and the idea of popular consent. In any case, the compulsion to preserve cultural values, a basic characteristic of southern progressivism, became more defensive and negative in the 1920s.

Although the postwar era changed the content and spirit of progressivism in the South, it failed to dampen the enthusiasm of southern businessmen and professional people for economic development. Indeed, the war stimulated the region's economic expansion and heightened the yearnings and expectations of its inhabitants for further "progress." The 1920s marked the triumph of the "Atlanta spirit," an era of commercial and industrial expansion, urban boosterism, and growth psychology. The good times of the new era encouraged this outlook, despite a series of agricultural crises and the straitened condition of the textile industry. The preoccupation with economic growth, the institutionalization of state services, and the achievement of administrative efficiency and professional standards, like the crusades for morality, represented an elaboration of older progressive themes. Southern progressives had always been strongly committed to what one scholar has called the need to "modernize the region through transforming its economic base."[2]

"Good government" and more adequate public services, southern leaders increasingly assumed, were as vital to economic progress as natural resources, abundant labor, and resourceful entrepreneurs. This ingredient in prewar progressivism reached early fruition during the 1920s in the politics and policies of several southern states and municipalities. It was evident in the leadership of a number of forceful and effective governors such as Cameron Morrison of North Carolina, John M. Parker of Louisiana, Austin Peay of Tennessee, Bibb Graves of Alabama, and Harry Flood Byrd of Virginia. These exemplars of "business progressives" stressed economy and efficiency. They reorganized and modernized the structure of their state governments, devised new administrative and tax systems, and expanded state services.

The development of public services, a significant but somewhat inchoate part of earlier progressivism, was a notable feature of state and municipal government in the 1920s. In the South dramatic advances were made in the construction of highways, the support of education, the expansion of public health facilities, and the growth of social welfare programs. State revenue and state debt increased sharply. All of these functions were associated with the themes of economic growth, efficiency, and modernization as well as concern over social problems, and they elicited strong backing from businessmen, professional groups, and the urban middle class generally. Chambers of commerce and other business organizations were devoted advocates of good roads; they increasingly identified the automobile as a vehicle of commercial development and urban growth. Professionals such as teachers, engineers, public health doctors and nurses, and social workers were also champions of the expanding role of government in providing what they regarded as essential services. With the growth of these governmental functions came, slowly and hesitantly, a conception of greater state responsibility for social welfare.

A more radical species of reform flared up briefly in Oklahoma, before collapsing in disarray and futility. In the immediate postwar years, an agricultural depression and a determined antilabor movement gave rise to the Farmer-Labor Reconstruction League of Oklahoma, which was organized in 1921. A coalition of agricultural and labor groups, Socialists, and other dissident elements, the League sponsored a program of radical reform measures, including government ownership of railroads and utilities, a guaranteed minimum price for farm commodities, and job security for workers. The new organization found a leader in John C. Walton, an entertaining and effective campaigner who was elected governor in 1922. "Our Jack" Walton soon plunged the state into bitter controversy; he interfered with the state institutions of higher education, made indiscriminate use of the state militia, and as a diversionary tactic launched a war on the Ku Klux Klan. The legislators reacted by impeaching and removing him from office in the autumn of 1923. Oklahoma Democrats were briefly divided into adherents of the Farmer-Labor Reconstruction League and partisans of the Ku Klux Klan. The League declined rapidly after Walton's fall, and the Klan also lost much of its influence soon afterward. Meanwhile, the Republicans made gains, winning a second U.S. Senate seat in 1924, carrying the state for Herbert Hoover in 1928, and making an impressive showing in legislative contests in the latter year. But the minority party was unable to take advantage of Democratic factionalism. In the 1920s, one student of the state's politics concludes, "a party of opportunism and negativism battled a party of factionalism and disorder."[3]

Remnants of the factionalism that had typified Democratic politics in the prewar South were still evident in some states, but most of the older political groupings had disappeared by the 1920s. In Texas, for example, the bifactional competition that characterized early twentieth-century Democratic politics was replaced by shifting political coalitions and a marked increase in the number of candidates in primary elections. Nevertheless, Texas politics in the 1920s continued to bear the imprint of earlier issues and divisions. One evidence of these fissures was the sharp division over prohibition; another was the survival from the Wilson era of the progressive-prohibition wing of the party. Though the faction was splintered by 1920, many of its adherents retained their commitment to prohibition as well as a general orientation toward reform. The bitter conflict among Texas Democrats over their party's presidential nominee in 1924 and 1928 testified to the continuing strength of this political element. Another carryover from the pre-1920 years was what Texans sometimes described as "Fergusonism"—the influence exerted by James E. Ferguson in state politics. Ferguson, a charismatic and colorful campaigner, may well have been the most important figure in Texas politics during the two decades after 1914. Either Ferguson or his wife was a candidate in every statewide election between 1914 and 1934, with the single exception of 1928. Between them they won the governorship four times during this period.

Ferguson was a forty-three-year-old farmer, lawyer, and small-town banker from east central Texas when he decided to enter the Democratic race for governor in 1914. Calling himself "Farmer Jim," Ferguson was presented as a "man who comes from the ranks of the people."[4] He promised to reform the rental system under which thousands of tenant farmers operated, while adamantly expressing opposition to any consideration of the controversial liquor question. He also poked fun at his Democratic opponent, a respectable prohibition leader. Ferguson proved to be a remarkable campaigner, and he won a surprisingly large victory in the primary. The new governor persuaded the legislature to pass a measure regulating farm rents, but the law was never enforced. In 1916 Ferguson was easily reelected. Then he blundered by getting into a dispute with the state university, an episode that opened the way to his impeachment on charges of misapplying state funds and improper interference with the university. When Ferguson was removed from office in 1917, he immediately began a campaign for his "vindication." Thousands of tenant farmers, small landowners, and day laborers—the "boys at the forks of the creek"—continued to have faith in Farmer Jim, who began to publish a paper he called the *Ferguson Forum*. It became a vital means of communicating with his rural flock. "Why, those old fellows out there know but two things," one observer remarked in 1918. "The first is that Levi Garrett & Sons make the best snuff in the world, and the second is that Friday is Forum day, the day the mails bring Ferguson's paper."[5]

Jim Ferguson's greatest political asset was his oratorical skill. He was emotional, reckless, and eloquent in his use of epithets and invective. Reinhard H. Luthin has described him as a campaigner. "Clad in a claw-hammer frock coat, he stuck his left thumb in trousers pocket, raised his right forefinger in the air, and shouted about his opponents' iniquity. Jim could go into a hostile crowd and leave with numerous converts."[6] A contemporary commented on Ferguson's effect on his audiences. "He swayed them like the storm sways the slender pines, and voted them in droves and platoons."[7] Campaigning frequently in the postwar period, Ferguson remained a factor of great importance in state politics. "Jim Ferguson," Will Rogers declared, "has 150,000 voters in Texas that would be with him if he blew up the Capitol building in Washington. They would say, 'Well, Jim was right. The thing ought to have been blowed up years ago.' "[8]

Indeed, Fergusonism was one of the three principal issues in Texas politics in the 1920s. The other two were prohibition and the Ku Klux Klan, both of which Farmer Jim strongly opposed. He also made war on old Wilsonian progressives like Thomas B. Love, who continued to wield power in party affairs. Since Ferguson was barred from holding state office, he adopted the stratagem of running his wife instead. In 1924 this scheme worked, and Miriam Amanda "Ma" Ferguson was elected governor. Jim Ferguson campaigned for his wife, vigorously attacking the role of the Klan in Texas politics. Once in office, Mrs. Ferguson, a quiet, home-loving body, deferred to her husband, who actually ran the administration. Controversy soon began to swirl around the administration, centering on Jim Ferguson's mischievous role in the awarding of highway contracts, in the governor's liberal issuance of pardons, and in the decisions of the state textbook commission. Some of these matters were investigated and challenged in the courts by Attorney General Dan Moody, a rising young political leader who defeated "Ma" Ferguson in her bid for a second term in 1926. Fergusonism, however, was far from dead. Jim Ferguson ran his wife again in 1930; she was defeated in her race for governor that year but was elected in the primary of 1932.

Jim Ferguson's perennial campaigns titillated and entertained the white masses of Texas, especially those who lived in rural areas. Political rallies, "speakings," and personalities remained a source of great interest and excitement in the South during the 1920s, despite the advent of the automobile, radio, and the motion picture. "Men of the people" like Ferguson, Theodore G. Bilbo, and Coleman L. Blease were marvelous exhibitionists with a distinctive mode of dress and a capacity for pageantry and entertainment. Their vivid personalities and brilliant campaign repertoires were often more important than their position on the issues in contributing to their political advancement. Bilbo once remarked that "there is no other entertainment for country folks except revivals and politics—and it is up to us politicians to do our share."[9]

Spectacular political figures and colorful campaigners were encouraged by the individualist and disorganized politics that existed in the one-party South. Factional division of the electorate around a powerful personality became characteristic of southern politics, sometimes providing an element of stability and structure in an essentially amorphous system. On occasion striking leaders of this type advanced the cause of reform, but more often they themselves became the central political issue. The emphasis on personality in political affairs was no doubt related to the longtime dominance of a rural, folk society in the region, to the social paternalism carried over from the Old to the New South, and to the mythology that enveloped the Lost Cause and Reconstruction in the minds of white southerners. Politics in such a culture was a prized pastime and a favorite source of entertainment. Campaign oratory in early twentieth-century South Carolina, Louis B. Wright has recalled, was "pungent and pointed, as candidates recommended themselves and damned their opponents. Nobody complained of apathy, for audiences turned out en masse to enjoy the fun, to cheer their favorites, to heckle the unfortunate, and now and then to shoot one another in the exuberance of partisanship."[10] Politics, in short, was a vital part of the regional culture, as familiar as evangelical Protestantism or the cultivation and marketing of cotton. As one southerner explained in 1922: "It is a recreation, a part of life, a thing in which all are interested, a medium through which men express themselves. A political meeting in a 'warm' year is to be anticipated as the coming of a circus. Men gather at the county seat from villages and farms miles away. The parking spaces are filled with buggies, wagons and automobiles. Most of those who come are men who work with their hands."[11]

While there were many manifestations of the "man of the people" phenomenon in the period between the two world wars, none was more dramatic than the case of Louisiana. Although the conservative

Democrats who ruled the Pelican State in the late nineteenth century were plagued by sharp factional divisions, they carried out the wishes of the planters, the commercial and financial interests centered in New Orleans, and the railroad and lumber companies. Resentment at this state of affairs fanned the fires of agrarian radicalism in the 1890s, but this evidence of class conflict was countered by the Bourbon Democrats' resort to an aroused racial animosity, and the insurgence proved abortive. Perhaps, as a noted scholar has written in another connection, "the religious, linguistic, cultural division of the people itself made it difficult for a leader to arise who understood both groups [the Creole-Catholic south and the Anglo-Protestant north], who constituted a denominator capable of giving full-throated voice to the common unhappinesses and aspirations of both peoples in rip-roaring political campaigns—after which everyone could go back to work."[12] John M. Parker, a planter and business progressive, won the governorship in 1920 by challenging the entrenched political machine and its allies in the state's political hierarchy. The Parker administration sponsored a moderately successful reform program, but it did little to alter the distribution of political power in Louisiana. When Parker left office, the state returned to its accustomed conservatism.

Then, toward the end of the 1920s, a remarkable new leader burst upon the political stage of Louisiana. His name was Huey Pierce Long, and within a few years, he had established the most complete mastery of politics at the state level in American history. Long was born in 1893, the seventh child in a family of middle-class hill farmers. He came from Winn Parish in the north central part of the state. A poor parish, Winn had a heritage of populism, Socialist party support, and political dissent. Leaving home at the age of sixteen, Long spent several years as a traveling salesman in Louisiana and surrounding states. Gregarious and resourceful, he sold household supplies, patent medicines, produce, and a lard substitute called Cottolene. After studying law for a year at Tulane University, he was admitted to the bar and began to practice in Winnfield. In 1918 he was elected to the state railroad commission as a vigorous critic of the Standard Oil Company and other corporations. As a member of the commission and eventually its chairman, he adopted a tough position in dealing with the utilities and was instrumental in securing lower telephone, gas, and electric rates, reduced railroad and streetcar fares, and a severance tax on oil. The audacious Louisianan already had his eye on the governorship, and in 1924, at age thirty, he entered the gubernatorial primary. Although Long lost that race, he could not be denied in 1928. Conducting a colorful, folksy campaign, he denounced the planter-business-New Orleans machine alliance and promised to increase state services. In 1928 he expanded his political base in the northern rural parishes into French Louisiana, including working-class districts in the cities.

Once in office, Long was able to get his legislative program enacted. It included new highway and bridge construction, increased appropriations for schools, public health, and welfare facilities, and cheap natural gas for New Orleans. Needing additional money for the new state services, Long demanded that the legislature levy an occupation tax on refined crude oil. This alarmed powerful interests in the state, and the governor's efforts to force the lawmakers to approve the tax were unsuccessful. Long's enemies then sought to remove him from office by charging him with several counts of misconduct. The house of representatives voted to impeach Long, but the senate failed to find him guilty of the charges. In fact, the impeachment move backfired, and Long steadily extended his control over the various agencies of state government. Unlike most southern reformers, Long set out not only to bring the political establishment in his state to terms; he intended to overwhelm the Louisiana hierarchy and to replace it with his own authority. He created a powerful and ruthless state machine. He also destroyed the old pattern of Louisiana politics and brought a new and enduring factionalism into existence. The struggle between "Longism" and "anti-Longism" would dominate the state's politics for a generation or more.

Huey Long, who moved on to the U.S. Senate in 1932 and was assassinated in September 1935, struck many Americans as a clownish fellow who liked the nickname "Kingfish," extolled the virtues of "potlikker," organized extravagant football trips for students at the state university, and sometimes received formal visitors while attired in green pajamas. He was full of what Wilbur J. Cash described as "the swaggering, hell-for-leather bluster that the South demanded in its heroes and champions; and in addition he had a kind of quizzical, broad, clowning humor, and a capacity for taking on the common touch that had characteristically been the stock-in-trade not only of the more successful demagogues but even of many of the best of the older leaders."[13] Like other southern demagogues, the Kingfish "stroked the ego of democracy,"[14] but, more than most of them, he made the masses feel important. He was, as Cash remarked, "wholly Southern in his capacity to represent all his deeds to himself as proceeding from the most splendid motives."[15] In his manners, values, and idiom, Arthur M. Schlesinger, Jr., has written, "Huey Long remained a backcountry hillbilly. But he was a hillbilly raised to the highest level, preternaturally swift and sharp in intelligence, ruthless in action, and grandiose in vision."[16]

If Long was unmistakably southern, he was southern with a difference. He himself once dismissed the speculation about his essential

character by saying that he was simply *sui generis*. It was an apt de-
lineation. The Louisiana leader was, for one thing, a realist rather
than a romantic in politics. He was, in the view of one critical observer,
"the first Southern politician to stand really apart from his people and
coolly and accurately to measure the political potentialities afforded
by the condition of the underdog."[17] Then, too, Long was adept in
the arts of power. He created his own political organization, overwhelmed an established party hierarchy, and replaced it with a state
machine based on the poor and disadvantaged and fueled by astute
use of patronage. Nor was that the end of it: he had a program, and
he kept his promises. Long was not basically a corruptionist, nor did
he employ "nigger-baiting" tactics to win elections. He had a populist
animosity toward concentrated wealth and upper-class privilege, tried
to promote greater equality, and insisted that government must be
responsive to social needs. He was, as one historian has suggested,
"democrat, demagogue, populist, capitalist, political boss"—and all
of these generic strains were "firmly rooted in the American political
tradition."[18] "Perhaps the lesson of Long," T. Harry Williams concluded, "is that if in a democracy needed changes are denied too long
by an interested minority, the changes, when they come, will come
with a measure of repression and revenge."[19]

In general, the years between World War I and the onset of the
Great Depression represented a period of consolidation in the evolving pattern of state politics in the South. Changes had occurred in
the factional politics of the individual states, the role of business and
industrial interests had grown larger, and the functions of state and
municipal governments in the region had expanded. But the basic
features of the one-party system were as solidly established in custom
and law as ever. It was this pattern of state politics that V.O. Key
illuminated so brilliantly in 1949 with the publication of *Southern Politics in State and Nation*. At the same time, southern politics in the 1930s
and 1940s was by no means static. Political leaders and issues, in the
South as in other regions, were strongly influenced by the impact of
the Great Depression, the leadership of Franklin D. Roosevelt, the
comprehensive legislation of the New Deal, the national realignment
of political parties in the 1930s, and the vast consequences of World
War II.

Three of the southern states—Virginia, Tennessee, and Georgia—
were distinguished by having fairly well-defined factions in their
Democratic parties. The median percentage of the total vote polled
jointly by the two top candidates for governor in the first Democratic
primary in Virginia during the years 1920–48 was an astonishing 98.3.
The factionalism among Virginia Democrats was grounded in the
dominance of a powerful machine. Although an independent Demo-

crat won the governorship in 1917 and Thomas S. Martin died in 1919, the Democratic organization retained control of the state's politics. Carter Glass, Virginia's most distinguished citizen and a longtime opponent of the Martin machine, made his peace with the organization in the early 1920s. In the meantime, Harry Flood Byrd, chairman of the state Democratic committee, emerged as undisputed leader of the organization. Byrd was elected governor in 1925. The organization suffered a defeat in 1928 when anti-Smith Democrats joined with Republicans to carry the state for Hoover. But the organization recovered quickly, winning the governorship the following year against a coalition of dissident Democrats and Republicans.

Led by Harry Flood Byrd and strengthened during his governorship in the late 1920s, the "organization" owed its success to effective management and a restricted electorate, which enabled its disciplined and well-organized campaigns to mobilize the requisite number of votes to win statewide primary elections. The machine enjoyed strong support from the business community and the well-to-do. Through Senator Byrd's leadership (he entered the Senate in 1933), the power of the legislature over key local officials, and the cooperation of circuit judges and other members of the "courthouse rings," the hierarchy could count on a network of outposts across the state. Although the Byrd organization was an oligarchy with a cavalier and aristocratic outlook, it insisted upon honest and efficient government, and it demonstrated some flexibility within the bounds of fiscal conservatism. Guided by Byrd and made more formidable by the support of such leaders as the venerable Carter Glass in the Senate and Everett R. "Ebbie" Combs, state comptroller and chairman of the state compensation board, the organization was almost always able to elect its candidates. The antiorganization faction was a loose alliance of Virginia Democrats generally identified as liberals. It was strongest in the tidewater areas, especially the cities, and in the southwestern mountain counties. In the 1930s and 1940s, these dissenters tended to support national Democratic leaders and their policies.

"A cohesive and continuing majority faction," V.O. Key observed in his analysis of southern politics, "tends to force most opposition elements into at least the semblance of a united minority faction."[20] That was the case in Virginia. It was also true of Tennessee, which experienced great political turmoil in the 1920s. In the immediate postwar years, political groupings took the form of extremely personalized and amorphous coalitions created by individual candidates. The nature of this party factionalism began to change in 1922 with the election as governor of Austin Peay, a business progressive whose administration reorganized the state government and provided new highways, educational facilities, and other needed public services.

One consequence of Peay's leadership was a realignment of Tennessee politics in which the rural areas, desperately in need of better schools and roads, were arrayed against the cities, which supplied most of the money to pay for the new services. Governor Peay and his allies led the rural faction. In addition, Peay's administrative innovations, designed to make for greater efficiency, concentrated power at the state level and in the hands of the governor. After Peay's sudden death in 1927, his political heirs, led by Luke Lea, the powerful publisher of the Nashville *Tennessean*, attempted to build a statewide machine, using the power in the governor's office and the allocation of state contracts and other favors. Meanwhile, an opposition faction, encouraged by corruption and scandal in the state administration, gained strength. The struggle between the two factions came to a climax in 1932 and brought a new political boss to power in the Volunteer State.

Edward Hull Crump entered politics early in the twentieth century as a typical urban reformer. He supported the new commission government in Memphis, became mayor of the city in 1910, and achieved an impressive record as an efficient administrator and successful sponsor of expanded municipal services. But he opposed prohibition and was ousted from office in 1916 for failing to enforce the state's dry law in Memphis. This setback was only temporary, however, for Crump proceeded to build a formidable political organization. He eventually controlled all of the major city and county offices as well as the party machinery in Shelby County. By the late 1920s, he had become the single most powerful politician in Tennessee. Crump's control of Tennessee's most populous city enabled him, when the opportunity came, to use that secure base as a springboard to statewide power. The collapse of the banking empire of Rogers Caldwell in late 1930 and the subsequent discrediting of Luke Lea for having misused state funds in Caldwell's speculative schemes undermined the administration of Gov. Henry Horton and the faction once led by Austin Peay. Crump moved quickly at this point to establish his own dominance over Tennessee politics. He advocated the impeachment of Governor Horton, and in 1932 succeeded in electing his own gubernatorial candidate, Hill McAlister. For the next sixteen years, the Memphis leader was the most influential factor in Tennessee politics. During this period his was frequently the determining voice in statewide elections for major office.

Edward Crump's dominant position was based on his thoroughgoing control of political affairs in Memphis and Shelby County and on the peculiarities of Tennessee politics. He saw to it that the people in Memphis received efficient and honest—but somewhat repressive—government, and his machine made sure that a large number of Memphians registered and voted. In a state with a perennially low voter turnout, Crump's dependable 50,000 or more votes in Shelby County could easily make the difference in statewide elections. Almost one-third of the total Democratic primary vote came from Shelby County, which was accustomed to giving Boss Crump's ticket a majority of about 85 percent. The Memphis leader was strongly supported by the business community, received the endorsement of conservative labor leaders, and controlled a sizable bloc of black voters. The Crump faction also received support from many Democrats in Republican East Tennessee, since they looked to Nashville and Washington for patronage. It was widely believed, moreover, that the Crump organization received some backing in Democratic primaries from East Tennessee Republicans in exchange for certain favors and acquiescence in local GOP control. The organization's control of the legislative process gave it considerable leverage with politicians in the various towns and counties, since in Tennessee local governments required a good deal of special legislation from Nashville. There were still other sources of strength for Crump and his friends. They controlled Democratic party machinery, could count on a friendly reception in the governor's office, had great influence in the legislature, and were allied with Sen. Kenneth D. McKellar, who was able to dispense a large amount of federal patronage to the right people in Tennessee.

Opposition to the Crump forces, though usually manifesting itself through shifting alliances rather than a coherent faction, was able to turn out a substantial vote. A degree of continuity was evident in the antiorganization wing, some of whose elements had been identified with the administration of Austin Peay. The anti-Crump faction was centered in Middle Tennessee, and its most vigorous newspaper support came from the Nashville *Tennessean*, whose publisher, Silliman Evans, directed a steady barrage of criticism at Crump and his tactics. The most prominent leader of this faction was Gordon Browning, who broke with Crump after receiving his support in the gubernatorial primary of 1936. As governor, Browning attempted unsuccessfully to reduce the power of Memphis, and therefore Crump, in statewide elections by introducing a county-unit system that would favor rural areas.

Georgia was another state in which the voters customarily were lined up in two Democratic factions. One wing of the party was made up of Eugene Talmadge's followers; the other was comprised of his opponents. As Key wrote, "The Talmadge personality and the vividness of his race and class appeals divided the Georgia electorate into two camps, whose struggles created a strong tendency toward bi-factionalism."[21] A political firebrand who called himself a "dirt farmer" and encouraged comparison with Tom Watson, Talmadge was a dynamic figure in Georgia politics for two decades. He ran in every statewide primary except one between 1926 and 1946 and won seven victories during that period. As commissioner of agriculture in the late 1920s, he fought the fertilizer "trust," misspent public funds on the Chicago hog market, and used his weekly agricultural bulletin to build a statewide political base. As governor between 1933 and 1937, he fought with the legislature, employed dictatorial tactics, and bitterly attacked the national government's deficit spending and welfare programs. After two unsuccessful campaigns for the U. S. Senate in 1936 and 1938, "Our Gene" was again elected governor in 1940. Talmadge's growing racism was a factor in his heavy-handed intervention in the affairs of the University of Georgia, a move that cost several units in the university system their accreditation and that contributed largely to the governor's defeat in his bid for reelection. When he died in December 1946, following a successful campaign for another term as governor, the leadership of his faction was transferred to his son Herman.

A contemporary account described Talmadge as "a dynamic and powerful stump speaker, a rabble-rouser with few equals among the piney-woods potentates of Dixie."[22] He delighted in a political fracas. Slender and wiry, with horn-rimmed glasses and a lock of dark hair that fell across his forehead, he would "shuck off" his coat at a rally, revealing a pair of red "galluses," roll up his shirt sleeves, and swing into a fiery tirade against his opponents—to the great approbation of his rural audiences. He pushed the "dirt farmer" theme hard and took advantage of the rural-dominated county-unit electoral system. "The poor dirt farmer," it was said, "ain't got but three friends on this earth: God Almighty, Sears Roebuck, and Gene Talmadge."[23] Although the "Wild Man from Sugar Creek," as he was often called, was a dominant leader in Georgia politics for many years, he had neither an organization nor a program. His flamboyant campaigns, personal magnetism, and race and class appeals brought him a loyal following from rural and small-town areas. But he offered no solutions to the economic and social problems of his supporters. He had no ideological direction beyond state rights, individualism, racial segregation, and an agrarianism that "blended the populism of Tom Watson and the parsimony of Jeffersonianism."[24] His social conservatism is captured in Numan V. Bartley's comment: "In the theater of the absurd that had become Georgia politics, the protection of rural and village usages and customs meant striking out at virtually anything that was not inherently native to the Georgia countryside."[25]

Talmadge's laissez-faire principles, fiscal conservatism, and opposition to organized labor eventually caused business interests to give him their quiet backing.

Eugene Talmadge's most enduring accomplishment was to divide the Georgia electorate into two camps that reflected a strong rural-urban cleavage and helped to create a structure of Democratic bifactionalism in the state. Opposition to Talmadge was stronger in urban places than in the countryside, and it was generally more prevalent in the northern part of the state than in south Georgia. With Talmadge or his personal candidate in a race, the opposition usually managed to consolidate against the common enemy.

North Carolina, like Virginia and Tennessee, had a dominant political organization and two fairly well-defined Democratic factions. The two top vote-getters in the Democratic primaries during this period normally received at least three-fourths of the total ballots between them. Following the defection of Sen. Furnifold M. Simmons in the presidential election of 1928 and the collapse of his long-entrenched organization, a new Democratic hierarchy gradually emerged under the leadership of Gov. O. Max Gardner. It came to be known as the Shelby Dynasty, since Gardner and several of the new organization's leaders came from the Piedmont town of Shelby. The predominant faction was strongest in the Piedmont and western section, and it was generally supported by the dynamic industrial and financial interests of the state. Unlike the Simmons organization, which relied upon a personal network of local politicians spread over the state, the Shelby Dynasty depended heavily upon the elective and appointive officers of the state administration, especially those heading the highway and revenue departments. Leaders of the controlling faction were in tune with North Carolina's moderate progressivism—with its commitment to industrial development, educational advancement, and harmonious race relations—and they favored the program of centralization and efficiency pushed through the legislature by the Gardner administration. North Carolina Republicans, concentrated in the western counties and normally polling from one-fourth to a third of the vote for governor, were strong enough to force a measure of coherence and discipline on the Democratic party. The result was an effort by the state's Democrats to create a genuine party organization with a statewide outlook.

Governor Gardner selected J.C. Blucher Ehringhaus as his successor. Ehringhaus was opposed in the gubernatorial primary of 1932 by Lt. Gov. Richard T. Fountain, who was viewed by many North Carolinians as the "little man's" candidate. Fountain was defeated, but the race was close. His electoral strength lay in the eastern tobacco belt and the coastal plain, where resistance to the established orga-

The Black Belt: Bedrock of Southern Solidarity

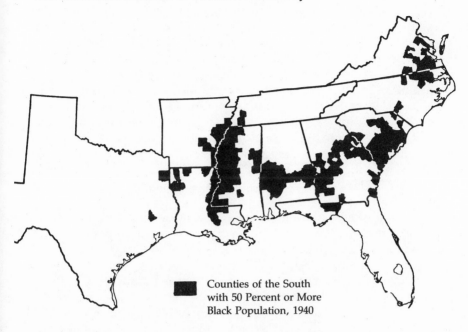

Counties of the South
with 50 Percent or More
Black Population, 1940

Reprinted with permission from V.O. Key, Jr., *Southern Politics in State and Nation*, new ed. (Knoxville: Univ. of Tennessee Press, 1984), p. 6.

nization was greatest. The insurgent Democrats were weakened in 1935 when Dennis G. Brummitt, an outstanding opposition leader in the legislature, died. Even so, Ralph McDonald, a former professor at Salem College, mounted a vigorous campaign in 1936 against Clyde R. Hoey, the candidate of the regular Democrats. Given support by most opposition leaders, McDonald attacked the Ehringhaus administration's sales tax, ran on a liberal-labor platform, and promised the state a "Little New Deal." But the regulars prevailed, as they continued to do during the next decade. McDonald challenged the dominant faction again in 1944, but he was defeated once more. By the time World War II had ended, however, there were signs that the Shelby Dynasty was beginning to lose its grip on state politics.

The factional organization in Alabama's one-party system was tenuous and shifting. In the absence of a stable and enduring bifactionalism, political groups were highly personal and amorphous, revolving around powerful state leaders. Factions were formed and reformed, as voters joined one faction and then another. Yet there was some continuity and rationality in the way Alabama Democrats aligned themselves during the 1930s and 1940s. One basis for such division was the state's traditional sectionalism, in which the northern and southeastern sections of the state were arrayed against the black belt–Birmingham "big mules." A pronounced localism found expression in the support political candidates received from friends and neighbors. There was also an ideological factor in the factional conflict among Alabamians. The Great Depression and the New Deal sharpened such ideological considerations by forcing new economic and political issues into the arena of state politics. Thus, Alexander Heard concluded in 1947, after interviewing a large number of Alabama politicians, that the "only consistent division" on matters of policy among the state's Democrats was the split between "liberal" and "conservative" individuals.[26]

Perhaps the most influential factional leader of this period in Alabama was Bibb Graves. A product of the progressive era in Alabama politics and a business progressive as governor in the late 1920s, Graves constructed a formidable personal following. Though not himself ideologically inclined, he became a strong New Dealer and as governor during the years 1935–39 assumed the leadership of the liberal Democratic faction in Alabama. Planning to seek another term as governor in 1942, he died on the eve of the primary election, leaving the liberals without a good candidate. Meanwhile, Frank Dixon, who served as governor from 1939 to 1943, represented the conservative faction.

In Louisiana Huey Long strengthened his political machine and extended his control over government during the early 1930s. He unveiled his "share-our-wealth" program in 1933, became increasingly critical of the Roosevelt administration's policies, and began to develop plans for his own presidential candidacy in 1936. His totalitarian regime was based both on mass loyalty and on the exercise of coercive power. Unlike earlier southern reformers, Long was not hamstrung by an uncooperative legislature; he elected his own legislature, forced it to enact his programs, and saw to it that the corporations paid for many of the new public services. Longism brought more people to the polls than ever before in Louisiana history. The Kingfish employed all of the techniques of the traditional machine, and he raised money to operate his organization from such sources as state control of petroleum production, gambling concessions, and "deducts" from state employees. Long's tight control was opposed by most of Louisiana's large newspapers and usually by the "better element," but this opposition was of no avail during Long's lifetime. The machine continued in power after Long's death. In 1936 Richard W. Leche, the Longite candidate for governor, was elected. Organization leaders entered into better relations with the federal government, and they seemed to become somewhat more conservative than in Huey's heyday.

The Long machine began to disintegrate in 1939 with a series of revelations of political corruption in the Leche administration and of extensive bribery, embezzlement, and other types of malfeasance involving Long's heirs. Leche soon resigned and finally went to prison, along with several of his cohorts. In the political reaction that followed these spectacular developments, a conservative named Sam Houston Jones won the governorship in 1940, defeating Earl K. Long, the late Kingfish's brother. Running on a clean-up platform but one that also promised a liberal program of public services, Jones emphasized such themes as good government, honesty, and efficiency in administration. Jones was succeeded by Jimmie H. Davis, another "reform" candidate who defeated the Long faction's candidate in the gubernatorial primary of 1944.

One of Huey Long's legacies was a durable bifactionalism in the state's one-party system. This dual factionalism exhibited a high degree of coherence and continuity. One evidence of remarkable cleavage was the use of "tickets" or "slates" in primary elections, with candidates of the two factions running together for state offices, party posts, and sometimes even parish positions. The Long tickets were normally strongest in northern Louisiana and generally among small farmers, workers, and the less affluent. The anti-Long or "good government" faction was usually supported by the business interests and the "better element," and its candidates fared best in the cities and larger towns and in the planter parishes. The two groups also differed in their orientation toward the national Democratic party, especially after 1940. The Long faction tended to support the policies of the national party, whereas the anti-Long grouping became increasingly hostile toward the New Deal, federal initiatives, and the politics of the national Democratic party. "Both sides were chastened and moderated by experience," George B. Tindall has written, "but they still presented Louisiana voters the dilemma of choice between buccaneering 'liberals' and standpat 'reformers.' "[27]

Kentucky also moved toward a more clearly defined state politics but in a very different way from Louisiana. During the 1920s Kentucky Democrats were divided and disorganized, while the so-called Bi-Partisan Combine ruled the state to the advantage of powerful racetrack, liquor, and coal concerns. Alben W. Barkley, a reform Democrat, challenged these interests in the Democratic gubernatorial primary of 1923, but he lost to a conservative candidate. Another reform candidate was defeated in 1927. These factional struggles, in which moral and economic reformers were pitted against conservatives acceptable to the established political and economic interests, enhanced the prospects of the state's Republicans, whose strength was increasing in this period. Republicans won the governorship in 1919 and again in 1927, and they carried the state in the presidential elections of 1924 and 1928. The Great Depression and the New Deal reversed this Republican trend and promoted a resurgence of Democratic strength, particularly among coal miners, farmers, blacks, and urban workers. These events also altered the factional lines in the state's Democratic party.

The administration organization, known locally as the Rhea-Laffoon machine, was defeated in 1935 by Albert B. "Happy" Chandler, whose governorship proved to be popular and successful. Although Chandler carried out some modest reforms, including administrative reorganization, he was not a New Dealer, and in fact, he failed in his attempt in 1938 to unseat Alben Barkley, a strong champion of the Roosevelt administration in the Senate. But the governor did succeed in building a robust political faction of his own, and it remained an important feature of the state's politics for many years. Democratic bifactionalism was reinforced by the absence of a run-off primary, a situation that encouraged party leaders to line up behind two major candidates. Kentucky politics, it was sometimes said, was really represented by three parties. One was the Republican party. The other were Democratic factions, one led by "Happy" Chandler, the other by leaders such as Earle C. Clements, who served as governor from 1947 to 1951. In that respect, at least, the state had developed a somewhat more stable political structure than in the first decades of the twentieth century.

Promising signs of an emerging two-party system in Oklahoma were obliterated by the Great Depression and the New Deal. With the Republican party reduced to impotence and the fade-out of earlier Democratic divisions over the Farmer-Labor Reconstruction League and the Ku Klux Klan, Oklahoma voters aligned themselves around strong personalities in state politics. Thus, they elected William H. "Alfalfa Bill" Murray to the governorship in 1930. Murray, an eccentric, outspoken, and unrepentant old agrarian, had played a leading role in framing the Oklahoma constitution and in Oklahoma's government during the early years of statehood. Murray had little success with his legislative proposals, opposed New Deal relief programs, and left office as a bitter critic of the Roosevelt administration in Washington. But "Murrayism" remained a divisive issue in the state's politics.

Murray's successor was Ernest W. Marland, the head of an oil empire that had collapsed in 1930. Marland promised to "bring the New Deal to Oklahoma," and as governor he sponsored an impressive program of public works, unemployment benefits, public power projects, and other state improvements. These proposals encountered determined resistance in the legislature, in the metropolitan press, and in business circles. Marland's inept leadership contributed to the failure of his administration and to the bankruptcy of his legislative program. The first of his legislatures was extremely economy-minded, while the second appropriated money lavishly for its own pet projects and for patronage purposes. Despite the weakness of the Marland administration, the New Deal was popular in the Sooner State, and in 1936 one of its strong advocates, Joshua B. Lee, was elected to the U.S. Senate. But there was also a growing movement against the New Deal among Oklahomans, and for a time a vague cleavage developed along New Deal and anti–New Deal lines. Leon C. "Red" Phillips, a conservative legislator and an opponent of Marland's proposals, won the governorship in 1938. By the early 1940s, a strong ideological conservatism had become ascendant in the Democratic party of Oklahoma. This sentiment was one reason for the defeat of Senator Lee in 1942 and the election of Ed H. Moore, a reactionary defector from Roosevelt's party.

Personal factions continued to be important in Texas politics during the 1930s and 1940s. The most notable of these were those identified with two rural demagogues: James E. Ferguson and W. Lee "Pappy" O'Daniel. Disqualified for state office himself, Jim Ferguson continued to use his wife as his political proxy. In 1932, in the depths of the depression, the Fergusons won again, and "Ma" served another term as governor. That was to be the end of the line for the Fergusons, although Mrs. Ferguson ran once more in 1940, but without success. O'Daniel, a flour salesman with a hillbilly band and a folksy and religious radio program, superseded Jim Ferguson as the hero of the rural masses. Taking advantage of his large radio following, he suddenly decided to run for governor and, to the surprise of most observers, won the Democratic primary in 1938. His platform included the Ten Commandments, abolition of the poll tax, a thirty-dollar-per-month pension for those over sixty-five, and opposition to a sales tax. O'Daniel was reelected in 1940 and won a special election to the U.S. Senate in 1941. James V. Allred, who served as governor from 1935 to 1939, gave Texas its most constructive administration during this period.

While not manifesting itself primarily in gubernatorial politics, an intense conflict gradually developed between pro– and anti–New Deal Democrats in the Lone Star State. This factionalism reflected economic and class differences. "The confluence of the anxieties of the newly rich and the repercussions of the New Deal in Texas," V.O. Key observed, "pushed politics into a battle of conservatives versus liberals, terms of common usage in political discourse in the state."[28] The scholar called attention to the fluid social structure in Texas: to the effects of rapid population growth, migration into and within the state, increasing urbanization, and the "wholesale manufacture" of new members of the upper economic orders. In such a volatile social milieu, one could find the promise of substantial change in the state's politics.

Democratic factionalism in the other southern states was even more fluid and unstable. The pattern of intraparty competition in these four states was a far cry from the clearly defined bifactionalism of Virginia and Georgia Democrats. In Arkansas, following the spectacular Jeff Davis early in the century, a succession of bland and generally conservative governors had come and gone without effecting any lasting change in the configuration of state politics. There was no statewide organization with either coherence or continuity. Given the small, homogeneous electorate, state politics developed few controversial issues. While the New Deal was an influential force in Arkansas politics, it did not create a durable division over economic policy among the voters. The most important political groupings were short-lived personal factions brought together by successful governors or other statewide candidates. Local leaders and machines played a central role in such statewide coalitions, while powerful economic interests such as the Arkansas Power and Light Company exerted great influence in state government. The most notable personal factions in the 1930s and 1940s were those led by two governors: Carl Bailey (1937–41) and Homer Adkins (1941–45).

South Carolina politics, like Arkansas's, was characterized by individualist, free-for-all intraparty fighting. The state's loose multifactional system revolved around the personal followings of strong governors. It also reflected a powerful localism and the long-standing animosity between the upcountry and the coastal plain (with the city of Charleston). The Palmetto State's preoccupation with matters of race inhibited the development of a more distinct bifactionalism along economic and sectional lines. Although Cole Blease retained his hold on his prewar constituency, the old Blease and anti-Blease polarity lost strength in the 1920s as the insurgent leader's popularity declined. The most noteworthy political factions in South Carolina politics during the years of the Great Depression and World War II were those of two governors: Olin D. Johnston and Burnet R. Maybank. One came from Spartanburg in the upcountry, the other from Charleston in the low country. Both men were later elected to the U.S. Senate.

Johnston, the upcountryman, served as governor during the years 1935–39. His administration was identified with a number of labor and welfare reforms, and he acquired a reputation as a "New Deal" governor. His rise to power was also based on traditional divisions and grievances in South Carolina: upcountry opposition to Charleston and patrician influence, alleged frauds in Charleston, reaction against some of the control exerted by a legislative clique known as the "Barnwell Ring," and Johnston's appeal to the state's mill workers. After losing contests for the Senate in 1938 and 1941, he was elected governor for a second term in 1942. Two years later he defeated the venerable Ellison D. "Cotton Ed" Smith in a campaign for the Senate. By that time Johnston had won the confidence of some conservative elements, and he seized on the race issue that arose with the outlawing of the white primary by the Supreme Court. Maybank, who succeeded Johnston as governor in 1939, was descended from a famous South Carolina family, headed a political machine in Charleston, and was himself something of a New Dealer. As governor he provided effective support for the Santee-Cooper power project, worked hard to obtain federal aid for the state, and placed great emphasis on the importance of economic development in the future of South Carolina.

An amorphous and transient multifactionalism also marked Mississippi politics in this period. The era of "redneck" control of the state government had apparently ended by the mid-1920s. By that time both James K. Vardaman and Theodore G. Bilbo had been defeated and repudiated. The old division between the delta and the hills still manifested itself occasionally in political campaigns and legislative debates, but it had softened and lost much of its intensity. The most important groupings were those that developed around the state's major political figures; few of these possessed much discipline or continuity. Although the New Deal became an issue in state politics, it did not provide the basis for a new and enduring factionalism among Mississippians. The only political faction possessing a semblance of stability and continuity in the 1930s and 1940s was the personal following of Theodore Bilbo.

Bilbo's influence in Mississippi politics lasted for almost forty years, from his emergence as a leader in the Vardaman faction early in the century until his death in 1947. Following his governorship, his political fortunes declined. Bilbo lost elections in 1918 and 1923, but then he was elected to a second term as governor in 1927. He had little success with the legislature, however, and when he left office early in 1932 the state was on the verge of bankruptcy. His career seemed to be at an end. Yet Bilbo was a resilient politician with a faithful following, and in 1934 he won a U.S. Senate seat. He was reelected in 1940 and 1946. Somewhat surprisingly, the Mississippi senator quickly became a staunch supporter of the Roosevelt administration's reform program. He was far more enthusiastic about many New Deal measures than his senior colleague, Byron Patton "Pat"

Harrison, an influential Senate chairman and himself one of the administration's congressional leaders. There was no love lost between the two senators, and in 1936 Bilbo tried unsuccessfully to defeat Harrison by supporting Martin S. Conner against him. This contest demonstrated how difficult it was even for Bilbo to transfer his personal following to the support of another candidate, particularly against a man as resourceful and popular as Harrison. "The Man" had more success in supporting two winning gubernatorial candidates: Paul B. Johnson in 1939 and Thomas L. Bailey in 1943. In the second of these primaries, the contest was infused with state-rights rhetoric and criticism of federal bureaucracy, and Bilbo was increasingly stamped as a racist demagogue. With his death, however, Mississippi no longer had a unifying personality around whom a faction could form.

In Florida the Broward and anti-Broward wings of the Democratic party gradually receded, while the personal following of Sidney J. Catts, the state's next "man of the people," did not survive his governorship as a strong force. Political coalitions, usually constructed by successful candidates for statewide office, were remarkably transitory, and there was a great turnover in the state's major political leaders. The gubernatorial primaries normally attracted a large number of candidates. No basic cleavage arose in the electorate over issues or principles, except for an imperfect sectional division between north and south and a tendency in some campaigns toward a conservative versus liberal dichotomy. In some respects, no doubt, the state's shapeless and shifting politics reflected its rapid urbanization, economic diversification, population growth, and influx of newcomers.

As in other southern states, the New Deal influenced the course of Florida politics in the 1930s and 1940s. For one thing, it provided the state with desperately needed federal assistance. David Sholtz, who served as governor during the years 1933–37, showed unusual resourcefulness in tapping these sources. Support for and opposition to the policies of the Roosevelt administration inevitably flowed into electoral politics in Florida. Sen. Claude Pepper, an ardent New Dealer, won reelection in 1938 and 1944. Rep. Lex Green became a strong supporter of the New Deal. But such a reputation was not necessarily an asset in Florida politics. In the gubernatorial primary of 1936, for example, Fred Cone defeated Raleigh Petteway, in part because the latter was accused of being a "reformer" bent on establishing a New Deal in the Peninsula State. Millard Caldwell won the governorship in 1944, taking advantage of Representative Green's reputation as a "liberal." "Floridians," two scholars observe, "have shown a persistent dislike of liberal, free-spending candidates at the state level."[29] By the same token, business leaders helped determine the outcome of statewide elections such as the gubernatorial primaries of 1940 and 1944. Florida was undergoing enormous change as mid-century approached, but no basic alteration of the state's politics had occurred since the time of Napoleon Bonaparte Broward.

By the end of World War I, the early twentieth-century patterns of Democratic factionalism in the southern states were disappearing. From the matrix of the 1920s, new patterns began to evolve that would become characteristic of southern politics in the 1930s and 1940s. With the coming of the Great Depression, the region's concern with the politics of morality associated with prohibition, religious fundamentalism, and the Ku Klux Klan receded. The search for industrial development and economic growth, on the other hand, continued to occupy southern governors and legislators. In Mississippi, for instance, Gov. Hugh L. White secured the adoption in 1936 of his "Balance Agriculture with Industry" program. One of the most important factors in the political affairs of the South after 1933 was the New Deal, which became a central issue in state politics and a stimulus to liberal ideas and leadership throughout the region. But the New Deal also brought a conservative reaction in the southern states, and in the 1940s this conservatism gained strength. Conservatives throughout this period continued to benefit from the overrepresentation of rural constituencies, from the restricted electorates in most southern states, and from powerful influence exerted by local elites, business groups, and other vested interests.

The state systems that emerged during these years were surprisingly diverse. They ranged across a spectrum from fairly clear-cut and stable dual factions in some states to loose and impermanent multifactional groupings in others. They included the well-ordered Virginia organization, Boss Crump's Tennessee, Gene Talmadge's personal faction in Georgia, Huey Long's lasting influence in Louisiana, and the free-for-all politics in Florida. Yet all of the thirteen southern states were one-party states. The Republican party did have some strength in the upper South and in Oklahoma. But the Solid South remained intact. Despite growing southern opposition to federal intervention and to the national party initiatives, prospects for the disruption of the region's Democratic solidarity were not very bright at the end of World War II. Significant changes in the pattern of state politics in the South seemed equally remote. Nevertheless, the New Deal had profoundly affected southern politics and the political role of the South in the nation.

5 The South and the New Deal

The onset of the Great Depression, the election of Franklin D. Roosevelt in 1932, and the popularity of the New Deal destroyed any hope the Republicans may have had of building on the southern defection in the presidential election of 1928. Roosevelt's leadership tended to broaden and nationalize the outlook of southern congressmen, in the manner of Woodrow Wilson, and the southerners, a goodly number of whom had been in Congress during the Wilson years, once again dominated committee chairmanships and parliamentary proceedings. Frank Freidel has summed up the contributions of the South and its congressional leaders to the enactment of the New Deal and to Roosevelt's foreign policy. "The South figured largely and indeed vitally in Roosevelt's political destinies. Most important of all, had it not been for Southern support, he would never have been nominated for President in 1932 and thus would never have reached the White House. It was Southern leadership in Congress that enacted the New Deal program and subsequently supplied to the President the requisite margin of votes to pass defense measures in the late thirties and early forties."[1]

Nevertheless, the South's response to Roosevelt and the New Deal was ambivalent. One disquieting development was the reconstruction of the Democratic party. While the South remained a vital part of the Democratic coalition, it was suddenly changed by the partisan realignment of the 1930s from a majority faction in a minority party to a minority faction in a majority party. The massive Democratic gains outside the South, which provided the foundation for the Roosevelt coalition of organized labor, urban ethnic groups, and blacks, drastically reduced the dependence of the national party on southern voters and threatened the traditional power of southern leaders in Washington. One of the South's longtime defenses—the two-thirds rule for making presidential nominations in national Democratic conventions—was abolished in 1936. Still, southern congressmen assumed a central role in the legislative history of the 1930s. On the

negative side, their powerful positions and skillful use of obstruc-
tionist tactics enabled them to turn back efforts to pass an antilynching
bill and to outlaw the poll tax as a voting prerequisite. Opposition to
Roosevelt's reform program gradually increased among southern congressmen, who helped bring the New Deal to a halt in the late 1930s
and some of whom entered into an informal conservative coalition
with Republican lawmakers.

During World War II and the early postwar years, the Solid South
remained intact. Southerners, in and out of Congress, rallied to the
support of Franklin Roosevelt's foreign and defense policies, and following the war the South strongly endorsed the nation's new international leadership. In the presidential election of 1944, southerners
gave Roosevelt 69 percent of their ballots, as compared to the 52
percent he received in the Northeast and to his 49 percent in the
Midwest. In Congress, as one scholar has observed, the devices of
the concurrent majority "had taken such deep root and were, on the
whole, protected so skillfully by the champions of the Southern position that the carefully constructed Southern mechanism did not fall
apart all at once like the wonderful one-horse shay."[2]

Franklin D. Roosevelt, who became governor of New York in
1929, was the principal beneficiary of Alfred E. Smith's overwhelming
defeat in the election of 1928. Most southerners viewed Roosevelt as
an attractive alternative to Smith, and the region's politicians provided
strong support for his nomination in 1932. The New Yorker, who
began to visit Warm Springs, Georgia, in the mid-1920s for the
strengthening of his withered legs, had established himself as something of "a Georgia farmer-politician." Having cultivated southern
political leaders, he impressed many of them in the aftermath of the
1928 debacle as a man who might bridge the sectional division among
Democrats and lead them to victory in 1932. As president, Roosevelt
struck a responsive chord among southerners, who had always
tended to personalize relationships and to approach politics on a per-
son-to-person basis. He soon captured the minds and hearts of the
southern people, including a substantial number excluded from any
part in the political process. During the 1930s his personality and his
programs were as popular in the southern states as in other parts of
the country.

Southerners welcomed the New Deal for several reasons: traditional attachment to the Democratic party, pride in the party's national
victories, the influential position of southern congressmen in Washington, Roosevelt's remarkable popularity, and their desperate need
of economic relief. The depression and the New Deal also revived the
voices of dissent and latent radicalism below the Potomac. They
brought the first modern stirring of the southern "proletariat"—of

submerged elements like the sharecropper, the textile worker, and the black domestic servant. Whatever their ideological inclinations, most southerners were disposed to regard Roosevelt and the New Deal as allies in the struggle to curb the economic imperialism of the Northeast: to regulate Wall Street, equalize freight rates that discriminated against the South, liberalize credit, and provide badly needed capital for economic development, not to mention saving the region's agricultural system and business enterprise. "The New Deal," two scholars have recently observed, "meant direct financial aid for many whites without a concomitant burden of heavy taxation since most of the recipients were too poor to pay much in taxes. By not supporting civil rights issues or programs that would provide substantial, obtrusive aid to blacks, the Roosevelt administration avoided entangling the national government in the one issue that would assuredly have infuriated white southerners."[3]

The lure of federal assistance was almost irresistible. As a southern political scientist wrote in 1931, "The seeking of Federal aid for southern highways, flood control, barge service, or cotton marketing, is only one aspect of the southern policy of looking northward for public and private funds for economic, scientific, and cultural development."[4] State rights in the depression seemed less essential than national subsidies, and especially so since many of the New Deal programs benefited the South more than other regions and since the benefits southerners received far surpassed their contributions to federal revenue collections. Even so, per capita federal expenditures in the South during the New Deal were lower than those of any other region, in part no doubt because the southern states found it difficult to raise matching funds and in part, one suspects, because guardians of the low-wage system did not want the money spent in the region.[5]

The new president looked to southern senators and representatives for leadership and cooperation in the enactment of his program. The response of these Dixie congressmen in 1933 and 1934 was all that Roosevelt could have hoped for. Like their Democratic colleagues from other regions, they gave the administration's proposals consistent and often enthusiastic support. They were moved by party loyalty, by Roosevelt's skill as a legislative leader, by their desire to ensure the success of the first Democratic presidency in twelve years, and by the terrible needs of their constituents. They were predisposed by experience and tradition to vote for such legislation as agricultural benefits and tariff reductions. Most of them liked the president. And they liked the power and prestige that came with responsible positions in a majority party.

A southern atmosphere was apparent on Capitol Hill in 1933 and the years that followed. Southerners dominated the committee structure and the parliamentary proceedings of the two chambers. The Texas delegation alone included nine chairmen of permanent committees. In the Senate the majority leader was Joseph T. Robinson of Arkansas, a veteran of twenty years in the upper house and a dependable advocate of administration interests. When Robinson died suddenly in the summer of 1937, he was succeeded as majority leader by a strong New Dealer, Alben W. Barkley of Kentucky. Two other key Senate leaders from the South were Byron Patton "Pat" Harrison of Mississippi and James F. Byrnes of South Carolina. In his capacity as chairman of the Senate Finance Committee, Harrison steered the passage of such important administration measures as the National Industrial Recovery Bill and the Social Security Bill. Byrnes, an astute and influential senator, was the president's liaison man in the upper house. Vice-Pres. John Nance Garner of Texas was also a significant figure in the Roosevelt administration's legislative plans, particularly during the early years.

The southern presence was equally forceful in the House of Representatives. Three southerners served in succession as majority leader and then speaker during the Roosevelt years: Joseph W. Byrns of Tennessee, William B. Bankhead of Alabama, and Sam Rayburn of Texas. Before becoming majority leader in 1937, Rayburn had been chairman of the Committee on Interstate and Foreign Commerce, a position he used effectively to help pass the Securities Exchange Act of 1934, the Public Utilities Holding Company Act of 1935, the Rural Electrification Act of 1936, and other New Deal legislation. Rayburn, George B. Tindall has written, "epitomized certain characteristics common among the southern leaders: 'small-townish, agrarian, nationalistic, individualistic, anti–Wall Street,' men of rural background and humble origin who had struggled hard for an education, who felt an instinctive sympathy for the 'little fellow,' who 'savored the honors and prestige associated with Congressional leadership,' and who observed party regularity as an article of faith."[6] Another southern House stalwart was Robert Lee "Muley" Doughton of North Carolina who, as chairman of the Ways and Means Committee, steered such key measures as the National Industrial Recovery and Social Security bills to passage in the lower house.

Southern congressmen gave the New Deal impressive backing during Roosevelt's first term. One scholar has found, after analyzing the Arkansas congressional delegation during the years 1933–36, that not a single negative vote was cast by the state's senators and representatives during that four-year period against measures that were central to the developing New Deal program. Like most other members of Congress, the Arkansas delegation generally exhibited more interest in legislation having a direct effect on their constituents—

Table 2. Southern Influence in Congress, 1933–1988

	House		Senate	
Congress	% of Committee Chairs[a]	% of Majority Party[b]	% of Committee Chairs[a]	% of Majority Party[b]
73d [1933–34]	71	37	50	43
77th [1941–42]	47	43	63	40
82d [1951–52]	58	49	53	53
87th [1961–62]	60	42	63	37
92d [1971–72]	43	34	53	33
97th [1981–82]	38	33	20	21
100th [1987–88]	27	33	50	33

SOURCES: *Official Congressional Directory*, 73d Cong., 1st sess.; 77th Cong., 1st sess.; 92d Cong., 1st sess.; *Congressional Quarterly Almanac*, vols. 7, 17, 37; *Congressional Index*, 100th Congress.

[a]Figures prior to 1951 are based upon *major* standing committees only; figures for 1951 to the present are based upon *all* standing committees.

[b]The Democrats were the majority party in both House and Senate in every Congress covered, with the exception of the 97th, when Republicans held a majority in the Senate.

matters such as agriculture, mortgages, relief, and social security—than on broad questions of political and economic philosophy.[7] Yet their concerted influence was remarkable. In the field of agriculture, for example, two historians assert that the southern lawmakers in this era shaped the substantive content of farm legislation "to an extent far greater than their numbers warranted." The authors attribute this to the southerners' "unmatched cohesiveness, continuity, parliamentary skill, and positions of power."[8] The journalist Turner Catledge, who covered the congressional scene for the *New York Times* in the 1930s, thought the southerners were "more closely knit" than legislators from other regions. "They were like a blood brotherhood," he later wrote. "They knew they were a minority and could have strength only by unity. They differed on details, but on the great issues—race, and a generally conservative approach to social and economic issues—they usually spoke with one voice."[9] Southern congressional delegations did gain strength because of their high degree of cohesiveness.

Some uneasiness was evident among southern congressmen about the implications of the New Deal, as well as scattered opposition to it, almost from the first. This was especially true of the Senate, where Carter Glass and Harry Flood Byrd of Virginia, Josiah W. Bailey of North Carolina, and Thomas P. Gore of Oklahoma spoke out against several of Roosevelt's legislative programs. Glass was the most vehement of these southern critics, for he quickly concluded that the New Deal represented a frontal assault on time-honored southern traditions such as state rights, individualism, constitutional government, and white supremacy. Another southern senator, Huey Long, gave the Roosevelt administration even more trouble than the conservatives. Until his assassination in 1935, the Louisiana senator condemned much of the New Deal as of little benefit to the poor and disadvantaged while serving the interests of the established and well-to-do. Early in 1934 Long began to promote his own Share-Our-Wealth program on a national basis. The New Deal provoked bitter controversy in the South, as in other regions. Not since the Populist Revolt had ideological divisions been of such central importance in southern politics. The labels "liberal" and "conservative" acquired a more substantive meaning, and the fiscal, regulatory, and welfare functions of government generated heated debate among southerners.

Perhaps the bitterest Democratic enemy of Roosevelt's New Deal in the South before 1937 was the conservative governor of Georgia, Eugene Talmadge, who by 1935 had set out to obstruct his state's participation in the president's new reform programs. "The New Deal," Talmadge declared on one occasion, "is a combination of wet-nursin', frenzied finance, downright communism, and plain damn-foolishness."[10] Having presidential ambitions of his own, the Georgia governor helped organize an anti–New Deal "Grass Roots Convention," which was held in Macon, Georgia, in January 1936. "Jeffersonian Democrats" were invited from seventeen southern and border states, and the convention was sponsored by the Southern Committee to Uphold the Constitution. The affair turned out to be a fiasco. "Our Gene" failed to control the Georgia delegation to the Democratic national convention in 1936, and he was trounced in his campaign for the Senate by Richard B. Russell, who defended the New Deal and his support of it.

Several southern governors became known as New Deal liberals. James V. Allred, who served as governor of Texas during the years 1935–39, brought that state into the national social welfare system and in other respects cooperated with New Deal programs. Although W. Lee O'Daniel, Allred's successor, was no New Dealer, he was an advocate of old-age pensions, and there was an aura of reform about his governorship. Bibb Graves, a liberal factional leader in Alabama, was closely identified with the New Deal during his tenure as governor (1935–39). In Georgia, Eurith D. "Ed" Rivers, a former supporter of Eugene Talmadge, was elected governor in 1936. He gave Georgia a "Little New Deal" and sponsored a series of measures that enabled the state to share in the Roosevelt programs. Rivers encountered revenue shortages, however, and his resort to martial law and liberal use of the pardoning power, along with an investigation of wrongdoing in the highway department, weakened his administration and caused him to leave office under a cloud. Still other politicians at the state level acquired reputations as New Dealers, including unsuccessful challengers of established Democrats such as Ralph McDonald of North Carolina.

Briefly in the late 1930s, the fortunes of New Deal supporters in Virginia assumed a rosy glow. Lt. Gov. James H. Price won the governorship in 1937 with the reluctant acquiescence of the Byrd machine. Price had been an organization man, but he approved of the New Deal, and his campaign was eagerly supported by most antiorganization leaders. The Price administration accomplished some of its objectives, but New Deal Democrats were unable to create a viable organization of their own in the Old Dominion, even with a measure of support from President Roosevelt. The ranks of the liberal, antiorganization faction soon dwindled in the face of the regulars' strength, their control of patronage, and the growing reaction against the New Deal. Roosevelt, increasingly concerned with developments abroad, made peace with Virginia conservatives after 1939.

The president's increasing emphasis on reform in the mid-1930s disturbed many southerners. Roosevelt knew that men like Joe Robinson and Pat Harrison were troubled "about the whole New Deal." They wondered, the president told Felix Frankfurter in the summer of 1935, "where that fellow in the White House is taking the good old Democratic party." Roosevelt went on to say, "I will have trouble with my own Democratic party from this time on in trying to carry out further programs of reform and recovery."[11] He had never lost sight of the importance of maintaining the support of southern congressional leaders. "I did not choose the tools with which I must work," Roosevelt explained to Walter White of the National Association for the Advancement of Colored People. "Had I been permitted to choose them I would have selected quite different ones. But I've got to get legislation passed by Congress to save America. The Southerners by reason of the seniority rule in Congress are chairmen or occupy strategic places on most of the Senate and House committees. If I come out for the anti-lynching bill now, they will block every bill I ask Congress to pass to keep America from collapsing. I just can't take that risk."[12] Still, FDR's patience was not unlimited, and following his triumphant reelection in 1936, he was not in a mood to make large concessions to southern Democrats. At the same time, he was not eager to challenge the dominant power structures in southern state politics.

The more conservative members of Congress from the South were torn between a desire to meet the pressing needs of their constituents and their dedication to a balanced budget, strong local government, and administrative efficiency. They were not unappreciative of their party's extraordinary success and of its leader's great popularity. But they were apprehensive and restless. Some of them had a vague fear that a liberalized party and a powerful executive would pose a threat to white supremacy. The Roosevelt coalition of 1936 frightened many southern leaders. As George Wolfskill and John A. Hudson have written, the traditional Democratic party "was yielding to one that was more northern than southern, more urban than rural; it was a new combination of forces which appealed to labor, to traditionally Republican Negroes, to the ethnic groups of the New Immigration, to women, and to the intellectuals attracted by the imagination and pragmatism of the New Deal. It was a new political edifice of which the South was the frieze, not the cornerstone."[13]

Despite such reservations, Franklin Roosevelt and the New Deal remained immensely popular in the South, and most southern congressmen continued to give the administration loyal support. But that began to change in 1937. Roosevelt's audacious plan to "pack" the Supreme Court created a great political crisis, gave his critics a weighty issue, and brought conservatives from both parties together in opposition. Although many southern congressmen backed the president in the court fight, large numbers of their colleagues from the South deserted him for the first time. The struggle demonstrated that Roosevelt was not invulnerable, and his opponents had found an issue on which they could openly attack him. By the autumn of 1937, an informal coalition of anti–New Deal Democrats and Republicans had developed. Southerners took a leading role in the coalescence of these congressional conservatives. The concern that united them was their opposition to much of the New Deal—to the growth of federal power and bureaucracy, to deficit spending, to industrial labor unions, and to most welfare programs. In a statement of principles drafted in December 1937 by Josiah W. Bailey and other leaders of this conservative coalition, the dissidents presented a ten-point list of demands, including a balanced budget, tax reduction in order "to free investment funds," a new labor policy, maintenance of state rights and local self-government, and reliance upon the "American form of government and the American system of free enterprise."[14] The coalition was a major factor in the failure of several New Deal measures in the late 1930s. During that period nearly half of the southern senators voted against the administration on key nonagricultural economic issues, while the percentage of southerners voting against such measures in the House was ordinarily greater than that of other members.

FDR and the Purge of 1938

Tom Little in the Nashville *Tennessean*. Courtesy of the Jean and Alexander Heard Library, Vanderbilt University

Other Roosevelt initiatives also provoked resentment and opposition from southerners in and out of Congress. One of these was Roosevelt's behind-the-scenes intervention in the contest to elect a Senate majority leader following Joe Robinson's death in the midst of the court fight. Alben Barkley, a staunch administration man, defeated Pat Harrison, a more conservative and less reliable New Dealer, by one vote. The Roosevelt administration was also identified with an outbreak of sit-down strikes in 1937 and 1938, and its Wages and Hours Bill threatened to wipe out regional wage differentials, against the wishes of many southern businessmen and politicians. Roosevelt's intervention in several southern primaries in 1938 and his effort to "purge" congressional opponents did not go down well with southerners. Nor did the president's reference to the South as the "nation's no. 1 economic problem," with the implication that the region's plight required liberal legislation and the election of liberal southerners to support the New Deal, increase his standing in the South. Furious over Roosevelt's court-packing scheme in 1937 and resentful of his endeavor to purge his congressional opponents in 1938, Carter Glass warned that the South had better "begin thinking whether it will continue to cast its 152 electoral votes according to the memories of the Reconstruction era of 1865 and thereafter, or will have spirit and courage enough to face the new Reconstruction era that northern so-called Democrats are menacing us with."[15]

The political scientist Marian D. Irish once suggested that Franklin Roosevelt found both "his staunchest supporters and his strongest opponents within the ranks of his own party south of the Mason-Dixon line."[16] This was a perceptive comment. There was mounting concern among the "county-seat elites" and other members of the governing class over the possible consequences of the national administration's welfare and labor programs, over the enlarged role of the federal government, and over the president's efforts to reform the courts and remove his conservative opponents from office. A recent study of North Carolina during this period concludes that the state was most influenced by a "conservative, business-oriented ideology that survived the changes wrought by the New Deal."[17] Congressional leaders like Carter Glass, Pat Harrison, and John Garner, reflecting the interests of the propertied establishment of their region, were determined "to secure and maintain the existing socioeconomic society at home in the South." In the opinion of George E. Mowry, they "came near to representing southern conservatism at its most informed and articulate best."[18] Many Democrats in the South, according to Raymond Clapper in 1936, saw the New Dealers as a "crowd of interlopers bearing strange and dubious ideas."[19] Writing in 1935, a South Carolinian informed Sen. James F. Byrnes of his dedication to the Democratic party and faith in President Roosevelt. "At the same time," he observed, "I have always felt that he was surrounded by an aggregation of parlor communists and socialists and that too many of this unpractical type was even placed in his cabinet."[20]

Roosevelt's New Deal did not transform southern politics, for conservative officeholders, attitudes, and institutions were too firmly entrenched at the state and local levels to be dislodged by the president's reform programs. The New Deal, being dependent on home-state authorities for the administration of its programs, did little to interfere with the distribution of political power within the region. "In effect," one historian says of the situation in Memphis, "the New Deal was filtered through the Crump machine."[21] This helps explain the Roosevelt administration's willingness to accept racial discrimination in the operation of its own relief agencies, to acquiesce in racial wage differentials, and to shy away from involvement in union-organizing efforts in the South. Influential southern liberals, moreover, were small in number and relatively weak, and Alan Brinkley has argued that they were further hampered by the fear they shared with conservatives of "federal interference in the South's right to manage its own affairs and chart its own future."[22] Noting the prevalence of rebellious forces in southern politics during the 1930s, Brinkley suggests that the dominant insurgency in the depression South "was not the weak and tentative group of southern liberals who identified with the New Deal. It was a force that drew from the region's own populist traditions, one that could produce both radical and reactionary demands, one that could find expression simultaneously in a Huey Long and a Eugene Talmadge."[23] There was also another aspect of the matter. While most southerners accepted New Deal activism and approved Roosevelt's work for "the common man," they were influenced by a deeply conservative culture. "It was obvious enough," W.J. Cash wrote in 1941, "that the basic Rooseveltian ideas, with their emphasis on the social values as against the individual, and on the necessity of revising all values in the light of the conditions created by the machine and the disappearance of the frontier, ran directly contrary to the basic Southern attitudes."[24]

Yet in some respects the Roosevelt presidency had a profound and lasting effect on politics and government in the southern states. This was most apparent in the altered relationship between the federal government and the states and in the composition of the revitalized Democratic party in the United States. The New Deal also aroused the political consciousness of millions of ordinary southerners—of poor farmers, coal miners, schoolteachers, blacks, and working people generally. "Negroes shud vote for Mistuh Roosevelt if they kin," a black day laborer and Works Projects Administration worker told an interviewer in 1940. "I been here twenty years, but since WPA, the Negro sho' has started talkin' 'bout politics."[25] Roosevelt and the New Deal remained popular with many of these southerners. During the court fight, a Gallup poll revealed that a majority of the respondents approved FDR's plan in every southern state except Kentucky and Oklahoma, while 53 percent of the national sample opposed it. In the election of 1938, to take another example, one study showed that in nine southern primaries pro–New Deal candidates had come out ahead of anti–New Dealers 53.4 to 46.6 percent.

Federal intervention during the 1930s was unprecedented in the modern South. Under the pressure from Washington, the southern states did a good deal to modernize their governmental structures, to extend public services, to develop more adequate social welfare systems, and even to improve the position of labor. The New Deal, while seldom displacing the dominant political factions, became a vibrant issue in the region's state politics. Still more consequential were the long-term effects of New Deal programs on the South. For the national reforms of the 1930s contributed to a series of deep-seated transformations that eventually changed the economic, social, and political character of the South and that were accompanied by the Second Reconstruction. The New Deal encouraged these developments through the changes it produced in the South's own social and economic institutions and through its impact outside the southern region: through its role in the vast migration off the southern land, massive out-migration of unskilled labor, the revamping of the agricultural system, the disruption of the "network of dependency relationships," the increase in the industrial wage level and the reduction of the North-South differential, and outside the region the creation of a new Democratic coalition that would ultimately demand more thoroughgoing federal action in areas such as civil rights.[26]

Franklin Roosevelt's leadership inspired and directed a hardy band of southern liberals in Congress—men like Hugo L. Black, Alben W. Barkley, Theodore G. Bilbo, Claude Pepper, and Morris Sheppard in the Senate and Robert L. Doughton, Maury Maverick, and Lyndon B. Johnson in the House of Representatives. There was a more numerous but less well-known aggregation of New Deal liberals in state houses and agencies throughout the South. Most of these Democrats shared Roosevelt's desire to liberalize the Democratic party in Congress and in their respective states. They tended to accept the reality of the colonial South and to believe that a reactionary ruling class at home, in combination with powerful outside interests, had hindered the economic and political advancement of the region. They supported efforts to repeal the poll tax, to create liberal coalitions in the South, to secure favorable labor legislation, and to equalize intersectional freight rates. There was a populist tinge to their political thought, tempered perhaps by their faith in progressivism and economic development. In his campaign for the Senate in 1934, Bilbo told his Mississippi audiences that many incumbent senators were "Tories of the first water," who were "shaking in their boots now. They have been forced by the lash of an outraged and indignant people to vote against their old masters."[27] Roosevelt's New Deal also encouraged a sprinkling of liberal and radical activism on the part of southerners bent upon investigating and publicizing the reform needs

of their region. These included such diverse enterprises as the High-
lander Folk School, the Southern Summer School for Women, the
Southern Policy Study, the Fellowship of Southern Churchmen, and
the Southern Conference for Human Welfare.

Try as conservative politicians might—by joining the New Deal
for a time, by endeavoring to water down its programs, by resorting
to subterfuge, disingenuous arguments, and clever appeals to old-
time shibboleths—the threat from Washington remained, and it
promised to grow larger in the future. Not only did it seem more and
more unlikely that the South could ever again dominate the Democratic party, but it was also increasingly apparent that the national
policies adopted during the 1930s would ultimately strengthen organized labor, farmers, blacks, and other disadvantaged elements
sufficiently to force concessions from those who had long had the
upper hand in the region. This was one measure of the New Deal's
challenge to southern conservatives.

But with the faltering of its domestic reform proposals and the
gathering war clouds in the late 1930s, the Roosevelt administration
moved toward a reconciliation with southern conservatives in Congress. Meanwhile, Republican gains in the midterm elections of 1938
had strengthened the position of southern congressional leaders. The
administration's approach to the tense international situation contributed substantially to the restoration of harmony between the president and southern conservatives. Although southern congressmen
had cast their share of votes for the neutrality legislation of the mid-
1930s, they rallied enthusiastically to the support of Roosevelt's foreign and defense initiatives after 1938. Party loyalty and economic
considerations involving foreign trade, as well as such factors as military tradition, ethnic composition, and psychological makeup, stimulated southern internationalism. The war boom, moreover, became a
mighty force in rejuvenating the southern economy and providing it
with a more substantial foundation than the old reliance upon cotton
and agriculture. In the late 1930s and early 1940s, southern Democrats
were more strongly in favor of intervention and internationalism than
any other regional or party group. Without their almost solid backing,
the administration would have been defeated on neutrality revision
in 1939 and 1941, Lend-Lease, extension of the draft, and authori-
zation for seizing foreign ships and arming American merchant ves-
sels.

President Roosevelt's wartime leadership was strongly supported
in the South, and southern congressional leaders were generally quite
satisfied to have "Dr. New Deal" replaced by "Dr. Win the War."
Southerners were also pleased with the federal expenditure of over
$10 billion below the Potomac during the war years, in part to com-

pensate the region for its loss of cotton and tobacco markets abroad. Southern influence grew in other ways as well. Large Republican gains in the congressional elections of 1942 tightened the grip of the southern delegations on the Democratic party in Congress and enhanced the role of the conservative coalition. The southerners' political independence was also heightened by wartime prosperity and suspicion of the Roosevelt administration's intentions in dealing with race relations.

The administration could take some satisfaction in the appearance of several new Democratic leaders at the state level. Oklahoma and Georgia provide examples of this new leadership. Robert S. Kerr, who was elected governor of Oklahoma in 1942, did a good deal to unify the Democratic party in that state. A popular and successful wartime governor, Kerr rallied Oklahomans around such themes as the need for economic growth, governmental assistance, and administrative efficiency. Though moderate in his liberalism, he was loyal to the national Democratic party and became the chief spokesman in Oklahoma for Democratic administrations in Washington. In Georgia Ellis G. Arnall, the state's young attorney general, emerged as leader of the anti-Talmadge faction. Taking advantage of Governor Talmadge's controversial interference in the system of higher education, Arnall defeated Talmadge in the gubernatorial primary of 1942. Arnall proved to be an able governor and a successful reformer. He restored the independence of the University of Georgia, reformed the penal and parole systems, spearheaded the adoption of a new state constitution, reduced the voting age to eighteen, took the lead in abolishing the poll tax, accepted Negro suffrage following the courts' invalidation of the white primary, and was partly responsible for the success of the regional movement against discriminatory freight rates.

In Washington, meanwhile, liberals suffered a series of setbacks on issues of domestic reform. In the Seventy-eighth Congress (1943–44), conservative southerners joined with their Republican allies in a concerted attack on surviving New Deal agencies. They eviscerated the Civilian Conservation Corps, Works Projects Administration, and National Youth Administration. They provided strong support for the South-Connally Bill, whose enactment in 1943 was designed to curb the freedom of labor unions to strike and also to prevent the use of union funds for political campaigns. They fiercely resisted an anti–poll tax bill, which was passed by the House but defeated in the Senate, and prevented the approval of a rule that would have liberalized the adoption of cloture in the Senate. They denied the administration's request for a simplified federal soldiers' ballot in the election of 1944, approving instead a state rights ballot. Rep. Hatton W. Sumners of Texas had warned in 1942 that the administration's recommendation would "strengthen the stranglehold of this great Federal bureaucracy upon the throats of the States."[28]

An early analysis of party loyalty in Congress during this period revealed that, whereas southern Democrats were more loyal, on the average, than their northern counterparts in the early 1920s and early 1930s, three-fifths of the northern Democrats were over 90 percent loyal to their party in 1944, as compared with less than one-twelfth of the southerners.[29] Nevertheless, the influence of the conservative coalition should not be exaggerated. V.O. Key's analysis of 598 roll call votes in the Senate for the period 1933 to 1945 showed that, while southern cohesiveness was slightly higher than that of nonsouthern Democrats and Republicans, on more than half of the roll calls in each of the seven sessions studied a majority of the southern Democrats disagreed with a majority of the Republicans. A majority of the Dixie Democrats joined with a majority of the Republican senators against a majority of the nonsouthern Democrats on less than 10 percent of the roll calls. Key's analysis of 275 roll calls in the House revealed similar behavior. He concluded that genuine southern solidarity in Congress existed only on the race question.

If international dangers and wartime mobilization led the Roosevelt administration to abandon its domestic reform agenda, southern conservatives soon learned that federal power and executive authority could also be expanded through the creation of new war agencies. The Fair Employment Practices Committee (FEPC), for example, was, in the opinion of Governor Arnall, an irritant to both liberal and conservative southerners, who regarded it as in the tradition of the Lodge Force Bill.[30] Many southern leaders were disturbed by the political activities of labor organizations and Negro groups and suspicious of their ties with the Democratic party. Feeling resentful and neglected, conservative Democrats in the South became increasingly outspoken and belligerent. In late 1942 and early 1943, Governors Frank M. Dixon of Alabama and Sam Houston Jones of Louisiana suggested that southerners might be forced to break the bonds of party loyalty. New Deal policies, Jones asserted, "have continued to kick an already prostrate South in the face."[31] A few months later, Sen. Josiah W. Bailey warned, "We can form a southern Democratic party and vote as we please in the electoral college, and we will hold the balance of power in this country."[32] In August 1943 Leon C. Phillips, a former governor of Oklahoma, denounced the New Deal for undermining the constitution, for attempting "to destroy individual initiative . . . through regimentation," and for permitting "labor racketeers" to become "the bosses of our people."[33] Phillips announced that he was joining the Republican party. Gessner T.

McCorvey, chairman of the Alabama Democratic executive committee, declared in September 1944, "I believe that the Southern people are finally waking up to the fact that by the South presenting a united front at our National Conventions we can regain in the councils of our Party the prestige which we formerly enjoyed."[34] Another Alabamian had written President Roosevelt two years earlier, complaining that "federal agencies have adopted policies to break down and destroy the segregation laws of . . . the entire South. Unless something is done by you, we are are going to . . . witness the Annihilation of the Democratic Party in this section."[35]

While these threats reflected a widespread and growing alienation among anti–New Deal southerners, they were not typical of the region's rank and file. A Gallup poll taken in the summer of 1943 revealed that 80 percent of the southerners questioned favored FDR's renomination for a fourth term. President Roosevelt, the journalist John Temple Graves remarked, was "the Democratic party, the rebel yell, Woodrow Wilson and Robert E. Lee rolled into one."[36] To defy him would be equivalent to repudiating the South's political heritage. One way to loosen Roosevelt's hold on the white masses of the region was to identify him and his administration with threats to white supremacy, and southern conservatives made the most of their wartime opportunities in this area. They expressed mounting concern over the FEPC, the anti–poll tax legislation in Congress, rumors of increasing racial violence, and the invalidation of the Democratic white primaries in *Smith* v. *Allwright* (1944). It is significant that almost all southern leaders condemned the FEPC and that even such a staunch New Dealer as Sen. Claude Pepper spoke out against the court's white primary decision.

As the presidential election of 1944 approached, sectionalism assumed a more prominent place in Democratic party affairs than at any time since 1928. By the summer of 1944, Roosevelt had indicated that he intended to revive the New Deal following the war. He had also advocated social welfare legislation, a federal ballot for soldiers, and noninterference with the rights of organized labor. The president's southern critics made much of the changing character of the Democratic party—of the part played by labor's Political Action Committee, urban bosses, and black organizations—and the South's diminished role in the party. They linked the administration with the challenge to the South's established racial order, with labor racketeering, with socialism, and with Communist sympathies. They charged Roosevelt with the construction of a gigantic federal bureaucracy and with a relentless assault on constitutional government, state rights, and local self-government. Meanwhile, conservatives had found their own hero in Sen. Harry F. Byrd of Virginia.

A Byrd-for-President Committee was established, and conservative revolts were launched in three southern states. In South Carolina the insurgents were turned back by Gov. Olin D. Johnston's faction, which controlled the state convention. The Mississippi Democratic convention placed a slate of uninstructed electors on the ballot, but they were replaced by a loyal slate after the party's national convention. A bitter struggle between pro- and anti-Roosevelt Democrats took place in Texas, which sent two delegations to the national convention. Later, after the pro-Roosevelt faction gained control of the state party, a group of conservative rebels known as the Texas Regulars managed to get an independent slate of electors on the ballot. It was pledged to vote for any Democrat other than Franklin D. Roosevelt. The Texas Regulars received only 11.7 percent of the vote, however, and Roosevelt won easily in the Lone Star State and throughout the South. He was too popular and too strong a wartime leader to lose in the South in 1944. But the president's critics could claim some credit in preventing the renomination of Vice-Pres. Henry A. Wallace. And they had pointed the way for future insurgents.

Roosevelt's reelection in 1944 did little to blunt the edge of the conservative coalition in Congress. Early in 1945 the president forced Secretary of Commerce Jesse H. Jones to resign and replaced him with Henry Wallace. The conservatives, led by Senators Bailey and Walter F. George, began an assault on this nomination. Distrusting Wallace, they succeeded in stripping the Commerce Department of its lending agencies (including the Reconstruction Finance Corporation) and then almost prevented the Iowan's confirmation. At about the same time, Senate conservatives refused to confirm the liberal Alabamian Aubrey W. Williams as head of the Rural Electrification Administration.

With Roosevelt's death in April 1945 and the accession of Harry S. Truman to the presidency, southern congressional leaders anticipated a more harmonious relationship with the White House and a revival of their influence in the Democratic party. Many of them thought Truman would bring an end to the New Deal. But those who savored such prospects were soon disillusioned. The new president antagonized the South by joining the advocates of a permanent FEPC, and in a special message on September 6, 1945, he called for an extension of wartime controls and of Roosevelt's domestic reforms. Truman made little headway with this program in the Seventy-ninth Congress (1945–46), however, thanks in considerable part to southern opposition. Southern Democrats and Republicans emasculated the wartime FEPC in 1945, defeated the proposal for a permanent commission by resorting to a long Senate filibuster in 1946, destroyed the effectiveness of the Office of Price Administration, drastically weakened the administration's full-employment legislation, and came close to overriding the president's veto of a stringent labor-control bill. In 1946, 43 of the 102 Democrats from the eleven ex-Confederate states in the House of Representatives cast less than 50 percent of their votes with a majority of their party members.

Since President Truman had clearly demonstrated his commitment to the concept of a dynamic chief executive and his desire to continue in the tradition of the New Deal, southern congressmen were not altogether unhappy with the Republican capture of Congress in the midterm elections of 1946. Although the southerners would lose their numerous committee chairmanships as well as the speakership of the House, they would constitute a majority of the Democratic membership in both houses during the next Congress. This would enable them to reorganize the party in Congress, dominate the Democratic caucus, and exercise greater bargaining power.

In the meantime, a politics of race and reaction had begun to manifest itself in the southern states, most noticeably in the deep South. Many state and local politicians in the region were upset by the Supreme Court's decisions striking at racial discrimination in interstate transportation and in labor unions, and they were appalled by the invalidation of the white primary and the prospect of a surge of black votes. Several of the southern states grudgingly accepted the *Smith* v. *Allwright* decision without further opposition, while a number of others set about tightening their voting requirements as a means of deterrence. The Alabama legislature and electorate approved the so-called Boswell registration amendment, whose requirements included a literacy test, a "good character" clause, and ability to "understand the duties and obligations of good citizenship." The white primary decision dominated the gubernatorial primary of 1946 in Georgia, a contest in which Eugene Talmadge lashed out at Gov. Ellis Arnall for not calling the legislature into session to repeal all primary laws, as South Carolina had done in 1944. Talmadge promised to preserve the white primary, and he was elected, with the help of his state's county-unit system and a divided opposition. Theodore G. Bilbo adopted Talmadge's tactics in his campaign for reelection in Mississippi, and his vituperative assault on black voters was also successful. In a number of other states, organized labor and particularly the Congress of Industrial Organizations was the focus of conservative attacks in 1946. The CIO organizing drive in Dixie and the alleged influence of its Political Action Committee alarmed conservative politicians, who depicted the CIO-PAC as a subversive threat to southern institutions. The following year witnessed the enactment of a number of right-to-work laws in the southern states.

Nevertheless, New Deal liberalism was still a strong force in southern politics. That was evident in the Alabama gubernatorial primary of 1946. With Bibb Graves dead and the liberals divided, Alabama conservatives anticipated success in 1946. But then a new political figure suddenly emerged in the person of James E. "Big Jim" Folsom, who won the governorship that year, frustrating conservative hopes and establishing himself as the state's most powerful politician. Folsom's greatest support came from northern Alabama and the southeastern Wiregrass section. A man of huge proportions—"the Little Man's Big Friend"—he toured the state in 1946 with a hillbilly band, "the Strawberry Pickers," and promised to use his "suds bucket" to clean out the statehouse. "Big Jim" was genial and kind-hearted, and he had a taste for strong drink and attractive women. He rejected the "courthouse ring" approach. While not cut from the same cloth as the old-time southern demagogue, his campaign performance was captivating. "He was every town's overgrown boy," one historian writes, "faintly bashful, full of mischief but easy to forgive. He exuded a sincerity of purpose and an integrity of intent that found ready adherents among those who heard him."[37] Folsom was basically a neo-Populist who appeared comfortable with the legacy of the New Deal and the direction of the national Democratic party. Alabama liberals, including Senators Lister Hill and John J. Sparkman, hastened to claim him as one of their own. Folsom was only partly successful in getting legislative approval of his program, which required increased revenues, and his proposals provoked determined opposition on the part of the black belt and the big mules. Nor was "Big Jim" an effective administrator. By 1948 the luster of his electoral triumph had faded, Alabama Democrats were locked in a struggle between state-rights advocates and those loyal to the national party, and conservative strength seemed to be increasing rapidly.

Back in Washington, civil rights for American blacks had become a national issue. An outburst of murders, lynchings, and violence directed at southern blacks brought pressure on the White House for national action of some kind. In December 1946 Truman established the President's Committee on Civil Rights, a panel made up of fifteen distinguished leaders. The committee's report, *To Secure These Rights*, was published in October 1947. It was a comprehensive set of recommendations for congressional and administrative action to overcome racial discrimination in the United States. Though these recommendations no doubt went further than Truman had expected, he sent a special message to Congress in February 1948 recommending passage of a broad civil rights law. He proposed that the Department of Justice be strengthened, that the poll tax be abolished, that a permanent FEPC be established, that citizens be protected against lynching, that segregation be outlawed in interstate transportation, and several other steps. Truman was the first modern president to recommend comprehensive civil rights legislation.

Most southern leaders were sharply critical of the president's civil rights proposals. The administration's proposals convinced the region's conservatives that Truman no longer had any real concern for the South and that he had become the spokesman of an urban coalition made up of intellectuals, labor unions, ethnic groups, and blacks. The national Democratic party could no longer be counted on to represent the South. Several southern governors, including Fielding L. Wright of Mississippi and J. Strom Thurmond of South Carolina, sought some kind of united action against Truman's civil rights program. They took their complaints to the Southern Governors' Conference and then to Washington, where they conferred with Sen. J. Howard McGrath, chairman of the Democratic national committee. Insurgents like Wright and Thurmond eventually decided that nothing was to be gained by talking with the Truman administration. Turning to the individual southern states, they undertook a movement of independence, seeking to persuade the party organizations to oppose Truman or any other liberal Democrat at the national convention, and, as a second step, the selection of uncommitted electors pledged to vote against a presidential nominee who supported the civil rights program. In the spring of 1948, the chances of a bolt became more likely in Mississippi, South Carolina, and Alabama, while the insurgents were optimistic about their prospects in Louisiana, Georgia, and Virginia.

Assuming that "the South can be considered safely Democratic," President Truman and his advisers had decided to emphasize the administration's reform program and to reach out to the party's urban constituency, partly as a means of countering the appeal of Henry Wallace's Progressive party.[38] At the same time, Truman made some effort to allay the discontent within the ranks of southern Democrats. Thus, administration forces in the party's national convention, which met in Philadelphia in July, pushed for the adoption of a platform reiterating the president's Fair Deal program but containing only a vague, general commitment to civil rights. This became the majority report of the platform committee, but it was challenged by a group of dedicated liberals, including Hubert H. Humphrey of Minnesota, and a bitter struggle ensued over the wording of the civil rights section of the platform. When the liberals finally won in a close vote, the Mississippi delegation and half of the delegates from Alabama walked out of the convention. While the other Dixie delegates remained, only

a handful of them voted for Truman's nomination. Most of the southerners cast their votes for Sen. Richard B. Russell in a symbolic protest
against Harry Truman and the leadership of the national party.

Within days a group of the more rebellious southern Democrats
convened in Birmingham, where they held their own convention.
Calling themselves States' Rights Democrats, they proceeded to nominate Governor Thurmond for president and Governor Wright for vice-
president. The insurgents were determined to retain the Democratic
party label, since it had been an instrument of white unity for generations and was too much a part of the South's political culture to
be discarded by southern voters. Taking advantage of their control
of state Democratic committees and party machinery, the States'
Righters were able to place their ticket under the Democratic label in
South Carolina, Alabama, Mississippi, and Louisiana. This tactic
failed in the other southern states, which were more reluctant to break
their ties with the national party and the Truman administration. It
was significant that in the Democratic primaries that year several liberal or reform-oriented candidates were nominated for governor:
W. Kerr Scott in North Carolina, Gordon Browning in Tennessee,
Sidney S. McMath in Arkansas, and Earl K. Long in Louisiana. Thurmond conducted an energetic campaign throughout the South, hoping to carry most of the region and to hold the balance of power if
neither Truman nor Thomas E. Dewey, the Republican nominee, received a majority in the electoral college. But the Dixiecrats polled
only 1,169,021 popular votes and won only the 39 electoral votes of
the four states whose Democratic label they had appropriated. In his
surprising national victory, Truman carried all of the other southern
states.

Some southerners supported the States' Rights Democrats because of their hostility toward New Deal economic policies. But despite its tender regard for business interests and its effort to refurbish
the arguments for state rights and constitutional government, the
Dixiecrat movement gathered most of its strength from the racism
and traditional sectionalism that had always frustrated political realignment within the region and perpetuated the Solid South. The
States' Righters enjoyed their greatest success in the black belt areas
of the deep South. Assuming that Truman would be defeated in 1948,
they seized upon the election as a favorable time to frighten the party
leadership into a more cooperative attitude. In the process they doubt-
less hoped to smash their liberal opponents in the South by forcing
them to endorse the unpopular side of the race issue and align themselves with the national party on that question. The outcome suggested that loyalty to the national Democratic party, particularly in
the peripheral South, was still strong among the region's white in-

habitants, that civil rights had not yet become an overriding issue in much of the South, and that the interests of many southerners were too diversified and too dependent on national politics and policies for them to join a rebellious sectional assault on Washington and the Democratic party.

Although the Dixiecrat revolt fell far short of its more ambitious expectations, it was a significant movement in the history of southern politics. For one thing, it led to a real political division in the South. The States' Rights party also provided, as Robert A. Garson has suggested, "a coherent and voluble vehicle" for channeling the region's growing sense of political isolation. The movement provoked an extraordinary political involvement by southerners, and it disrupted the Solid South. "Whatever courses southerners subsequently took," Garson writes, "the Democratic party was never again upheld as the embodiment of race, country, God, and southern womanhood."[39] By the end of the 1940s, another scholar observes, the South was no longer a part of the New Deal coalition. The New Deal party—"the party of the urban masses, union labor, Negroes, civil rights, and social reform"—had become "an affront to the conservative, rural-minded and rural-dominated, if no longer rural South."[40]

When V.O. Key analyzed southern politics in the late 1940s, the supporting institutions he identified—disfranchisement, malapportionment, one-partyism, and the elaborate structure and pervasive ethos of Jim Crow—were all still in place. Yet there were growing doubts about the future course of southern politics. The New Deal had sharpened class lines in the region's politics, the traditional system of plantation agriculture had been dealt a savage blow by the depression, swelling the stream of black migrants flowing out of the South, and the war had greatly stimulated and diversified the southern economy. Even more important, in the short run, was the emergence of civil rights as an issue in national politics, the identification of the Democratic party with that issue, and the Dixiecrat revolt of 1948. With the passage of time, it became clear that overwhelming southern fidelity to the Democratic party had come to an end in the presidential election of 1948. Since 1948, William C. Havard remarked in 1980, the South has been "in a more or less active state of rebellion against its great symbol of sectional political unity—the Democratic party."[41]

Developments in the 1930s and 1940s encouraged the eventual fragmentation of the Solid South. The changing character of the national Democratic party and the shrinking importance of the South in the party began to eat away at the old assumption that Democratic control and defense of the "southern" position were synonymous. The growth of centralized government and the creation of a welfare state disturbed conservative southerners, who were inclined to attribute their apprehensions to the leadership of Franklin Roosevelt. But if they expected Roosevelt's successor to turn aside from the path charted by the New Deal, they were soon disillusioned. In fact, the reforms Harry Truman sponsored after the war promised not only to expand the welfare program of the 1930s but also to enter boldly into the field of federal civil rights legislation. The result was the States' Rights rebellion of 1948. While racial fears were at the heart of the Dixiecrat revolt, the movement was also a manifestation of a broader regional conservatism promoted by rapid economic and social change as well as tradition. By mid-century the foundation had been laid for the "massive resistance" of the 1950s.

6 The Politics of Massive Resistance

In the 1950s southern politics entered a period of chronic disorder. With racial issues threatening to become all-encompassing, an increasing number of white southerners were alienated from the national Democratic party, and Republicanism grew more attractive in the South. The disruption of the Democratic South in 1948 was repeated in the national elections that followed, and presidential Republicanism became an enduring feature of politics below the Potomac and the Ohio. New factional patterns began to emerge in the region's state politics. In some respects, such as the growth of the Republican party, the entry of black voters into Democratic primaries, and the rapid pace of economic and social change, particularly in the cities, the decade's developments seemed to betoken significant alterations in southern politics. Meanwhile, however, the epochal Supreme Court decision of 1954 in *Brown* v. *Board of Education* provoked a movement of "massive resistance" to public school desegregation. That movement dominated southern politics in the late 1950s, fostered an intensified politics of race, and debilitated the New Deal–liberal factions in the Democratic party.

As for the Dixiecrats, their fortunes declined in the aftermath of Harry Truman's startling victory in 1948. While the insurgents created a National States' Rights Committee in 1949, the Dixiecrat movement as an organized effort soon spent itself. Most Democratic officeholders and professional politicians in the South were careful not to break their ties with the national party. Democratic officials in Washington showed little disposition to punish the southern bolters, although the national committee did remove Dixiecrat members from four deep South states and the Truman administration denied patronage to Sen. James O. Eastland of Mississippi and other disloyal southern congressmen. Southern Democrats in the tradition of Roosevelt's New Deal and Truman's Fair Deal could take heart from several electoral successes in 1948, including the victories of W. Kerr Scott in North Carolina, John J. Sparkman in Alabama, Estes Kefauver and Gordon

Browning in Tennessee, Earl K. Long in Louisiana, Sidney S. McMath in Arkansas, and Lyndon B. Johnson in Texas. In 1950 Sen. Olin Johnston turned back a campaign challenge by Strom Thurmond, while Benjamin T. Laney, chairman of the Dixiecrat national committee, failed in a bid to regain the governorship of Arkansas. Senators Sparkman and Lister Hill led a successful effort in Alabama to regain control of the Democratic executive committee from the States' Rights Democrats.

Although state politics in the late 1940s and early 1950s continued to reflect the economic and class alignments stimulated by the New Deal, the racial apprehensions that gave rise to the Dixiecrat movement did not dissipate. The Truman administration, pressing its Fair Deal program in Congress, struggled in 1949 and 1950 to secure passage of a Fair Employment Practices Commission Bill and other measures. By that time the National Association for the Advancement of Colored People had begun a direct attack on the separate but equal doctrine in the federal courts, and in 1950 the Supreme Court in *Sweatt* v. *Painter* and other cases ruled against segregated facilities in higher education and interstate transportation. These decisions pointed toward the elimination of segregation in southern graduate and professional schools and seemed to threaten the inviolability of white supremacy in the region. Senators Claude Pepper of Florida and Frank P. Graham of North Carolina, two of the South's best-known liberals, were defeated in hotly contested primary campaigns in 1950. Racist charges and innuendos were used with telling effect against both men, and Graham probably suffered because the Democratic primary occurred only a short time after the *Sweatt* decision.

Racial protest was a factor in the reelection of Gov. Herman Talmadge of Georgia and in the gubernatorial victory of James F. Byrnes in South Carolina. While refusing to join the Dixiecrats in 1948, Talmadge had exploited the race question in his successful campaign that year. During his second term, he emerged as the most ardent gubernatorial defender of segregation. "As long as I am Governor," he declared, "Negroes will not be admitted to white schools."[1] In 1951 the Georgia governor secured the enactment of legislation denying public funds to any state institution that allowed racial desegregation. Byrnes, who had served as secretary of state under President Truman, returned to South Carolina in the late 1940s eager to restore the rights of the states and the South. After his election in 1950, he sought to defend segregation by providing black South Carolinians with "substantial equality in school facilities." His administration made considerable progress in this endeavor, and it helped secure the adoption of a constitutional amendment to permit the conversion of public schools into private institutions. Byrnes assured his fellow citizens that South Carolina would not "mix white and colored children in our schools."[2]

Southern disaffection with the national Democratic party manifested itself in the presidential election of 1952, as it had four years before. Democratic leaders, confronted with the candidacy of Gen. Dwight D. Eisenhower and a revitalized Republican party, adopted a conciliatory approach toward the restless southerners. In late July at the party's national convention in Chicago, the efforts of liberals to impose a "loyalty pledge" on all delegates and to adopt a strongly worded civil rights plank were defeated. The party's unifiers prevailed. A resolution was passed that merely pledged the delegates to use their influence to see that the national ticket was placed on their respective state ballots under the Democratic label. A moderate civil rights plank was adopted, and Gov. Adlai E. Stevenson of Illinois and Sen. John J. Sparkman of Alabama were nominated for president and vice-president. Most of the southern delegates supported the candidacy of Sen. Richard B. Russell, but his bid for the nomination failed to gain strength outside the South. Two liberal candidates—W. Averell Harriman of New York and Estes Kefauver of Tennessee—were also unable to develop broad support. Yet Kefauver had attracted a national following and had entered the convention as the leading candidate in terms of committed delegates. Indeed, he was the first southerner since Woodrow Wilson to mount a genuine national campaign for his party's presidential nomination.

The Solid South was again disrupted, this time by Republican victories in five of the region's states. Building upon the traditional Republicanism of the upper South, Eisenhower ran well in the region's cities and larger towns. His southern victories represented an important breakthrough for presidential Republicanism in the South, and it gave the minority party a new respectability among southerners, particularly middle-class and affluent urbanites and suburban dwellers. While he failed to carry any of the deep South states, Eisenhower made an impressive showing in Louisiana and Mississippi, and he attracted conspicuous support in the black belts and plantation areas, the historic strongholds of the Democratic party. This reversal was clearly related to the rising tide of racial protest in the lower South. The Republicans owed part of their southern success to the collaboration of several Democratic leaders. Governors Robert F. Kennon of Louisiana and Allan F. Shivers of Texas were leaders in a "Democrats for Eisenhower" movement, while Governor Byrnes of South Carolina spearheaded an "Independents for Ike" campaign that tried to place its own electors on the ballot. After a lengthy silence, Sen. Harry F. Byrd of Virginia announced that he could not support the Stevenson-Sparkman ticket, but he did not endorse Eisenhower.

While much of this new Republican sentiment was based on mounting southern distaste for New Deal–Fair Deal economic and welfare policies, it also rested in no small part on racial concerns.

Several factors contributed to a pervasive mood of conservatism and foreboding among white southerners in the 1950s. One disturbing development was the new leadership and direction of the national Democratic party, which for all its conciliatory gestures during presidential years was apparently committed to a policy of civil rights and an extension of New Deal reform. White southerners were also concerned over increasing federal intervention: in the invalidation of the white primary, desegregation of the armed forces, and the challenge to segregated hospitals, graduate and professional schools, and transportation facilities. They were alarmed by the growing assertiveness and mounting demands of blacks, both within the South and in Washington. The Supreme Court's school desegregation decision of 1954 and the gradual coalescence of civil rights reformers seemed to confirm their worst racial forebodings.

New white sensibilities in the South were in part the product of the region's rapid economic and social change during the postwar years—of its industrial expansion, quickening urbanization, large-scale migration, swelling middle class, and declining farm population. By the 1950s the South's center of political gravity was shifting from rural and small-town voters to residents of urban places. Yet the political culture remained highly individualist. Widespread economic growth and prosperity dampened southern interest in New Deal–type programs and nurtured the role of "entrepreneurial individualists" dedicated to modernization and economic progress.[3] Though eager to obtain federal subsidies, these business promoters strongly opposed governmental restraints, welfare programs, and higher taxes.

Southern alienation and defection in the presidential elections of 1948 and 1952 did not necessarily denote any major change in the dominant pattern of southern politics. Indeed, the salient characteristics of the state patterns portrayed by V.O. Key in 1949 continued to be evident for some time. In Virginia the Byrd organization retained its control of state politics, despite the opposition of an independent faction. But the organization seemed less sure of itself in the early 1950s than in the past. It was challenged by independents from within and Republicans from without. Francis Pickens Miller, an independent Democrat, ran a spirited race in the gubernatorial primary of 1949 against the organization's candidate, John S. Battle, who managed to eke out a victory. The state went Republican in the presidential election of 1952, and in the next year's general election an attractive Republican named Theodore R. "Ted" Dalton waged a surprisingly close race for governor. In the legislative session of 1954, the organization was forced to compromise when a band of "Young Turks" from its own ranks demanded that surplus state funds be spent for expanded public services. By the mid-1950s, the Byrd faction was showing signs of decline.

Tennessee, another state with a durable bifactional structure, experienced more significant change. The most important new developments were the weakening influence of Edward H. Crump and the rise of new state leaders. Crump, who supported the Dixiecrats in 1948, was jolted that year when his candidates for the governorship and the U.S. Senate were defeated by Gordon Browning and Estes Kefauver. Four years later his ally, Sen. Kenneth D. McKellar, was denied reelection by Congressman Albert Gore, and the state was captured by General Eisenhower. Crump had endorsed Frank G. Clement, the successful candidate for governor in 1952. The aging boss died in 1954, and his powerful role in state politics came to an end. Meanwhile, Kefauver, Clement, and Gore emerged as the most prominent politicians in Tennessee; the electorate expanded with the invalidation of the poll tax; and organized labor and black voters became influential factors in the state's politics.

Georgia and Louisiana, two other states with strong bifactional politics, demonstrated both continuity and change in the 1950s. Following the death of his father, Herman Talmadge soon rose to a dominant position in Georgia politics. He won the governorship in a special election in 1948 and was elected to a four-year term two years later. He prolonged and broadened the Talmadge organization. His rural strength lay with the poorer farmers, nurtured on what one historian has called a Gene Talmadge "blend of racial demagoguery and reaction."[4] The younger Talmadge firmly opposed Negro voting, resisted the desegregation of the state's universities, and sought to preserve the sanctity of the county-unit system. Yet his program included a "New South" as well as a neo-Bourbon emphasis, and his administration attracted business and urban support with its commitment to the development of education, highways, mental health, and economic growth. In many respects Talmadge was a far more constructive governor than his father. The anti-Talmadge faction, led by former governors Ellis G. Arnall and Melvin E. Thompson, was a competitive force in the state's politics until the mid-1950s, when it swiftly disintegrated in the face of Talmadge's predominance and the mounting racial crisis.

In Louisiana, meanwhile, Longism continued to provide the basis for a bifactional division among the state's Democrats. The anti-Long faction, generally characterized by its conservatism, opposed both the local radicalism of the Longs and the liberalism of the national Democratic party. Both factions enjoyed some success. Earl K. Long was elected governor in 1948, the conservative Robert F. Kennon succeeded him in 1952, and Long was returned to the governorship in 1956, despite his affronts to respectability and an odor of scandal in his previous administration. The state's anti-Washington sentiment was reflected in the large vote Dwight Eisenhower received in 1952 and in his success in carrying Louisiana four years later. By the mid-1950s, the state-rights issue had shifted heavily to an emphasis on race.

Alabama's Democratic factionalism was less clear-cut and less stable than that of Louisiana, but "a progressive-conservative cleavage" in the state's politics persisted into the 1950s. The personalizing of leadership continued to operate in conjunction with class and sectional divisions, as well as growing racial alarm among white Alabamians. As Numan V. Bartley and Hugh Davis Graham have written, "The black belt and the suburbs stood broadly for the status quo, or perhaps the status quo ante, while the hills and the wire grass and the working-class districts in the cities demonstrated a distinct liberal bias."[5] Momentarily in the early 1950s, the liberals appeared to be ascendant. Gordon Persons, a Democratic loyalist, won the governorship in 1950, and earlier that year regulars had taken control of the party machinery. James E. Folsom was elected to a second gubernatorial term in 1954, and the state's liberal U.S. senators, Lister Hill and John Sparkman, turned back conservative challenges in this period. A knowledgeable Alabama journalist, writing on the eve of Folsom's second inauguration, commented on his uniqueness "in the line of Southern mob spellbinders": his appeal both to "the 'nigger hater' element and the Negro himself."[6] Nevertheless, Folsom faced strong opposition in the legislature, and his reform proposals during his second administration were largely unsuccessful. Although Folsom, Hill, and Sparkman were all liberals, they campaigned independently, and their constituencies, while overlapping, differed in some respects. "Big Jim" made an effort to fashion a statewide faction in his own image, but he was unable to transfer or perpetuate his popularity, which eventually fell victim to the rising tide of racial hysteria and his own personal and administrative weaknesses.

Postwar developments in Texas gave some support to V.O. Key's assertion in 1949 that the state's voters were beginning to "divide broadly along liberal and conservative lines."[7] The 1950s were marked by sharp factional struggles in the state's politics, with a fairly distinct division along economic lines. Allan Shivers, a forceful conservative, succeeded to the governorship in 1949 when Beauford Jester died. Shivers, who supported Eisenhower in 1952, was elected three times in his own right, serving until early 1957, when Price Daniel, another conservative, assumed office. Lyndon B. Johnson, a moderate liberal who had been elected to the U.S. Senate by a handful of votes in 1948, was reelected in 1954. He then became Democratic majority leader. The most pronounced liberal among Democratic leaders in the 1950s was Ralph W. Yarborough, a neo-Populist who elicited enthusiastic support from "liberal-labor-loyalist" elements in the Texas electorate. He also appealed to blacks and generally to lower-status whites. Yarborough lost a series of close gubernatorial contests between 1950 and 1956, before winning a Senate seat in a special election in 1957. The year before, in a contest for the chairmanship of the Texas delegation to the Democratic national convention, Senator Johnson defeated Governor Shivers. On the whole, however, the conservative wing of the party maintained firm control of politics and policies in the Lone Star State.

Factional alignments among North Carolina Democrats at midcentury were less ideological in origin than those in Texas. But they differed from the factional pattern of the prewar period. No leader or organization arose to dominate state politics in the manner of the Simmons machine or the Shelby Dynasty. W. Kerr Scott, a rural progressive, served as governor from 1949 to 1953, while Luther H. Hodges, a businessman and a political moderate, held that office from 1954 to 1961. Democratic groupings in North Carolina were shifting and indistinct during the postwar era, although the state's Democratic politicians in the early 1950s tended to divide into what has been described as "the conservative, urban-oriented, establishment wing of the Democratic party leadership and the progressive, farm bloc followers of Kerr Scott."[8]

Two aspects of South Carolina politics emphasized by V.O. Key continued to characterize political affairs in that state in the 1950s. One was the Palmetto State's loose multifactional system; the other was the ever-present factor of race in politics. South Carolinians were affected by such considerations as the traditional cleavage between upcountry and low country, by a broad division along liberal versus conservative lines, and by sympathy for the New Deal and national Democratic initiatives as opposed to support of the Dixiecrat revolt in 1948. The careers of two South Carolina leaders embodied these differences. Sen. Olin D. Johnston's political base was the Piedmont Plateau, where he attracted strong support from mill workers and lower-class whites in the cities. He was identified with the New Deal and remained loyal to the national Democratic party. Gov. Strom Thurmond, on the other hand, found his greatest strength in the low county. He became a symbol of anti–New Deal politics in South Carolina and bolted the national party in 1948. Both Johnston and Thurmond were outspoken advocates of white supremacy, and in 1950

the senator defeated the governor in the latter's campaign to replace
him in Washington. Four years later, however, Thurmond won a
suprising election as a write-in candidate to succeed Sen. Burnet R.
Maybank, who had died. The politics of race clearly contributed to
James F. Byrnes's election as governor in 1950 and to the selection of
George Bell Timmerman to succeed him four years later.

Mississippi politics in this period was also marked by shifting
factions in the Democratic party and mounting racial apprehension.
In the absence of "a unifying personality around whom a faction may
form, and against whom the anti's can unite," Key had written, "Mississippi politics tends to disintegrate into a multifactionalism."[9] The
nearest thing to "a unifying personality" in the prewar period had
been Theodore G. Bilbo, who died in 1947. In the years that followed,
the state's two U.S. senators, James O. Eastland and John C. Stennis,
won reelection with monotonous regularity. But their constituencies
were highly personal. The governors during the 1950s—Fielding L.
Wright, Hugh L. White, and James P. Coleman—were unable to extend the embryonic factions that began to develop during their administrations. Coleman, who defeated an ardent segregationist in
1956, was a moderating force in the state's politics. He resisted extremist legislation and continued to support the national Democratic
party. But white militants condemned his moderation and soon
brought his administration under siege. Meanwhile, a pervasive conservatism and heightened fears of racial change steadily debilitated
the growth of neopopulism and an inchoate liberal versus conservative division over economic issues.

Two other southern states, Arkansas and Florida, showed fewer
signs of political change in the early 1950s. The leader of the reform
forces in Arkansas, Gov. Sidney S. McMath, was reelected in 1950
but lost his bid for a third term two years later. In 1954 McMath
unsuccessfully challenged John J. McClellan for his Senate seat. Party
factions in Arkansas, as in many other southern states, were personal
and impermanent, and they seldom assumed the dimensions of a
statewide organization that lasted beyond a particular election or gubernatorial administration. The same was true of Florida in the years
after World War II. Despite the enormous economic and social
changes that were transforming the state, it remained a one-party
state with a fluid multifactional competition among Democratic politicians. LeRoy Collins, an attractive newcomer to statewide politics,
won the governorship in 1954 and served for six years. He sponsored
a forward-looking program in such areas as educational opportunity
and economic development and sought to steer a moderate course
through the troubled waters of racial politics. Collins's efforts to secure
legislative reapportionment and constitutional revision were blocked

by the rurally oriented legislature. By the mid-1950s, the legislature had become polarized, with each house being divided between a dominant small-county bloc known as the "pork choppers" and a minority urban bloc called the "lamb choppers."

In the peripheral states of Oklahoma and Kentucky, established patterns of political behavior continued in the 1950s. The Republican party remained weak in Oklahoma, even though the state voted for Eisenhower in 1952 and 1956. The party's unflinching conservatism, dictated by wealthy oil producers, limited its appeal in state and local politics. The Republican party in Oklahoma, one historian suggests, was "a political Wizard of Oz, all head and no body."[10] As for the Democratic party, its factions took shape in large part as a result of gubernatorial campaigns and administrations. The state's best-known and most formidable campaigner was former governor Robert S. Kerr, who was elected to the U.S. Senate in 1948. Although Gomer Smith and his protégé William O. Coe represented an insurgent strain in the state's politics, attacking the "money hogs" and the political establishment, they were repeatedly defeated by a strong Democratic coalition made up of businessmen, rural interests, labor leaders, and professional elements. The success of this coalition was finally interrupted in 1958, when a young, urban-oriented candidate named J. Howard Edmondson was elected governor on a "reform" platform.

The political scene in Kentucky was considerably different from that in Oklahoma. For one thing, the Republicans in Kentucky posed a stronger threat to Democratic control. While the Democrats held the governorship throughout the 1950s, the Republicans carried the state for Eisenhower in 1956 and won both U.S. Senate seats in the same election. The Democratic party's dominant wing—the so-called administration faction—was headed by a series of governors: Earle C. Clements, Lawrence W. Wetherby, and Bert T. Combs. This faction was based on a sturdy organization in western Kentucky, with strongholds in the eastern mountains. Albert B. "Happy" Chandler's large following comprised the other major party faction. The Chandler faction was built around the personality of its leader; it was particularly strong in central Kentucky but enjoyed the allegiance of able lieutenants in many counties. Chandler, a superlative campaigner and kind of Kentucky folk figure, captured the governorship in 1955. As one close observer of Kentucky politics has written, "While representing the traditionally conservative faction of the party, Chandler cultivated a populist image, though his was not a populist record."[11] In general, the administration Democrats tended to have a more liberal and national orientation than the Chandler wing of the party.

Few events in the postwar period had a greater effect on southern politics than the Supreme Court's momentous decision in *Oliver Brown et al.* v. *Board of Education of Topeka, Kansas* (1954), which overturned the "separate but equal" doctrine and declared separate educational facilities in the public elementary and high schools on the basis of race to be "inherently unequal." The *Brown* decision in May 1954 and the court's implementing decree a year later provided a rallying point for the forces of reaction in southern politics. It precipitated an outburst of political demagoguery, organized resistance, and powerful pressure to coerce conformity among white southerners. The result was the infusion of politics, especially in the lower South, with racial concerns, an obsession that threatened to blot out older factions and divisions that had evolved in the various southern states.

Southern reaction to the Supreme Court's school desegregation decision ranged from the moderation and cautious optimism of Gov. Thomas B. Stanley of Virginia and Gov. LeRoy Collins of Florida to the outspoken defiance expressed by a number of deep South politicians. Gov. Talmadge of Georgia asserted that the court had reduced the constitution to a "mere scrap of paper," while Sen. Richard B. Russell condemned the *Brown* decision as "a flagrant abuse of judicial power." Sen. James O. Eastland of Mississippi predicted that the South "will not abide by or obey this legislative decision by a political court."[12] Writing in the period of massive resistance to school desegregation, one southern historian remarked that "it is safe to attack the Supreme Court, the National Association for the Advancement of Colored People (NAACP), 'nigger lovers,' both local and outsiders, sociologists, and meddlesome Yankees."[13]

Most of the border state region, including the District of Columbia, Maryland, West Virginia, Missouri, and Kansas, soon began to comply with the *Brown* decision. Although the states to the south were not prepared to desegregate their public schools "with all deliberate speed," as the Supreme Court decreed in May 1955, they were restrained in their reactions for several months. The reason was that the desegregation decision had no immediate effect on southern schools, which remained segregated. This state of affairs did not last long. Local school boards, particularly outside of the deep South, were soon being petitioned by black parents to admit their children to previously all-white schools. The NAACP encouraged these petitions. In 1955 and 1956, the federal courts ordered the admission of black students to a number of public schools in Kentucky, Tennessee, and Texas. The courts also issued an injunction to prevent interference with the desegregation program worked out by an Arkansas school district.

These court orders resulted in a series of riots and what the *New York Times* described as "actions of violence and the unleashing of malevolent moods."[14] Angry mobs and ugly scenes surrounded efforts to desegregate public schools in Clinton, Tennessee, Mansfield, Texas, and Sturgis and Clay, Kentucky. In February 1956 a mob of students and townspeople forced the expulsion of Autherine Lucy, a young black woman who had just been admitted to the University of Alabama by court order. In the fall of 1956, Gov. Shivers of Texas exercised the state's police power to prevent violence and maintain order—and to preserve segregation—in two communities under court order to desegregate public schools. Mob rule was quickly terminated in Kentucky and Tennessee when Governors Albert B. Chandler and Frank G. Clement sent in state police and national guardsmen to restore order and enable desegregation to continue. Despite Shivers's intervention more than a hundred Texas school districts, beginning with San Antonio, were desegregated by the end of 1956. Meanwhile, a score of judicial decisions had begun to dismantle racial segregation in such areas as transportation, housing, and recreational facilities in the South. Even so, school desegregation had made little progress in the region. By September 1956 only 723 of the South's 10,000 school districts had been desegregated, and the eight South Atlantic and Gulf Coast states—from Virginia through Louisiana—remained completely segregated at the primary and secondary school levels.

By the early part of 1956, an organized resistance movement had taken shape in these eight states. "The atmosphere of violence, boycott, reprisal, and caste solidarity," Numan V. Bartley has written, "both set the stage for and announced the arrival of the Citizens' Council movement."[15] The Citizens' Council soon became the most vocal of all pressure groups opposing desegregation. First organized in July 1954 in the delta town of Indianola, Mississippi, the Council soon spread to surrounding counties and shortly afterward formed a state association. The movement quickly dominated political life in Mississippi. The Council was also powerful in Alabama, and it became an influential movement in Louisiana and South Carolina. Virginia, the fifth state with a strong white supremacy organization, was represented by the Defenders of State Sovereignty and Individual Liberties. A variety of other segregationist organizations, including the Patriots of North Carolina, the States' Rights Council of Georgia, and the Ku Klux Klan, appeared in other parts of the South. Citizens' Councils existed in most southern states, and at the movement's height in 1956 the Councils had about 250,000 members.

Generally, the segregationist groups were strongest in the black belts and rural areas, but they also attracted support from working-class residents of the region's cities. The growth of these groups was promoted by racial strife and fears of social change, as well as strident appeals to the southern white masses to oppose desegregation. At the same time, leaders of the Citizens' Councils renounced violence and pledged themselves to preserve white supremacy through peaceful and lawful means, thereby appealing to the "respectable" elements of southern society. The Citizens' Councils and allied organizations used economic retaliation against desegregationists, worked for the passage of legislation to frustrate their opponents, endeavored to "purify" voting lists and prevent further black registration, and sought to rally white southerners to their cause. They contributed to a spreading mood of white defiance in the region. "It was a frightening thing to go into a small city," Pat Watters of the Southern Regional Council recalled, "and to realize that not merely the semi-literate poor white gas station attendant, but also the bankers, the mayor, the editor, even some of the preachers, all those who are personages in such a place supported it [resistance] fervently."[16]

School desegregation became an absorbing issue in the politics of some southern states even before the Supreme Court's implementation decree in the spring of 1955. The *Brown* decision was a factor in several Democratic primaries in 1954, and it dominated the state campaigns in Georgia and South Carolina. Marvin Griffin, a lieutenant of Herman Talmadge's and an outspoken critic of the desegregation decision, won the governorship in Georgia. George Bell Timmerman, Jr., who was identified with the Byrnes-Dixiecrat wing of the party in South Carolina, swept to victory in that state's gubernatorial primary. Later in the year, former governor Thurmond was elected to the U.S. Senate. Nevertheless, race was not always a major issue in the 1954 elections, and in North Carolina and Tennessee, senatorial and gubernatorial candidates were elected over opponents who tried to exploit the threat of racial change.

South Carolina and Georgia foreshadowed the development of racially dominated politics in the deep South and several other southern states. Both states were led by determined, resourceful, and influential politicians: South Carolina by Strom Thurmond and James F. Byrnes, Georgia by Herman Talmadge. All three were powerful transitional figures in the shift to a politics of massive resistance. Thurmond symbolized the Dixiecratic insurgency of 1948, and his leadership served to link that movement with the rising opposition to the *Brown* decision. As governor, Byrnes used his considerable prestige to resist social change and to promote regional political independence. In some respects Talmadge was the most significant of the three, for he came to dominate his state's politics, virtually destroyed the anti-Talmadge faction, and appealed strongly to the racial sensibilities of his constituents. Race was an important issue in the younger Talmadge's gubernatorial campaigns of 1948 and 1950, and as governor he assumed a fiercely antagonistic position toward any change in race relations. The Georgia governor was a harsh critic of the *Sweatt* decision and other court decrees resulting in the admission of black students to southern graduate and professional schools, and he was a vociferous opponent of desegregation at the college level. Talmadge sought unsuccessfully, in 1950 and 1952, to secure voter ratification of a constitutional amendment to formalize the county-unit system, and his administration succeeded in 1954 in securing voter approval of an amendment permitting the substitution of a private school system for the public schools.

Beginning in the lower South, state legislatures soon laid down a barrage of defensive enactments. The Louisiana lawmakers, who were in session when the *Brown* decision was handed down in May 1954, quickly censured the Supreme Court, created a joint legislative committee to devise strategy for the maintenance of segregation, passed a measure requiring segregation in all primary and secondary public schools, and enacted a pupil assignment law, authorizing local superintendents to assign individual students to public schools. Similar bills and constitutional amendments, including measures authorizing the abolition of entire public school systems and a variety of other segregationist legislation, were adopted later in the year by Georgia, South Carolina, and Mississippi. Several other southern states enacted local pupil assignment laws in 1954 and 1955.[17]

In August 1954 Gov. Thomas Stanley of Virginia appointed a thirty-two-member Commission on Public Education. Headed by state senator Garland Gray, the Commission was created to study how best to avoid desegregation of the public schools in the Old Dominion. The Gray Commission took more than a year to prepare its report, which was presented to the governor in November 1955. The Commission recommended, as part of a comprehensive plan, the adoption of a pupil assignment law, modification of the state's compulsory attendance requirement, and the payment of tuition grants to any student refusing to attend a public school with members of another race. Broadly speaking, one historian concludes, the plan "represented a compromise between the extreme white supremacy sentiment of black-belt Virginia and the more moderate attitudes evident elsewhere in the state."[18]

Although Governor Stanley praised the Commission's work and called a special session of the legislature to act on its recommendations, the Gray Plan encountered strong opposition. The recommendations of the Gray Commission were criticized as being too moderate by key figures in the Byrd organization, by the Defenders of State Sovereignty and Individual Liberties, by the Richmond *News Leader*, and by white leaders in the black belt. Senator Byrd himself soon joined the assault. By the autumn of 1956, a militant segregationist program known as "massive resistance" had been adopted, despite the efforts of moderates who argued in favor of the milder Gray Plan. In the late summer of 1956, the Virginia general assembly, meeting in special session, approved a series of antidesegregation bills, including a measure denying state appropriations to any public school attended by black and white children. The most important massive resistance law was an interpositionist statute declaring that the "Commonwealth of Virginia assumes direct responsibility for the control of any school, elementary or secondary, . . . to which children of both races are assigned and enrolled by any court order." Virginia, a part of the upper South, had demonstrated the possibilites of massive resistance to the *Brown* decision. The movement soon spread through the deep South. As one perceptive scholar has noted, "The southern mood made massive resistance possible; Citizens' Councils provided the working cadres and crusading fervor; and entrenched southern politicians contributed much of the leadership, direction, and strength."[19]

A dramatic indication of the South's mounting political defiance came in March 1956, when 101 of the 128 congressmen from the ex-Confederate states issued a "Southern Manifesto." Originally proposed by Senator Thurmond and quickly endorsed by Senator Byrd, the "Declaration of Constitutional Principles," as it was formally known, was revised by a committee headed by Sen. Richard Russell. Byrd explained that the manifesto was "a part of the plan of massive resistance we've been working on and I hope and believe it will be an effective action." The document denounced the *Brown* decision as "a clear abuse of judicial power." It commended the motives of those states "which have declared the intention to resist forced integration by any lawful means."[20] The manifesto's signers pledged themselves to use all lawful means to reverse the desegregation decision and to prevent its enforcement. Only three senators from the states of the Confederacy failed to sign the Southern Manifesto: Albert Gore and Estes Kefauver of Tennessee and Lyndon B. Johnson of Texas. Critics of the Tennessee senators in their home state tried to make the most of their apostasy. As one of Kefauver's constituents wrote him in 1957, "You are of the South, yet the 'mouth-men' of your enemies see fit to whisper around behind the back of their hands 'He is Pink' 'He is a nigger-lover'—'He has nothing in common with the South,' 'He leans towards Communism.' "[21]

One of the signatories was Sen. James O. Eastland of Mississippi, who was perhaps the most relentless crusader for massive resistance in the 1950s. Dedicated to the principles of racial purity and state rights and alarmed by the threat of a Communist conspiracy, which he suspected might be at the bottom of the Supreme Court's mischievous attack on white supremacy, the Mississippi senator soon emerged as one of the most resourceful and influential of the new Bourbon leaders in the South. "Defeat," he declared in 1954, "means death, the death of Southern culture and our aspirations as an Anglo-Saxon people. With strong leadership and the loyalty and fortitude of a great people, we will climb the heights."[22] Eastland was one of the architects of the Federation of Constitutional Government, established in December 1955 as a coordinating agency for the resistance movement in the South and as a means of carrying the fight to the North. Although the Federation failed to live up to its promoters' expectations, it served an important role in helping shape the rising tide of southern opposition to desegregation. Eastland and other opposition leaders soon turned to the Citizens' Council of America, which became a center for the formulation of massive resistance strategy.

The doctrine of "interposition" provided massive resistance with a theory and a rallying cry. Reviving constitutional concepts associated with Thomas Jefferson and John C. Calhoun, advocates of interposition invoked the state-rights tradition, the compact theory of the Union, and a strict constructionist view of the Constitution. They argued that, by consolidating public school authority in the state government and interposing the "sovereignty" of the state between local school officials and federal courts, the *Brown* decision could be reversed. Interposition would be valid, they insisted, until other states secured the adoption of a constitutional amendment declaring segregated schools to be illegal. First resurrected by Governor Talmadge and endorsed by such votaries as the Richmond *News Leader* and the *Citizens' Council*, the proposition had become a leading legislative proposal in the southern states by early 1956. It seemed to offer a marvelous strategem to turn back federal intervention in the South's traditional pattern of race relations and a solution to the region's problem resulting from *Brown v. Board of Education*.

Early in 1956 Virginia's general assemby adopted a joint resolution "interposing the sovereignty" of the state "against encroachment upon the reserved powers" of the Old Dominion. The five states of the deep South soon followed Virginia's lead, and by mid-1957 eight southern commonwealths had approved interposition resolutions. Two others had adopted resolutions of protest. Formal adoption of interposition provided a pretext for additional resistance legislation. Meanwhile, the peripheral South had become the scene of a crucial struggle to solidify the region in support of massive resistance. Led by moderate, business-oriented chief executives, most of these states stopped short of massive resistance tactics, while they strengthened their opposition to complying with desegregation rulings. They enacted local option school closing laws, authorized tuition grants to students attending private schools, and passed various other segregation measures. Only Kentucky and Oklahoma, and to a lesser extent Texas, demonstrated a willingness in the mid-1950s to comply with the *Brown* decision.

Public opinion polls in late February 1956 suggested the extent of sectional polarization over school desegregation in the United States. Over 70 percent of northern whites who were interviewed supported the Supreme Court's rulings of 1954 and 1955, while 80 percent of southern whites were opposed. In national politics, as well, the South seemed to be increasingly alienated from the rest of the nation. Approximately one out of every three recorded votes in Congress during the mid-1950s found a majority of the southern Democrats voting against the Democratic majority from other regions. The "southern" position on many votes was also different from that of congressional Republicans, although the two groups tended to agree on issues having to do with domestic welfare spending and state rights. Southern congressional attitudes toward world affairs were also becoming more distinctive. While continuing to champion "cold war" patriotism, a growing number of southern senators and representatives had abandoned their support of active international involvement, with the major exception of military defense and alliances.

Despite the gathering strength of massive resistance, there was no Dixiecrat revival in the presidential election of 1956 nor, for that matter, even a southern protest in the manner of Richard Russell's candidacy in 1952. Indeed, Russell actively campaigned for the Democratic national ticket in 1956. The explanation for this state of affairs is apparent. The national Democratic party, including its presidential nominee, Adlai Stevenson, was far more conciliatory toward the South than it had been in 1948, and the party's national convention was unusually harmonious. Southerners had no difficulty in accepting the mild loyalty pledge and in agreeing to see that the party's nominees were placed under the Democratic party label on the ballot. The party platform omitted a direct endorsement of the *Brown* decision and specifically rejected the use of force in implementing the desegregation decree. An even more important consideration was the fact that the political power structure of the southern states and localities had a strong vested interest in Democratic loyalty. That interest included not only its domination of local and state politics in the South— massive resistance won one victory after another in Democratic primaries—but also the enormous influence exerted by southern congressmen in the committee system and the considerable role southern

Table 3. The Conservative Coalition in Congress, 1957–1985

Year	Congress	% of Appearances	% of Victories	Average Coalition Support Scores among Southern Democrats	
				Senate	House
1957	85th	14	89	NA	NA
1959	86th	17	71	63	82
1961	87th	28	55	67	61
1963	88th	17	50	61	58
1965	89th	24	33	60	61
1967	90th	20	62	62	65
1969	91st	27	68	67	68
1971	92d	30	83	70	63
1973	93d	23	61	64	63
1975	94th	28	50	70	63
1977	95th	26	68	64	63
1979	96th	20	70	67	64
1981	97th	21	92	71	70
1983	98th	15	77	62	65
1985	99th	14	89	68	64

SOURCE: *Congressional Quarterly Almanac*, vols. 13–41.

NOTE: Coalition support scores are based upon an analysis of all roll call votes on which a majority of Republicans and southern Democrats voted in opposition to a majority of nonsouthern Democrats and represent the proportion of such voes on which an individual congressman voted in agreement with the conservative coalition.

Democrats played in their party's national campaigns. Southerners, moreover, were reluctant to abandon their traditional identification with the Democratic party.

The presidential election year did bring threats of Democratic party defection in the South. Two interstate meetings of southern Democrats were held in the summer of 1956, presumably as a means of safeguarding sectional interests in the forthcoming election, and a National States' Rights Conference was convened in Memphis. Independent campaigns were undertaken in several southern states, but they fared poorly even in South Carolina and Mississippi, whose voters cast 29.4 and 17.3 percent of their ballots, respectively, for Sen. Harry Byrd and Rep. John Bell Williams of Mississippi. But the Democrats carried both states, in addition to North Carolina, Georgia, Alabama, and Arkansas. Nevertheless, the Republicans won Louisiana and the other six southern states. They clearly benefited from southern disaffection with the national Democratic party. And President Eisenhower was popular in his own right. He ran well in the cities, in the upper South hill country, and in such traditional Democratic strongholds as East Texas and the hill parishes of Louisiana. The Democratic ticket won 50 percent or more of the vote in only five of the former Confederate states, receiving only 47.6 percent of the total regional vote.

Federal intervention and the prospect of radical changes in "the southern way of life" encouraged "a sense of beleaguered solidarity" among white southerners in the 1950s. The advocates of massive resistance were quick to exploit this sensibility. They hoped to unite white southerners on the basis of state rights and the maintenance of segregation. They also sought to undermine their opponents and to discredit the black equal rights movement. Citizens' Councils and other resistance groups disseminated a great mass of literature promoting segregation and the "southern" position. These zealous defenders of the traditional South set up speakers' bureaus, sponsored radio and television programs, and tried in various other ways to create conformity in the outlook of white southerners. The Charleston *News and Courier*, the Jackson (Miss.) *Daily News*, the *Citizens' Council*, and numerous other newspapers spoke out in support of the segregationist cause. Although some of the region's major newspapers opposed the politics of massive resistance, most of the southern press reflected the white South's strong opposition to school desegregation. The crusade for conformity also resorted to political pressure: through lobbying, candidate questionnaires, the purging of "unqualified" black voters, and the election of outspoken segregationists.

State authority was, of course, the ultimate reliance of segregationist leaders in their quest for conformity. Legislation was one major objective. State legislatures in the eleven ex-Confederate states passed, by one count, no fewer then 450 prosegregation measures during the decade following the *Brown* decision. Since the burden of initiating litigation to force school desegregation fell on the National Association for the Advancement of Colored People, segregationists singled out that organization and its allies by special legislation and legal harassment. "Attacking the NAACP in the South," Professor Bartley observes, "was politically analogous to assaulting the Communist Party in the rest of the nation."[23] Several states required the organization to register and provide membership lists and the names of contributors. Other statutes stipulated that no member of the NAACP should be employed by a state agency. Criminal sanctions were also directed at the association, including efforts in six states to curtail the organization's access to the courts. Southern lawmakers did not stop with the NAACP. Several states required their employees to take antisubversive oaths and to list all organizations to which they belonged.

Governmental harassment of dissenters and coercion of the uncommitted were most extreme in the investigations and other activities of state sovereignty commissions and special legislative committees created throughout the region. These groups did their best to prevent any deviation from orthodox thinking and behavior among southern educators, launched harsh probes of black institutions such as South Carolina State College in Orangeburg, and severely restricted academic freedom and civil liberties in many parts of the South. State attorneys general like Eugene Cook of Georgia used their positions to further the assault on the NAACP and to promote the cause of massive resistance. Hearings held by congressional subcommittees headed by Senator Eastland and Rep. James C. Davis of Georgia, allegedly to investigate the relationship between the black equal rights movement and Communist activities in the South, supplemented the work of state officials.

The politics of massive resistance was sustained by a social and political philosophy characterized by one scholar as "neobourbonism."[24] While emphasizing the centrality of white supremacy and state rights, the neo-Bourbons appealed to the values of rural and small-town life, to the tradition of southern resistance, and to the leadership of the local elites. Since their greatest strength lay in the black belts and rural areas, they were determined in their resistance to legislative reapportionment. In national politics they condemned the intrusion of big government and opposed the welfare state, federal aid to education, and protective labor legislation. They tended to be nationalists in foreign policy, usually of the "unilateralist" type. The most reactionary among them seemed willing to sacrifice the public school system in their states if such a step would maintain segregation.

Massive resistance reached the limits of its power in 1957–58. In the early fall of 1957, the movement was tested in a dramatic confrontation that developed over the desegregation of Central High School in Little Rock, Arkansas. The Arkansas capital city was an unlikely scene for such a confrontation, given its lack of political extremism in race relations and its early formulation of plans to desegregate Central High. But the breakdown of community leadership and the pressure exerted by such elements as the Citizens' Council, not to mention the surging tide of massive resistance in the South as a whole, led Gov. Orval Faubus to intervene with state militiamen in order to prevent desegregation. When a federal court enjoined this action and a frenzied mob surrounded the school, President Eisenhower sent in federal troops to remove the obstruction.

News of the Little Rock crisis electrified the South and placed Arkansas in the forefront of massive resistance. Orval Faubus was suddenly transformed into a heroic southern leader. Some southerners, white as well as black, were no doubt reassured by the president's decision to enforce the law. But the immediate effect of Little Rock was to embarrass or silence southern moderates and to strengthen extremist elements. It also brought the collapse of "Operation Dixie," an ambitious plan to rebuild the Republican party in the southern states. The crisis stiffened resistance to desegregation in the upper South and slowed the trend toward "moderation" in several states where school districts were moving cautiously to comply with court orders to open white schools to black pupils. State governments throughout the region were galvanized into action, reinforcing barriers to desegregation and stepping up their attacks on the NAACP. In 1958 Gov. J. Lindsay Almond of Virginia and Governor Faubus challenged federal authority in the courts; Almond closed the nine schools in his state under federal court order to admit black students, while Faubus closed all of the secondary schools in Little Rock. Another measure of southern hostility was an intensified assault in Congress on the Supreme Court, although this attack was also encouraged by conservative opposition outside the South to the liberalism of the Warren Court. Five proposals to curb the Court's authority passed the House of Representatives in 1958, only to die in the Senate.

"Remember Little Rock!" might be a red flag in the eyes of southern recalcitrants, but it was also a warning they could hardly miss. Thoughtful segregationists were beginning to understand that the power of the national government could now be expected to enforce the decrees of the federal courts. After Little Rock it was scarcely possible to use violence to nullify decisions of the federal courts. Courtroom conflicts over school desegregation during the years 1957–61 proved to be a significant factor in the undermining of massive resistance. The federal courts eventually ruled that a state had no right to close some but not all of its public schools; they also refused to accept the subterfuge of publicly subsidized private schools. Thus, early in 1959 a federal court found that Virginia's action in closing nine public schools under orders to desegregate was unconstitutional. In June of the same year, the courts struck down Arkansas's school-closure laws and ordered the Little Rock school board to proceed with its original plan of desegregation.

Still, the politics of massive resistance had not yet run its course. In the election of six southern governors in 1958, the conservative trend in the region's politics was unmistakable, and the position of the victorious candidates generally supported the doctrine of massive resistance. By the end of 1958, ten southern states had adopted school-closing laws, and eight states had provisions for substituting private schools for desegregated public schools. Nevertheless, the course of the upper South remained uncertain, and in the lower South Governors James E. Folsom of Alabama and Earl K. Long of Louisiana attempted to move politics in their states toward economic issues. Both of these rural liberals were finally overwhelmed by the forces of massive resistance, Folsom in 1956 and Long in 1958. In Louisiana the segregationists, led by state senator William M. "Willie" Rainach, made a concerted effort to purge blacks from the voting lists and to enact a new registration law that would deny them the ballot in the future. In Washington Parish 1,377 of the 1,510 registered blacks were removed from the rolls. The controversy over voter registration was the first in a series of events that made race a salient issue in the gubernatorial election of 1959.

The first decisive political setback in the massive resistance campaign occurred in Virginia, where a shift away from interposition had become apparent by the fall of 1958. Some Virginia leaders had begun to weigh the relative importance of traditional white supremacy and public education. An open-schools movement was launched, and influential business interests raised questions about the wisdom of massive resistance. When the courts overturned the state government's school-closure policy in January 1959, Virginia was forced to reconsider its position. Governor Almond, a committed advocate of massive resistance, gradually moved to a more moderate stance, and under his guidance the general assembly finally adopted a series of measures compatible with token desegregation. The closed schools were reopened, and three cities were soon desegregated. Senator Byrd and most of the leaders of his organization strongly opposed these steps. But the outcome of the Democratic primary elections in July 1959 confirmed the demise of massive resistance, although these and later elections did not weaken Byrd's personal popularity.

Massive resistance was also turned back in Arkansas in 1959, again with the assistance of an unfavorable court decision. The balance of political pressures was narrow, but, as in Virginia, a coalition of educators, citizen supporters of the schools, and business elements was successful. This success only came, however, after a bitter and divisive struggle in Little Rock during the first half of 1959. The public high schools of the Arkansas capital were peacefully desegregated in August 1959. And the elections of 1960 confirmed the arrival of moderation in Arkansas, even though they resulted in Governor Faubus's reelection.

"Massive Is in the Cold, Cold Ground"

Newton Pratt in McClatchy Newspapers. Reprinted by permission.

Although massive resistance had collapsed in Virginia and Arkansas, the compromises that were effected in those two states suggested the feasibility, from the segregationist point of view, of shifting from all-out defiance to a more moderate position and a willingness to accept token desegregation. That seemed preferable to most southern leaders when faced with the necessity of choosing between segregation and traditional values, on the one hand, and social stability, pecuniary pursuits, and "progress," on the other. Meanwhile, the process of school desegregation had slowly continued in the outer

South. By the end of the decade, only the five states of the deep South remained completely segregated. Yet they, too, succumbed in the early 1960s. Georgia and Louisiana acted first, under court orders. The University of Georgia opened its doors to black students in 1961, and Atlanta, eager to preserve its image as a progessive metropolis of the New South, began the desegregation of its public schools in the same year. The process was more difficult and painful in Louisiana, but New Orleans took the first step in 1960. The other states of the deep South followed during the next few years, employing the conservative solution of token desegregation.

School desegregation among white southerners was almost universally unpopular. As Anthony Lewis wrote in 1964, segregationists "have invested their cause with a searing emotional impact. It has been made to appeal to the most susceptible tribal impulses: patriotism, racial purity, religious dogma, group solidarity, status and personal pride."[25] One needs to remember, however, that the South was not uniformly preoccupied with the politics of massive resistance. The peripheral South, save for Virginia and Arkansas, did not yield to a racially dominated politics. Nor were most white men and women, even in the deep South, consumed with a resolve to support massive resistance. Most southerners, white and black, were primarily concerned with the pressures and necessities of their daily lives. For most whites racial segregation provided the most feasible means of maintaining an orderly society in which the two races could coexist in relative peace, and their fears, however exaggerated, stemmed not only from racial prejudice but also from anticipation of the consequences that would come with the overthrow of long-established patterns of racial separation. If life went on more or less as usual for most southerners in the 1950s, the same was true in the exercise of political power by the organized interest groups and the county-governing class, though the distribution of that power would soon change.

The collapse of massive resistance did not immediately lead to a new politics for the South, even though almost all southern politicians by the early 1960s had reconciled themselves to the inevitability of token school desegregation. The shift to a policy of moderation in dealing with the pressures to desegregate the schools was motivated by expediency and conservative purposes. Though the South had changed enormously in the 1950s, its racially obsessed politics had blurred the lines between legality and illegality, weakened the sources of dissent and independence, and sapped the strength of economic liberalism in the region. The 1950s had not brought an emerging class politics, as V.O. Key had anticipated. Instead, the school desegregation issue provoked an intense preoccupation with the maintenance of white supremacy and a fixation on racial themes in politics, particularly in the deep South. That does a good deal to explain why the structure of political power in the individual southern states had not undergone much change during the decade.

7 The Second Reconstruction

The failure of massive resistance did not instantly jeopardize the South's traditional politics. Political currents in the various southern states continued to reflect the influence of well-established interest groups and local elites as well as the basic conservatism of most white southerners. The region's congressional delegations, overwhelmingly Democratic, still constituted a powerful force for the protection of the South's special interests in Washington. Although southerners approached the presidential election of 1960 in a mood of uncertainty, many of them hoped that the outcome would enable the South to retain a large measure of political autonomy and to ease the threat of still further racial change.

These hopes were soon dashed, not so much by the initiatives of John F. Kennedy's administration as by black protest and the civil rights movement. Southern white leaders—and the Kennedy administration—were thus overtaken by events, and the ensuing process of interaction between the protest movement and the national government brought the so-called Second Reconstruction into full flower. It led to momentous changes in the South, including black enfranchisement, but it also produced a strong white reaction in the form of Democratic division, Republican gains, and the rise of a new champion of the white masses. The divergent tendencies of the Second Reconstruction came to a climax in the presidential election of 1968, by which time the seeds of profound political change had been sown in the South.

Both of the major parties looked to the South in 1960 for vital support in a national election that promised to be extremely close. While the Republicans were less formidable than in 1952 and 1956, with the absence of the popular Dwight Eisenhower from the ticket, they undertook a vigorous campaign in the South under the leadership of the party's nominee, Vice-Pres. Richard M. Nixon. In some respects southern Republicans were inhibited in exploiting the troubled racial situation in the region, since the Eisenhower administration was identified with the use of federal troops at Little Rock and the passage of the civil rights laws of 1957 and 1960. As an Alabama newspaper warned, in listing the results of the southern defection to Eisenhower in 1952: "What did we gain by . . . dereliction? We got Earl Warren and the NAACP; we got Little Rock and Federal troops on Southern soil again; we got the rights of the individual states here in the South ground under foot, and if Slick Dick Nixon has his way, we will have carpetbag rule all over again."[1] Furthermore, the GOP platform in 1960 contained a strong civil rights plank. Although Nixon seemed to be a moderate on racial issues, he hoped to attract conservative voters on the basis of his party's economic position and state-rights attitude. In any case, the vice-president made a fervent appeal for southern support, campaigning in every southern state. Speaking in Atlanta in late August, Nixon was given an enthusiastic reception by almost 200,000 people. Ralph McGill, editor of the *Constitution*, wrote that it was "the greatest thing in Atlanta since the premiere of *Gone With the Wind*." Mayor William B. Hartsfield suggested that one reason for the spectacular Nixon reception was that "the South has been a one-party section for so long it has a sort of feeling of adventure like a gal out late at night."[2]

Southern interest in the election of 1960 was heightened because of the prominent role assumed by Sen. Lyndon B. Johnson of Texas. Johnson sought his party's presidential nomination on the basis of his strong congressional support and his success as Senate majority leader. In an effort to transcend his regional base, he stressed his western orientation and reached out for delegate support in other parts of the country. One reason he helped enact civil rights legislation in 1957 and 1960 was his desire to "nationalize" his southern image. Some Democrats, particularly liberals from outside the South, were suspicious of the Texan's solicitude for the oil and gas industry and of his cooperation with the Eisenhower administration. On the other hand, Johnson had worked hard as majority leader to keep the race question from becoming a disruptive barrier between the two major geographical divisions of the Democratic party. Nevertheless, he was widely viewed as the *southern* candidate, receiving backing in the national convention from virtually all of the South except Florida. His strength in other regions proved to be limited, and he was unable to prevent the nomination of Sen. John F. Kennedy of Massachusetts on the first ballot. Johnson's loss embittered many of his southern supporters. One Texas delegate asserted, "They crammed a civil rights plank down our throats, a liberal for president, then asked us to help sell the deal to the South with Johnson's aid."[3] This resentment was alleviated when Kennedy persuaded Johnson to join the ticket as the party's vice-presidential nominee. During the following campaign, the Texan devoted much of his time to the South. Touring the region by rail on the "LBJ Special," Johnson traveled almost 3,000 miles, made about sixty speeches at southern stops, and worked with his accustomed political flair to secure the cooperation of Democratic leaders. Near the end of the campaign, he concentrated a great deal of attention on his home state.

Kennedy himself campaigned in six southern states. Although the Democratic platform included a forthright endorsement of civil rights, the Massachusetts senator adopted a conciliatory approach to southern whites. He was concerned about the religious as well as the racial sensibilities of white southerners, since his Roman Catholicism had revived memories of the divisive campaign of 1928. Southern Baptists, the largest religious group in the region, were particularly aroused over this issue, and some observers predicted that it might tip the balance against the Democrats in Tennessee, Kentucky, and Oklahoma. Kennedy tried to minimize his potential losses by confronting the question directly. He reassured many southern Protestants when he appeared in September before the Greater Houston Ministerial Association to assert his belief in the separation of church and state. He also seized an opportunity to telephone the wife of Martin Luther King, Jr., when the civil rights leader was convicted on a technicality and ordered sent to a Georgia penitentiary. This dramatic gesture enhanced his appeal to black voters.

The Democrats carried a majority of the southern states, winning 50.47 percent of the vote in the former Confederate states, as compared to 47.76 percent in 1956. Yet the election in the South was almost as close as in the nation at large. Nixon won most of the rim states—Virginia, Kentucky, Tennessee, Florida, and Oklahoma—and he came within a few thousand votes of carrying Texas. The Republican nominee led his Democratic opponent in the metropolitan counties of the South, and he did better than Eisenhower had done in the black belts of six southern states. This impressive Republican showing was in part the result of the party's strong campaign throughout the region. But it also reflected the accumulating distrust of the national Democratic party felt by many white southerners, a distrust that was exacerbated by the civil rights movement and by Kennedy's Catholicism. The intense opposition to the Kennedy-Johnson ticket was illustrated in Texas, where a Texans-for-Nixon organization was sparked by former governor Allan Shivers.

Still, the Democrats could claim victory in the South. Though their winning margin was extremely close in Texas and South Carolina, they carried the rest of the South except for Mississippi and part of Alabama, where unpledged Democratic electors voted for Sen. Harry F. Byrd.[4] The religious issue clearly hurt the Democratic ticket in

Table 4. Party Identification in the South, 1952–1984

Party Identification	1952	1960	1968	1976	1984
All southerners					
Democrats	76	60	58	52	40
Independents	14	18	31	32	35
Republicans	10	22	11	16	25
Whites only					
Democrats	78	61	50	47	33
Independents	13	18	36	35	38
Republicans	9	21	14	19	29

SOURCE: Adapted from Earl Black and Merle Black, *Politics and Society in the South* (Cambridge: Harvard Univ. Press, 1987), p. 237, by permission.

NOTE: These statistics refer to the eleven ex-Confederate states only.

several states, and the Survey Research Center at the University of Michigan estimated that the defection of Protestant Democrats from Kennedy in the southern and border states represented 17.2 percent of the two-party vote in those states. Yet Kennedy was popular among many southerners; his stand on civil rights appeared moderate, he was dynamic and eloquent, and he seemed to have a genuine interest in the South. His impressive support from black southerners was an important factor in the outcome in several southern states.

While it is difficult to determine the relative importance of black as opposed to white voters in the Democrats' southern success, many observers believed, with Sen. John C. Stennis of Mississippi, that Lyndon Johnson "made the difference in the 1960 campaign."[5] Not only did Johnson's moderate record and southern background reassure the region's whites, but his strenuous campaign and strong influence among southern Democratic leaders made an indispensable contribution to his party's victory. One of the notable aspects of the Democratic campaign in the South was the support it received from state leaders and party organizations, a situation that had not existed since World War II. Among prominent Democrats only Senators Byrd and Thurmond, Rep. Howard W. Smith of Virginia, and Gov. Ross R. Barnett of Mississippi failed to endorse the Kennedy-Johnson ticket. Soon after the election, Sen. Richard B. Russell of Georgia explained his role in the campaign. "I am afraid that I go too much on personalities for when my friend Lyndon Johnson called me the third time and said that he was really in trouble and I could help, I stopped weighing issues and went out."[6] At about the same time,

Russell wrote a constituent: "I have seen many Senators come and go—practically all of them good men. A very few of them have been great men. In my opinion Lyndon Johnson is the ablest legislator who has served in the Congress in the past half century."[7]

The prospect of federal appropriations and patronage from a new Democratic administration was undoubtedly an important consideration in the minds of southern politicians. Democratic success in state and congressional contests was as great as ever. But the Republicans did make one breakthrough. In a special election held in May 1961 to fill Lyndon Johnson's Senate seat, a young Republican named John G. Tower won a close race against William A. Blakley, an extreme conservative, with the help of liberal Democrats.

John F. Kennedy's election raised the hopes and expectations of Americans who wanted significant advances in the movement for civil rights. During the campaign of 1960, Kennedy had expressed sympathy for the equal rights cause and had promised an "innovative and vigorous" administration in this area. But the new president soon disappointed those who expected him to pursue a bold and vigorous civil rights program. The reasons for his cautious approach soon became obvious. Realizing how narrow his margin of victory was in 1960 and that Richard Nixon had attracted more votes from southern whites than he had, Kennedy was unusually solicitous of those southerners, whose support he coveted in Congress and in the election of 1964. Of more immediate import was the powerful presence of southern congressmen in the committee structure and leadership of the Senate and House of Representatives. Kennedy needed the cooperation of these southerners in order to get his legislative program enacted. As the young president said to an aide, "If we drive [John] Sparkman, [Lister] Hill and other moderate Southerners to the wall with a lot of civil rights demands that can't pass anyway, then what happens to the Negro on minimum wages, housing and the rest?"[8] Finally, while the president agreed with the general objectives of the civil rights movement, he was not yet convinced of the need for or the desirability of comprehensive federal involvement in the struggle.

Rather than sponsoring a broad civil rights program in Congress, the Kennedy administration emphasized executive action in such areas as voting rights, employment, transportation, and education. The administration helped secure a two-year extension of the Civil Rights Commission in 1961, established the President's Committee on Equal Employment Opportunity, under the chairmanship of Vice-President Johnson, and endorsed two voting rights proposals in 1962. Kennedy's use of executive power was also evident in his appointment of a considerable number of blacks to high-level positions and in other employment gains in the federal government. The president lent his support to the civil rights division in the Department of Justice, which was headed by his brother, Robert F. Kennedy. During the Kennedy years, the number of voting rights suits initiated by the Justice Department was greatly increased. On the other hand, the chief executive refused to act on a recommendation that nondiscrimination be made a condition of federally aided programs in the states. Pressured by southern senators, he appointed several staunch segregationists to federal judgeships in the South. And despite his campaign promise to ban discrimination in federally subsidized housing, he delayed such action for almost two years, and even then his executive order was cast in a narrow and ineffective form. The administration sought to encourage the voluntary acceptance of the civil rights of black people in the South, but it studiously avoided even the appearance of federal coercion.

By the time of Kennedy's election, the civil rights movement had entered a new phase, a phase manifested in sit-ins by college students and other kinds of direct protest that spread rapidly over the South in 1960. Although these direct-action campaigns employed the nonviolent tactics advocated by Martin Luther King, Jr., they led to heightened tension and bitter confrontation in many southern cities. The writer John Egerton later described the almost apocalyptic nature of these events in the region below the Potomac and the Ohio. "The civil-rights movement was a traveling road show that held center stage before massed crowds of the hopeful and the hostile during a twelve-year run in the South. For sheer drama, it was unsurpassed; the emotional fervor whipped up by fire-eyed evangelists on the Sawdust Trail in an earlier day seems by comparison as quiet and placid as a Sunday night vespers. The Movement had all the elements of a great folk epic—heroes and villains, triumphs and tragedies, martyrs and prophets, a supreme cause (integration), and a cast of thousands."[9]

The wave of antidiscrimination demonstrations soon confronted the Kennedy administration with troublesome problems. One of the first incidents was that of the so-called Freedom Riders, an interracial group sponsored by the Congress of Racial Equality (CORE) as a means of implementing the Supreme Court's decision declaring segregated restaurants and other public facilities in bus terminals to be unconstitutional. Setting out from Washington, D.C., the Freedom Riders got as far as Anniston, Alabama, before a mob attacked their bus, burned it, and beat the demonstrators. Later on the same day, the riders were beaten by a group of Ku Klux Klansmen in Birmingham, at which point the venture was abandoned. The Kennedy administration was reluctant to get involved, in spite of the failure of local authorities to protect the demonstrators, since Gov. John Patterson, a dedicated segregationist, had been the first southern political leader to endorse John F. Kennedy for president. But when a new group recruited by the Student Nonviolent Coordinating Committee (SNCC) resumed the ride to Montgomery, Attorney General Kennedy managed to persuade Governor Patterson to guarantee the safety of the bus as far as the Montgomery city limits. At the downtown terminal, however, an angry mob of whites viciously attacked the riders. When a second riot developed during the evening of the next day outside a black church where Martin Luther King was leading a rally in support of the Freedom Riders, the president sent 400 federal marshals to Montgomery; Governor Patterson finally acted as well, declaring martial law in the city and mobilizing the National Guard. As the Freedom Riders traveled on to Jackson, Mississippi, the Justice Department was able to secure their safety by agreeing not to interfere in the arrest of the riders, who were found guilty, fined, and given two-month suspended sentences. The demonstrators all went to jail rather than pay their fines.

One result of the Freedom Rides was the Kennedy administration's decision to file a petition with the Interstate Commerce Commission to compel the desegregation of all bus and railroad terminals in the United States. The ICC approved that petition in September, to become effective on November 1. This administrative action represented a major defeat for southern segregationists because, for the first time, desegregation was decreed for an entire class of institutions in the region. In the meantime, the administration attempted to persuade black leaders to shift their emphasis from demonstrations to voter registration drives, and SNCC and several other organizations did devote much of their time to that task, especially in the deep South. Mass protests and civil disobedience continued, however, as in Albany, Georgia, where, beginning in November 1961 and lasting more than a year, thousands of blacks led by King endeavored to win the franchise and to secure the complete desegregation of public facilities. Many of the demonstrators were arrested, but city authorities were careful to maintain order. In the end, the Albany campaign collapsed. Meanwhile, the Kennedy administration refused to become involved, in part because it wanted to enhance the chances of Carl Sanders, a moderate candidate in the Democratic gubernatorial primary of 1962.

As the pressure for change in racial practices mounted, the White House was eventually drawn into a dramatic confrontation with intransigent white supremacists in Mississippi. The federal courts had ordered the admission to the state university of a black Mississippian named James H. Meredith in the fall of 1962. Gov. Ross Barnett, who had been elected with strong Citizens' Council support, aroused the public with demagogic rhetoric and talk of nullification. He defied the court orders and denied Meredith's enrollment in the University of Mississippi. The Kennedy administration tried persuasion with Barnett, and the president addressed the nation over television, urging the students and people of Mississippi to comply with the court ruling. Such pleas were unavailing. Meredith's appearance on campus was greeted by an outbreak of violence, and only after a night of terror and a pitched battle involving thousands of students and segregationist sympathizers, on the one hand, and 400 federal marshals and a small contingent of army troops, on the other, was the lone black man enrolled. Kennedy moved to quell the riot by sending in regular troops and federalizing the state's National Guard. Much of the nation applauded the president's actions.

While the crisis over Meredith's admission to Ole Miss forced the Kennedy administration to intervene and brought a triumph of great symbolic importance to the equal rights struggle, it did not dethrone Jim Crow in the deep South. The token desegregation of schools and universities had been accepted by even the most recalcitrant of the region's states, but segregation and other forms of racial discrimination were still solidly entrenched in most of the lower South. The failure of the Albany demonstrations made unmistakably clear how much remained to be done in the civil rights struggle. What was desperately needed, Martin Luther King and other black leaders decided, was a dramatic new confrontation that would capture the attention and the sympathy of the American public and bring civil rights gains, including federal action.

Massive demonstrations in Birmingham, Alabama, led by King in the spring of 1963, provided the needed confrontation. When the black leader and his associates defied an injunction barring racial demonstrations, they were subjected to police brutality and mass arrests. But the demonstrators, including black children, persisted for almost a month. When the Birmingham police, under the leadership of the notorious segregationist T. Eugene "Bull" Connor, met the peaceful demonstrators with clubs, fire hoses, guns, and police dogs, vivid pictures of the brutal repression were seen on television screens throughout the country. The president finally sent federal troops to restore order in the city. By early May Birmingham business leaders had become more determined in urging negotiations with King and the Southern Christian Leadership Conference (SCLC), and, after a series of discussions, an agreement was reached. The protesters won their demands for the desegregation of lunch counters, rest rooms, and certain other facilities, as well as the hiring and promotion of blacks "on a nondiscriminatory basis throughout the industrial community of Birmingham." Even so, the end of the Birmingham protests was marked by two bombings and a Ku Klux Klan rally.

By the time the Birmingham demonstrations finally ended, the Kennedy administration was moving rapidly toward a new position in its response to the gathering momentum of the equal rights movement. When Gov. George Corley Wallace threatened to defy a court order admitting two black students to the University of Alabama, Kennedy acted quickly, federalizing the state's National Guard and forcing the governor to stand aside when he personally sought to prevent their registration. In an eloquent television address soon after this episode, on June 11, the president declared that America was confronted "primarily with a moral issue." The nation would not be fully free, he warned, "until all its citizens are free." A week later, Kennedy sent Congress a comprehensive civil rights bill. The movement for black equality now seemed to be moving inexorably toward the enactment of a broad civil rights law. The Birmingham demonstrations in the spring had sparked one black protest after another, and by the summer almost 800 demonstrations, involving growing numbers of whites, had taken place in some 200 southern cities and towns. The culmination came when more than 200,000 blacks and whites staged a great March on Washington on August 28, which the president praised for its "deep fervor and quiet dignity."

Prospects for early passage of the administration's civil rights bill were uncertain, but Kennedy's assassination in November altered the situation and identified the equal rights movement with the tragic death of the young president. The new president, Lyndon B. Johnson, made a point of stressing his commitment to the realization of Kennedy's New Frontier. Johnson seemed determined to push ahead with civil rights legislation, almost as if that alone would demonstrate his loyalty to his predecessor and certify his own liberalism. When the second session of the Eighty-eighth Congress convened in January 1964, the Johnson administration mobilized all of its powers behind the effort to enact an omnibus civil rights law. The threat of a discharge petition persuaded the House Rules Committee to clear the measure for floor action by late January, and the bill was passed with strong bipartisan support on February 10. Ninety-two southern Democrats voted against the bill, while only eleven of the region's Democratic representatives supported it. Meanwhile, thousands of people poured into Washington to press for congressional approval, and scores of national organizations participated in the movement through the Leadership Conference on Civil Rights.

In the Senate the outlook was much less encouraging, given the strategic positions of southern leaders in that body and the difficulty of overcoming filibusters. Southern senators hoped to bury the House-approved bill in James O. Eastland's Judiciary Committee, but administration leaders skillfully avoided that trap and on February 26 managed to have the measure placed directly on the Senate's calendar. Senate leaders of both parties and administration spokesmen carried on intensive negotiations in an effort to work out an agreement that would make it possible to halt debate and pass the bill. President Johnson was a pivotal figure in these negotiations. Finally, on June 10, the Senate adopted a cloture resolution, and for the first time in its history the upper house had voted to close debate on a civil rights bill. Twenty-one southern senators voted against cloture; five senators from the peripheral South supported it. Senator Russell, who spearheaded the opposition, and his southern colleagues had made a strategic error in demanding unconditional surrender. Had they sought an agreement with Republican moderates earlier in the debate, they might have obtained significant concessions and seriously weakened the final enactment. Yet by late spring the mood of the country clearly favored passage of the administration's proposal. After adopting cloture the Senate approved a few minor amendments, voted down a large number designed to weaken the measure, and passed the bill on June 19 by a roll call vote of 73 to 27. Twenty-one southern senators voted no.

The Civil Rights Act of 1964 was the most sweeping affirmation of equal rights and the most comprehensive commitment to their implementation ever made by a U.S. Congress. The law contained new provisions to help guarantee black voting rights; assured access to public accommodations such as motels, restaurants, and places of amusement; empowered the federal government to bring suit to desegregate public facilities and schools; extended the life of the Civil Rights Commission for four years and gave it new powers; provided that federal funds could be cut off when programs were administered discriminatorily; required most business firms and labor unions to follow equal opportunity procedures in employment; and authorized the Justice Department to enter into pending civil rights cases. Compliance was not universal, but the act was generally obeyed throughout the South, in part because of careful preparations by federal and local officials. A startling change in the daily behavior, if not the thinking, of millions of southerners took place almost overnight.

Taking advantage of a more sober and supportive mood in Congress and the public, Lyndon Johnson adroitly maneuvered to break the long congressional deadlock that had held up reform legislation year after year. The results were impressive, not only in the passage of civil rights legislation, but also in the approval of several other major proposals urged by the Kennedy administration. Advocates of equal rights for American blacks applauded the Johnson administration's role in the passage of the Civil Rights Act of 1964, which seemed to demonstrate the depth of the president's commitment to liberal reform. Hoping to attract broad support for his comprehensive program of domestic reform and to win an overwhelming triumph in the election of 1964, Johnson pursued the politics of consensus with great energy and skill. In approaching the campaign of 1964, Johnson stressed his role as the national leader of *all* the people. But he faced a serious problem in his own region, where many white southerners reacted strongly against the new civil rights legislation and were disturbed by Johnson's liberal policies. The party images of southerners changed sharply between early 1961 and late 1964. One analysis of interviews conducted in 1964 by the Survey Research Center at the University of Michigan revealed that the proportion of southern blacks with strongly pro-Democratic party images had more than doubled during this period, from 24 to 52 percent, while the proportion of southern whites with strongly pro-Republican party images had doubled, from 9 to 18 percent.[10] During the campaign the president appealed for unity and party loyalty on the part of southern Democrats, and on one occasion, in New Orleans, he sought to call forth the South's "finest instincts" in defending his administration's support of civil rights. "Race should not be the issue," he declared, "only 'equal opportunity for all, special privileges for none.' "[11]

While Johnson was consolidating his national leadership, the two political parties were making preparations for the presidential election of 1964. The Republicans, racked by internal conflict and frustrated by the resurgence of Democratic strength in the late 1950s and early 1960s, turned abruptly from the moderate course followed by their presidential nominees since 1940 and launched a militantly conservative campaign for control of Washington. Over the years a variety of right-wing organizations had sprung up, among them the John Birch Society, the Christian Anti-Communist Crusade, the Citizens' Council, and the Minutemen. In general, these groups emphasized economic freedom; "strict" construction of the Constitution; opposition to governmental intervention, welfare programs, and heavier taxes; and unrelenting hostility toward international communism, which they interpreted as a pervasive and subversive threat within the United States. The radical right found a political figure to rally around in Sen. Barry M. Goldwater of Arizona.

The South and the "heartland" of the Midwest were vitally important in the movement for Goldwater's nomination. Conservative sentiment in the South, frustrated by the civil rights demonstrations and increasingly opposed to the liberal Democratic administrations in Washington, was strongly attracted to Goldwater. An early indication of this conservative disaffection came in the midterm elections of 1962, when Sen. Lister Hill of Alabama was almost defeated by James D. Martin, a staunch Republican conservative, and Sen. Olin

D. Johnston of South Carolina was given a serious challenge by another Republican conservative, William D. Workman, Jr. Significantly, much of Martin's support came from the traditionally Democratic black belt.[12] Southern Republicans such as John Grenier of Alabama and Peter O'Donnell of Texas were leaders in the task of capturing the party machinery for the senator from Arizona. The outspoken Goldwater, an advocate of state rights and an opponent of federal civil rights legislation, elicited enthusiastic support from white southerners, particularly in the deep South. When the GOP national convention met, Goldwater received the vote of virtually every southern delegate and was nominated on the first ballot. He ran on a platform that was decidedly more conservative than that of the Democrats.

In some respects President Johnson was successful in holding the Democratic party together in the South. When the regular Mississippi delegation to the national convention was challenged by the insurgent, largely black Mississippi Freedom Democratic party, Johnson's lieutenants worked out a compromise permitting the regular delegates to take their seats if they would sign a party loyalty pledge and give two convention seats to the challenging group.[13] Most of the party leaders in the South endorsed the national ticket. Among these supporting leaders were Senator Russell of Georgia and Governor Faubus of Arkansas. But there were exceptions. Sen. Strom Thurmond of South Carolina left the Democrats and joined the "Goldwater Republicans party." No major Democratic politician in Mississippi spoke out in favor of Johnson's election. Governor Wallace of Alabama was so disillusioned with the Johnson administration that he challenged the president's nomination in several northern primaries. He eventually gave up this fruitless venture, apparently in order to allow southern conservatives to rally behind Senator Goldwater in the November election.

Johnson won the election by a landslide, carrying forty-four states and 61 percent of the popular vote. He captured eight southern states. The president was aided by the endorsement he received from the party organization in several southern states, and he was given overwhelming support by the region's black voters. Many southerners, black and white, were impressed by Johnson's record of accomplishment and were put off by Goldwater's impulsive pronouncements about the desirability of selling the Tennessee Valley Authority, abandoning farm subsidy and social security programs, and undertaking a more vigorous war in Vietnam.

Nevertheless, Goldwater made his best showing in the South. He received 87 percent of the votes in Mississippi and also carried Alabama, Georgia, South Carolina, and Louisiana. Goldwater's popularity in the deep South swept seven new Republican congressmen into office, five in Alabama and one each in Georgia and Mississippi. Race was an ever-present concern in the lower South. As one historian has written of Louisiana, the state "seemed engulfed by a wave of pro-segregation and anti-Johnson feelings that fall."[14] The perception of Goldwater as the segregationist candidate clearly influenced many white voters in the deep South, although the continuing rebellion against the national Democratic party was a significant consideration. Unlike the Republican pattern in the three previous elections, Goldwater's greatest southern strength was in the old Dixiecrat belt and in the rural areas. He was weaker in the urban counties, in the traditionally Republican areas, and in the upper South. Eisenhower and Nixon had made their best showing in the peripheral South, whereas Goldwater carried none of the states in that subregion. On the other hand, the Arizona senator won 61.8 percent of the deep South's popular vote to Nixon's 35.9 percent in 1960. Goldwater won a majority of the white votes in all of the ex-Confederate states except Texas. In 1964 a great many southerners supported the Republican party for the first time in their lives. As a perceptive student of the Goldwater campaign points out, "The Republican presidential party, for the first time in history, played the role of the 'traditional' party of the South."[15]

Encouraged by his electoral triumph in 1964, President Johnson soon decided to seek additional legislation in the field of voting rights. Ancient obstructions such as literacy tests, discriminatory treatment by local officials, economic pressure, and intimidation were still prevalent in much of the South, particularly in the lower part of the region. Perhaps a million black southerners had registered to vote by 1952, but in the face of stiffening white resistance fewer than half a million new Negro registrants were added to the voting lists during the next ten years. In 1962 less than 30 percent of the South's black adults were registered. In moving to sponsor a federal voting rights statute, the administration was influenced not only by the slow progress of registration campaigns in the deep South during recent years but also by the strong support of the black community and by the leaders and tactics of the evolving civil rights movement.

By the time of the March on Washington in the late summer of 1963, many equal rights leaders had come to believe that enfranchisement was probably of more immediate importance to southern blacks than desegregation. The vote, they assumed, would gradually improve the condition of the black masses and provide a political means of attacking both racism and poverty. Southern blacks themselves showed a growing interest in the ballot. Shortly before the November election of 1963 in Mississippi, SNCC leaders devised a Freedom Election to prove that Afro-Americans wanted to vote. On the same day that white Mississippians voted, nearly 80,000 disenfranchised blacks cast "freedom ballots." Registration drives were supported by national foundations and by such organizations as the Southern Regional Council's Voter Education Project (VEP). CORE concentrated its registration efforts on Florida, Louisiana, and South Carolina, while SNCC turned its attention to Alabama and Mississippi.

The success of these registration campaigns was limited. Setbacks in Mississippi during the early 1960s persuaded voter registration leaders to concentrate on exposing the hazards of trying to register blacks in the Magnolia State. "The whole of Mississippi became the stage," Neil R. McMillen has written, "its public officials and law-enforcement personnel unwitting, but perfectly cast, villains, its 400,000 disfranchised adult Negroes the principal players, and the nation at large the audience to which 'live' television presentations were offered each evening with the news."[16] In 1964 the Council of Federated Organizations (COFO), a coalition of equal rights groups, conducted what was called the Mississippi Summer Project, a voter registration campaign that enlisted over 700 student volunteers and resulted in fierce opposition by local whites and the death of 3 volunteers. Gains were few. While COFO staff members and volunters, working in 25 communities, brought perhaps as many as 17,000 black applicants to courthouses across the state, only some 1,600 were able to register, and most of them in Panola County under a federal court order.[17] Soon afterward the Voter Education Project reported that 688,800 blacks had qualified to vote for the first time in the eleven states of the old Confederacy between April 1, 1962, and November 1, 1964, but most of that impressive increase came in urban areas and in the upper South. While 38 percent of the adult black population in the region was registered by 1964, the percentage ranged from less than 7 in Mississippi to almost 70 in Tennessee. Less than half of the potential black electorate was registered in eight of the southern states. The white registration in the ex-Confederate states was 73.4 percent.

In late 1964 Martin Luther King, Jr., and other members of the Southern Christian Leadership Conference developed plans to arouse the nation to the need for a national voting rights law. The SCLC leaders planned a series of demonstrations in Selma, Alabama, in the heart of the black belt. Speaking in Selma early in January 1965, King announced, "We will dramatize the situation to arouse the federal government by marching by the thousands to the places of registration."[18] Dallas County, in which Selma is located, had a black majority, but only 325 Negroes were registered to vote as compared with 9,800 whites. In some other black belt counties, not a single black man or woman was enfranchised. King and his associates spent several weeks leading black people to the courthouse to register and staging demonstrations. Few blacks were able to register, and hundreds were arrested. Frustrated by these developments, King called for "a march on the ballot boxes throughout Alabama," moving from Selma to Montgomery, the state capital, fifty-four miles away. Governor Wallace refused to permit such a march, and when the demonstrators tried to proceed without his approval, they were met with clubs and tear gas. The president finally stepped in, federalizing the Alabama National Guard, and the march, involving a large number of black and white participants, was completed between March 21 and 25. The violent clashes that took place in the Selma area provoked national outrage and set the stage for congressional action on voting rights legislation.

Lyndon Johnson addressed a nationally televised joint session of Congress on March 15, 1965, to urge the prompt passage of a strong voting rights act. Having committed itself to this legislation, the Johnson administration submitted a carefully developed proposal on March 17. From March until August, the voting rights coalition never lost its momentum. It was a bipartisan effort, with stalwart administration support and important assistance from the Leadership Conference on Civil Rights and other groups. After a compromise anti–poll tax provision was approved, the Senate adopted a cloture motion on May 25—the second one in two years. The major opposition came from southern senators. The bill was passed on the following day. The House passed a similar measure on July 9, and after a conference committee worked out an agreement reconciling the differences between the two houses, the revised measure was signed by the president in early August. While most of the negative votes on final passage were cast by southerners, thirty-six representatives and a few senators from the South voted for the bill.

The Voting Rights Act of 1965 authorized direct federal action to enable blacks to register and vote. It empowered the attorney general to appoint federal examiners to supervise voter registration in states or voting districts where a literacy test or similar qualifying devices existed and where fewer than 50 percent of the voting-age residents had voted or were registered to vote in the presidential election of 1964. This brought the federal registration machinery to bear on seven southern states—Alabama, Georgia, Louisiana, Mississippi, South Carolina, Virginia, and twenty-six counties in North Carolina. To register under the new law, an applicant merely had to fill out a simple form (with assistance from a registrar if necessary), giving name, age, length of residence, and whether he or she had ever been convicted of a felony. Stiff penalties were provided for interference with voter rights.

Justice Department officials moved rather circumspectly to implement the new statute, hampered in the beginning by subterfuge and lack of cooperation on the part of many local officials in the deep South. In Mississippi, the state with the most disfranchised blacks, U.S. examiners were sent to twenty-four "noncompliance" counties; they accounted for over 70,000 of the aproximately 140,000 Negroes registered in that state by September 1966.[19] Federal intervention was never very extensive. Between 1965 and 1980, federal registrars entered no more than 60 of the 533 southern counties covered by the Voting Rights Act. Most of those counties were in Mississippi, Alabama, and Louisiana. Still, this statute has been aptly characterized as "the grand turning point in modern times for the reentry of blacks into southern politics."[20]

Meanwhile, the ratification in 1964 of the Twenty-fourth Amendment to the Constitution, which invalidated the poll tax as a prerequisite for voting in federal elections, and a Supreme Court decision in 1966 outlawing the poll tax as a requirement for voting in other elections also gave impetus to the enfranchisement of blacks and whites in the South. The number of black voters in the southern states steadily increased during the next few years. More than 400,000 blacks were registered in the ex-Confederate states during the first year following passage of the Voting Rights Act. In Mississippi the percentage of registered blacks rose from 7 to 59 between 1964 and 1968, and in Alabama from 24 to 57. During that period the number of southern black voters increased from fewer than 2 million to 3.1 million, 62 percent of the black voting-age population. Thus, the federal statute of 1965 seemed to be rapidly changing the face of southern politics. Writing about this phenomenon in 1966, the political scientists Donald R. Matthews and James W. Prothro spoke of "a revolution in process—the growing participation of southern Negroes in the politics of the 1960's."[21] But if a sharp increase in black voter registration resulted from the passage of the Voting Rights Act of 1965, that development was in turn a major reason for an even larger increase in white registration. About six million names were added to the voting rolls of the ex-Confederate states during the 1960s, of which 70 percent were white. Many of these white registrants became supporters of George Wallace and other insurgent leaders.

The dramatic increase in the voter registration of southern blacks after 1965 was only one result of federal intervention in the 1960s. That intervention included, in addition to the civil rights laws of 1964 and 1965, the invalidation of the poll tax and the widespread reapportionment of legislative and congressional seats in the wake of the Supreme Court's "one man, one vote" principle in *Baker* v. *Carr* (1962).

These external forces were destined to have an enduring influence on southern politics. Meanwhile, more subtle developments such as the region's growing economic diversification, urbanization, and changing migration patterns were also contributing to the reconstruction of southern politics. The evolving shape of southern politics was significantly affected by still another factor: the nature of the political and civic response within the South to these pressures. That response varied from one state to another and thus helped shape the political behavior of region and subregion. One notable reaction to the challenge of the civil rights movement was that of the business community in most southern cities. Even in the 1950s urban leaders like Mayor Hartsfield of Atlanta were concerned about a closed public school system and its effect upon the image of their individual cities. Massive resistance and the equal rights demonstrations were a sobering experience for these leaders. As two scholars have written, "When businessmen became convinced that sustained racial upheaval would imperil economic development, they provided a climate for change in southern customs by taking a stand on upholding 'law and order.' "[22]

Perhaps the most spectacular political changes precipitated by the new dynamics of the 1960s took place in Virginia. Although the Byrd organization survived the failure of massive resistance and entered the 1960s in control of the state's politics, it proved to be too inflexible to accommodate itself to the Great Society of Lyndon Johnson, who carried Virginia in 1964, to mounting opposition within the Democratic party at home, and to a stronger Republican challenge in the Old Dominion. Legislative reapportionment in 1964 shifted a number of seats in both houses of the general assembly and clearly showed that future redistricting would increasingly reflect the state's impressive urban growth. The rising tide of black voters, who tended to vote as a bloc, made their support frequently decisive, both in Democratic primaries and in general elections. The changing political environment began to have its effect as early as 1965, when state senator Mills E. Godwin, Jr., an organization man who had supported massive resistance, won the governorship with strong backing from black voters. Responding in a positive way to the new political and economic currents, Godwin set the state on a new course by sponsoring a progressive program and effecting a shift from traditional state policies. Senator Byrd's failing health led him to resign in late 1965, and the next year brought the defeat of two machine stalwarts, Sen. A. Willis Robertson and Rep. Howard W. Smith. Unfortunately for the new Democratic leadership, the party was soon divided into conservative, moderate, and liberal factions, which contributed to the election of

A. Linwood Holton, a moderate Republican, as governor in 1969. The long period of stability provided by the Byrd organization had given way to political upheaval, conflict, and uncertainty.

Economic and social change, intense factionalism in the Democratic party, and voter susceptibility to the race issue quickened the pace of change in Florida politics during the 1960s. The remarkable growth of urban centers in central and south Florida, the sharp increase in voter registration and turnout, and the reapportionment of the legislature in 1969 all brought added pressure on the traditional political system. Politics became more competitive. Although President Johnson carried the state in 1964, the Democrats soon fell to fighting among themselves. In 1966 Mayor Robert King High of Miami, who had defeated Gov. Haydon Burns in the Democratic gubernatorial primary, was himself overcome by Republican Claude R. Kirk, Jr., who campaigned as a conservative and pictured his opponent as a Great Society liberal. Two years later Florida Republicans won another victory when Edward J. Gurney defeated former governor LeRoy Collins for a Senate seat. Once again the GOP nominee sought to appeal to the conservative and racist sensibilities of the voters by portraying Collins as an extreme liberal and a champion of equal rights for blacks. The Republican beachhead, in a state experiencing rapid economic growth and demographic volatility, promised still greater political change in the future, regardless of the party in control.

Change was less striking in Tennessee than in Florida, but even so the politics of the Volunteer State shifted noticeably during the 1960s. A revived Republican party, continuing urban growth, and an increasingly significant black vote all had their effect. The relative position of the two parties began to shift. The death of Sen. Estes Kefauver in 1963 seemed to mark the beginning of the Democratic party's disintegration in the state, although Frank G. Clement and Buford Ellington alternated as governor throughout the decade. Intense Democratic factionalism, an enlarged electorate, and an expanding middle class worked to the advantage of the state's Republicans. After *Baker* v. *Carr*, the legislative dominance of rural and small-town elements was broken, and the cities began to wield greater influence in political affairs. This transfer of power enhanced the political importance of the growing suburbs and in some respects deepened the conservatism of Tennessee and the South. In 1966 Howard H. Baker, Jr., was elected to the Senate, and in 1970 the Republicans won the other U.S. Senate seat and the governorship. Tennessee seemed to be on the threshold of two-party politics.

The political scene in Texas was characterized by strong continuity and limited but prophetic change. As might have been expected,

Texas politics in the 1960s reflected the state's extraordinary economic expansion, the ideological orientation of its voters, and the fact that racial questions were normally not a salient political concern. The state's Republicans made an important breakthrough early in the decade with the election of John G. Tower as Lyndon Johnson's successor in the Senate. Tower received the help of a substantial number of Democratic voters who preferred a conservative Republican to a reactionary Democrat. Thus, as in many other southern states, Democratic factionalism opened the door to the Republican party in statewide elections. Although Texas politics in the 1960s was dominated by conservatives such as three-term governor John B. Connally, a liberal movement gained strength by recruiting blacks, Mexican-Americans, and blue-collar workers. Johnson's Great Society also gave a boost to the state's liberals. The liberals' leading spokesman was Ralph Yarborough, who was elected to the Senate in 1957 after losing several earlier statewide races. Johnson succeeded in holding the feuding Democrats together for a time, but in the long run, the prevailing conservatism among white Texans and the strong reaction against the liberalism of the national party could be expected to strengthen the Republicans.

Meanwhile, the Republican party was becoming more competitive in two other states of the peripheral South—Kentucky and Oklahoma. In the postwar period, Kentuckians elected a succession of strong Democratic governors: Earle C. Clements, Lawrence W. Wetherby, Bert T. Combs, and Edward T. Breathitt, Jr. Breathitt, who assumed office in 1963, was, in the words of one historian, "identified with a new breed of Southern Democrats, men who accepted the broad directions of the New Deal and Fair Deal, who viewed state government as a proper tool with which to address social, economic, political, and human problems, and who rejected the traditional demagoguery of race and states' rights."[23] The factionalism that revolved around Earle C. Clements and Bert Combs, on the one hand, and "Happy" Chandler, on the other, became somewhat less acrimonious in the 1960s. Nevertheless, it persisted, sometimes weakening the Democrats and strengthening the Republicans, who held both Senate seats during the 1960s and gained the governorship with the election of Louie B. Nunn in 1967. In Oklahoma the decade began auspiciously for the Democrats with the election of a young, urban-oriented governor named J. Howard Edmondson. But he suffered a series of setbacks, and in 1962 Henry Bellmon became the first Republican governor in the state's history. The minority party was broadening its appeal. Bellmon was succeeded four years later by another Republican, Dewey Bartlett, and in 1968 Bellmon was elected to the U.S. Senate. The state also voted for the GOP ticket in presidential elections, except for 1964. The Democrats, while less faction-ridden than in earlier years, found it difficult to work together effectively. They did send a strong congressional delegation to Washington, led by Robert S. Kerr (until his death early in 1963), A.S. Mike Monroney, and Carl Albert. Yet Oklahoma, like Kentucky, was becoming a two-party state.

During the decade between the mid-1950s and the mid-1960s, North Carolina politics and government seemed to reflect the progressive image for which it was famous. Governors Luther H. Hodges and Terry Sanford adopted a cautious and moderate approach to desegregation and civil rights, and their administrations were largely concerned with economic development and, especially in Sanford's case, educational reform. Nevertheless, the debate over racial questions led to violence in the early 1960s, and many white North Carolinians were attracted to the segregationist pronouncements of Dr. I. Beverly Lake, who sought the Democratic nomination for governor in 1964. Although Lake was defeated, the progressive faction's candidate was turned back by the conservative Dan K. Moore. North Carolina Republicans also went fishing in these troubled waters. James C. Gardner, the GOP gubernatorial nominee in 1968, stressed the race issue and appealed to the supporters of Beverly Lake. But Gardner was defeated by a Democratic moderate, Robert W. Scott. North Carolina Republicans had reason to be optimistic, however. They expected to gain new strength from the rapidly growing urban corridor that stretched from Raleigh to Charlotte. In 1968 they elected more legislators than at any time since the days of Herbert Hoover— 29 of 120 in the house and 12 of 50 in the senate.

State politics in Arkansas during the 1960s assumed a different pattern. The racial reaction identified with Gov. Orval Faubus's leadership during the Little Rock school crisis, while somewhat muted in the mid-1960s, persisted until 1966, when Faubus decided not to run for a seventh term. Faubus, a skillful administrative and political manager, got along well with special interest groups. His successor as the Democratic gubernatorial nominee was James D. Johnson, an outspoken segregationist. Johnson's nomination drove many liberal Democrats to vote for the Republican candidate, Winthrop Rockefeller, who had run against Governor Faubus two years before. Rockefeller, a refreshing change in Arkansas politics, was a moderate on the race question and a strong advocate of the state's economic development. He played a key role in changing the state's economic and political direction. In 1966 his well-organized and well-financed campaign was successful. He received strong support from black voters, an important new factor in Arkansas politics, and from disaffected liberal Democrats. But this Republican breakthrough was hardly the wave of the future. Two years later Arkansas voters reelected Rockefeller, returned J. William Fulbright to the Senate, and gave the state's presidential electoral votes to George C. Wallace.

The situation was somewhat different in the deep South. In South Carolina Senator Thurmond's shift to the Republicans gave the minority party an established figure around whom to rally. As could have been predicted, South Carolina Republicans appealed to voter disaffection with civil rights legislation and the liberal policies of Democratic administrations in Washington. Democratic leaders, somewhat surprisingly, made the decision to open their party to blacks and to sponsor more liberal social programs. As upper-income elements and an increasing number of blue-collar whites began to vote Republican, the Democrats worked harder to attract black voters, who made up about 20 percent of the heavy turnout in the election of 1966. By the fall of 1968, over 200,000 blacks had registered, almost a quarter of the state's voters. The Democratic strategy of seeking to build a black and white coalition seemed to work in gubernatorial elections. Beginning with Ernest F. Hollings in 1959, one moderately liberal Democrat after another served as governor for the next sixteen years.

Politics in the other states of the deep South showed how the social upheavals of the decade were encouraging "the darker strains in southern politics."[24] Developments in Louisiana illustrate the trend. By 1960, when Earl Long died, the Long era seemed to be ending. Race had become the major political issue, and the electorate was divided less by economic questions than by racial concerns, north versus south, and Protestant against Catholic. Mayor deLesseps S. Morrison of New Orleans, a moderate on the race question, was twice defeated for governor by segregationist opponents, first by Jimmie H. Davis in 1959 and then by John J. McKeithen in 1963. McKeithen and several other Louisiana politicians, one scholar writes, "had been running hard against the 'feds' in general and the Kennedys in particular."[25] McKeithen, who was reelected in 1967, was able to project three contradictory images—those of reformer, progressive Longite, and segregationist. Yet as racial tensions mounted and as conflict within the Democratic party increased, McKeithen's legislative program foundered, his popularity declined, and he announced that he would not campaign for his party's presidential nominee in 1968. The results of that election seemed to indicate Louisiana's continued swing toward conservatism.

Georgia began the decade on a more promising note, only to succumb to racist fears. The official acceptance of token desegregation, the ending of the county-unit system, and the election of Carl Sanders, a racial moderate and a spokesman for urban Georgia, as governor in 1962 pointed toward a reorientation of Georgia politics. "The urban

victory over rural areas in the school desegregation controversy,"
Numan V. Bartley writes, "symbolized the transfer of the focus of
power in Georgia from plantation elites to uptown metropolitan
elites."[26] The altered political situation brought former governor Ellis
G. Arnall out of political retirement in 1966. But the progressive Arnall
was defeated in a run-off primary by Lester G. Maddox, a fanatical
opponent of civil rights who ardently defended free enterprise and
Protestant fundamentalism. In the meantime, Republicans launched
their first real campaign to win the Georgia governorship. Their candidate, Howard H. "Bo" Callaway, came within a few thousand votes
of defeating Maddox. Since neither man received a popular majority,
the election was thrown into the legislature, which voted along party
lines in favor of Maddox. A colorful and flamboyant advocate of rural
and small-town values, Maddox was, in one writer's words, "the
symbol of poor white protest in the tradition of Tom Watson and the
Talmadges."[27] His election reflected the same basic concerns that led
Georgians to give the state's electoral votes to Barry Goldwater in 1964
and George Wallace in 1968.

Ross Barnett, Paul B. Johnson, Jr., and John Bell Williams—all
ardent segregationists—served as governors of Mississippi in the
1960s. In 1963 former governor James P. Coleman was tellingly portrayed by Paul Johnson as a moderate, a racial liberal, and a pro-
Kennedy candidate. In 1967 another moderate, state treasurer William
Winter, found his chances similarly destroyed. In that contest even
Ross Barnett, trying to make a comeback, was apparently perceived
as insufficiently firm on the race issue, since he finished far back
among the contestants. By the late 1960s, there was some evidence
of a fear among the state's more sensitive citizens that racial violence
and political demagoguery would hinder badly needed industrial and
economic development. The national Democratic party had become
an anathema to a large number of whites in the Magnolia State. A
statewide survey of white Mississippians in 1967 revealed that the
image of the Republican party was more favorable than that of the
Democratic party.

In neighboring Alabama the politics of race was equally predominant. The most powerful factor in the state's politics was the leadership of George C. Wallace, who won the governorship as a
champion of white supremacy in 1962. Wallace quickly emerged as
the most influential and unrelenting opponent of the civil rights movement in the South—as the defender of the faith against the protest
demonstrations led by Martin Luther King, Jr., and the equal rights
policies of the Kennedy and Johnson administrations. Since Wallace
was constitutionally ineligible to succeed himself, he arranged for his
wife, Lurleen, to run instead in 1966. She won a decisive victory.

When she died of cancer in 1968, Lt. Gov. Albert P. Brewer assumed the governorship. He tried to pursue a moderate approach to racial questions and to concentrate on economic development. But in 1970 Wallace narrowly defeated Brewer in the Democratic primary by resorting to a demagogic campaign based on racial accusations and fears. Meanwhile, James B. Allen, a conservative critic of the national Democratic party, was elected in 1968 to succeed Sen. Lister Hill. The Republican party had made some headway in the state. Goldwater won 69.5 percent of the popular vote in 1964 and was instrumental in the election of five Republican congressmen in Alabama, three of whom retained their seats in the midterm elections of 1966.

Governor Wallace proved to be the most compelling politician in the South during the 1960s, and he was possibly the most influential popular leader to appear in the region since Huey Long. Marshall Frady, one of his biographers, refers to the Alabamian as "the palpable, breathing articulation into flesh of Willie Stark in Robert Penn Warren's *All the King's Men*."[28] Politics was his life. A fellow politician once described him as a man "who has no other desires, no hobbies. Doesn't waste any of his time drinking. Doesn't waste any of his time doing anything, except talking politics every waking hour."[29] Wallace began his career as a supporter of "Big Jim" Folsom, in the state legislature and in the Folsom campaigns. But the young politician voted for the Dixiecrat ticket in 1948 and eventually broke with Folsom over patronage and the segregation issue. As a state circuit judge, Wallace gained a certain notoriety for his truculent behavior in dealing with the federal courts in civil rights matters. After running unsuccessfully for governor in 1958, he was elected to that office four years later. His inaugural address was a fiery "Segregation Now! Segregation tomorrow! Segregation forever!" The fire-eating governor proceeded to involve himself in several dramatic confrontations with the federal government, including his "stand in the schoolhouse door" at the University of Alabama in an effort to prevent the admission of black students. He quickly became the dominant figure in politics and a symbol of white-supremacy defiance throughout the South.

The Alabama governor was described as "a stumpy little man with heavy black eyebrows and bright black darting eyes and a puglike bulb of a nose who looked as if he might have stepped out of an eighteenth-century London street scene by Hogarth."[30] He existed, one of his biographers wrote, "as the very incarnation of the 'folks,' the embodiment of the will and sensibilities and discontents of the people in the roadside diners and all-night chili cafés, the cabdrivers and waitresses and plant workers, as well as a certain harried Prufrock population of dingy-collared department-store clerks and insurance salesmen and neighborhood grocers."[31] His appeal was especially powerful among white southerners deeply committed to rural and traditional values in the midst of an industrializing and urbanizing region. Wallace himself explained his appeal as resulting in part from his role in restoring confidence and pride to southerners, who had long resented the criticisms, sneers, and patronizing attitude of outsiders. Southerners, he remarked, "were talked about. You know, rednecks, hill billies, backward, ignorant, illiterate, racist. And the people developed a complex. They knew it wasn't true, but they had a hard time proving it. . . . And when I became the governor of the state of Alabama we still had that viewpoint about our region. . . . And I think they feel that my position as governor was used to help restore . . . [a sense of pride]."[32] In some respects a latter-day Populist, Wallace's politics struck a responsive chord by appealing to morality, apprehensions over rapid social change, and antiestablishment feelings. The governor's exploitation of racial fears was the means that made it possible for much of his constituency to override their traditional identification with the Democratic party and the ideological orientation of lower-class status.

In 1964 Wallace challenged Lyndon Johnson's consensus politics by entering three presidential primaries in the Midwest and East—Wisconsin, Indiana, and Maryland. "Here was a boy from the Deep South," the political scientist Donald S. Strong remarks, "who was going up to play ball in the major leagues." Strong suggests that this gesture probably "brought emotional gratification to large numbers of Alabamians."[33] It appeared that Wallace might resort to the Dixiecrat strategy of running as a third-party candidate. He did surprisingly well in his presidential primary ventures outside the South, receiving 43 percent of the vote in Maryland and about a third of the ballots in Indiana and Wisconsin. But the Alabama governor retired from the presidential scene when Senator Goldwater won the Republican nomination. Nevertheless, Wallace had demonstrated his vote-getting potential, and during the next few years he became the ultimate expression of the appeal to racism in southern politics. Despite his racial demagoguery, the Alabamian believed in using the powers of government to assist lower-income people, and as governor he sponsored a series of costly programs in vocational education and other fields.

For a time it seemed that Lyndon Johnson's Great Society would not only strengthen the Democratic party throughout the country but also rehabilitate it in the South. In 1965 the Great Society swept aside all restraints, as the Johnson administration scored one legislative triumph after another in civil rights, medical insurance, federal aid to education, urban renewal, and so on. But Johnson's reformism provoked opposition and disaffection among many white southerners. While there was strong southern support for the administration's course in Vietnam, in the nation as a whole Johnson's escalation of the war following the election of 1964 made his presidency increasingly vulnerable. As U.S. involvement deepened and as more and more Americans perceived a credibility gap between what Johnson said and what was actually happening, the president lost popularity steadily. Plagued by ghetto riots, campus unrest, rising inflation, and bitter divisions over Vietnam, the administration was eventually threatened with paralysis. Early in 1968 it was dealt a series of heavy blows, including the Tet offensive by the enemy in Vietnam. Then, on March 31, came Johnson's shocking announcement that he would not seek reelection in 1968.

As the election of 1968 approached, Democratic prospects in the South were dimmed by a number of unfavorable developments. In the deep South, the war against the national party was being carried on by Governors Wallace, Maddox, and Williams. In Congress southern Democratic dissidence manifested itself in hostility to urban social and welfare programs, opposition to increased federal spending and growth of federal services, and concern for state control of various programs. This southern defiance of national Democratic policies also found expression in the growing strength of the conservative coalition in the late 1960s. As Democratic party unity declined in Congress, the percentage of coalition victories over the administration increased. Controversies over the recognition and seating of Alabama, Georgia, and Mississippi delegations to the national Democratic convention, leading to the unseating of some regular delegates, as well as the nomination of Vice-Pres. Hubert H. Humphrey and Sen. Edmund S. Muskie as the party's standard-bearers, alienated many southern Democrats, as did the platform's strong endorsement of civil rights. Even more portentous was the decision by George Wallace to bolt the Democratic party and run for president at the head of the American Independent party. Southerners who continued to think of themselves as Democrats were dispirited. "I have about given up hopes of really reforming the Democratic Party," Richard B. Russell informed a constituent late in the campaign. "We have to live with it as it is. It has been an oil and water mixture and, if Humphrey wins . . . I am afraid that you will not see a housecleaning job but only the spreading on of several new layers."[34]

Wallace's new third party also alarmed GOP leaders in the South, where the minority party had high hopes for electoral success in 1968. Many southern Republicans were attracted to Gov. Ronald Reagan of California, an outspoken conservative, and that fact made former vice-president Richard M. Nixon, who became the party's presidential nominee, unusually solicitous of the South. Nixon dealt with the chal-

lenge from Reagan by holding private talks with a number of important southern Republicans in Atlanta on May 31 and June 1. He
assured Senator Thurmond and other Republican leaders of his sympathy for their position on questions like the use of busing as a means
of achieving school desegregation and a get-tough policy against crime
and disorder. Southern influence was clearly an important factor in
Nixon's nomination and also in the choice of Gov. Spiro T. Agnew
of Maryland for vice-president. The Republican platform emphasized
an "all-out" campaign against crime, reform of the welfare laws, an
end to inflation, and a stronger national defense.

In contrast to the Republicans, who enjoyed a substantial lead in
the public opinion polls, the Democratic party seemed to have disintegrated, torn apart by controversy over Vietnam and a divisive
preconvention campaign. The assassination of Sen. Robert F. Kennedy and the Democrats' strife-torn convention in Chicago cast a pall
over the party. Wallace's third-party candidacy also contributed to
the Democrats' gloomy outlook. Well financed by wealthy conservatives and many grass-roots donations, the new party was able to get
itself listed on the ballots of all fifty states. Wallace developed surprising strength, not only among white southerners, but also among
blue-collar groups and the lower-middle class in other regions, where
there was often rising tension between white and black America.
Displaying a quick wit and a folksy speaking style, the Alabamian
campaigned throughout the country. He had become a national figure. He liked to assert that there was not "a dime's worth of difference" between the two major parties. His jibes at the "pointy-headed
bureaucrats" and the "intellectuals who look down their noses at you"
were calculated to appeal not only to the "white backlash" but also
to the growing sense of alienation, resentment against war demonstrators, and frustrations of powerlessness felt by blue-collar workers,
rural dwellers, and hard-pressed members of the lower-middle class.
He hoped to prevent either Humphrey or Nixon from getting a majority of the electoral votes and thus to throw the election into the
House of Representatives, where the South might hold the balance
of power. Early in the fall this appeared to be a possibility, since
Wallace was receiving more than 20 percent of the preference votes
in the public opinion polls.

After their slow start, Humphrey and Muskie began to gather
strength, having managed to bring a measure of unity to the party
and to mount an effective appeal to labor unions and working-class
people, often at the expense of George Wallace. By early November
the Humphrey surge had brought the Democrats almost abreast of
the Republicans in the polls. But Nixon won a narrow victory, receiving 31.7 million votes to 31.2 million for Humphrey and 9.9 million

'THERE'S SOMETHING ON THAT LINE!'

G.O.P.

SOUTHERN WATERS

NO FISHING — DEM. PARTY

· Roy Justus

Reprinted with permission from the *Star Tribune:* Newspaper of the Twin Cities.

for Wallace. The South played a major role in Nixon's election. He carried six states in the peripheral South, plus South Carolina, while Wallace won Georgia, Alabama, Mississippi, Louisiana, and Arkansas. Humphrey captured only one southern state—Texas, where President Johnson's vigorous support no doubt made the difference. Nixon, with 34.7 percent of the popular vote in the ex-Confederate states, did best in the upper South and appealed to higher-income and middle-class voters on the basis of economic conservatism and law-and-order rhetoric. Wallace, with 34.3 percent of the southern vote, showed his greatest strength in the deep South and attracted impressive support from rural and blue-collar voters. Humphrey, with 31 percent of the vote, was strongly supported by southern blacks and did well in Jewish and Chicano precincts. Wallace's southern vote in 1968 correlated positively with that of Goldwater in 1964, although there were significant differences in their constituencies. Economic and class distinctions were much less marked in 1968 than in earlier elections. Wallace's effect on the outcome in the South was even greater than was evident in the five states he carried: his campaign influenced Republican leaders throughout the South to move closer to the positions assumed by the third-party candidate. Finally, the election of 1968 represented a momentous departure in southern politics, since it produced an almost solid non-Democratic South. A completely solid non-Democratic South would come in 1972.

The Second Reconstruction, like the First Reconstruction, had a profound effect upon the thinking and behavior of southerners. Once again, federal intervention on behalf of black southerners brought bitter protest and opposition from much of the region's white population. But in some respects the reforms of the Second Reconstruction promised to be far more lasting than those of the First. This was particularly true of the institutional changes made in the 1960s: the overturning of Jim Crow, disfranchisement, malapportionment, and the one-party system. The traditional pattern of southern politics simply disintegrated. The Second Reconstruction led to the enfranchisement of millions of southern blacks—and whites—to more democratic political machinery and to a more open and competitive politics. "By settling the principle of racial segregation," two scholars have recently observed, "federal intervention indirectly encouraged the region's politicians to concentrate more single-mindedly on stimulating economic development."[35] Whether it would also lead to a genuine two-party system remained unclear as the 1960s ended and the 1970s began. Only time would tell how the most striking political divisions of 1968—white Republicans, black Democrats, and third-party rebels—would sort themselves out.

8 Toward a Two-Party South

In the aftermath of the presidential election of 1968, it was hard to tell what direction party politics in the South would take. The three-way cleavage in 1968 seemed to reflect a politics that was more volatile and unpredictable than ever. While Republicanism had apparently taken a giant step forward, the future course of the five million southerners who voted for George Wallace remained imponderable. One thing was certain: the Democratic party was in a shambles, having been reduced to an impotence it had not experienced since Radical Reconstruction.

Although Democratic loyalties persisted, many southerners were distancing themselves from the party of their fathers and grandfathers. In a survey of Mississippi whites conducted in the summer of 1967, for example, 46 percent of those questioned identified themselves as Democrats, 6 percent as Republicans, but no less than 39 percent as independents. A survey of the Oklahoma electorate by a team of political scientists in 1972 revealed that only 20 percent of the voters identified themselves as "strong Democrats," while 9 percent characterized themselves as "strong Republicans" and 26 percent as independents.[1] Still, a good deal of truth was contained in the observation of a South Carolinian on the Republican vote during the 1960s. "There ain't that many Republicans in South Carolina, just a lot of mad Democrats."[2] Democratic leaders in the South could take some comfort in the rapid enfranchisement of southern blacks after 1965. By 1970 the number of blacks registered in the eleven states of the Old South had reached 3.3 million. But this development was accompanied by a dramatic increase in white registration, part of which involved blue-collar and low-income southerners who comprised a significant part of Wallace's constituency.

Richard Nixon lost no time in appealing to the Wallace supporters and to other white southerners. Calculating the best means of assuring his own reelection, Nixon pursued a "southern strategy" from the time he entered the White House in January 1969. His immediate purpose was to counter the Wallace movement, to attract as much southern support as possible in and out of Congress, and thus to enhance his chances of carrying the South against the Democratic nominee in 1972. Conceding the loss of black votes and those of white liberals, Nixon made a determined bid for the support of white southerners, suburbanites, and ethnic workers troubled by the threat of racial equality and social disorder. His strategy was designed to attract southerners by combining law-and-order appeals with economic conservatism. The latter was an important factor in attracting middle-class white southerners to the Republican philosophy in national politics. Despite the lip service he paid to racial justice, the Republican president launched a wide-ranging campaign to exploit the racial fears and prejudices of white Americans, particularly in the South. He attempted to slow the pace of school desegregation, weakened civil rights offices in the Justice Department and in the Department of Health, Education, and Welfare, tried to undermine the fair-housing enforcement program, opposed the extension of the Voting Rights Act of 1965, and urged Congress to impose a moratorium on court-ordered busing. In other respects, Nixon followed a policy of willful neglect in dealing with civil rights questions. Meanwhile, he nominated three conservative "strict constructionist" southerners to the Supreme Court.[3] And he made extensive use of Vice-Pres. Spiro Agnew's slashing rhetoric in presenting his case to the South.

Although Nixon's "southern strategy" heightened the sectional sensibilities of many white southerners and elicited their strong approval, it did not result in substantial Republican gains in the South in the elections of 1970. Administration leaders conducted a vigorous campaign that year, giving particular attention to congressional contests. A central theme in the president's appeal was that southerners should elect Republicans to Congress so that they could support his firm stand against busing to achieve racial balance in the schools. According to two southern newspaper editors, "It was a cynical strategy, this catering in subtle ways to the segregationist leanings of Southern voters—yet pretending with high rhetoric that the real aim was simply to treat the South fairly, to let it become part of the nation again."[4] The results were disappointing—in the South and elsewhere. Except in Tennessee, where Winfield Dunn was elected governor and Rep. William E. Brock defeated the liberal senator Albert Gore, the Republicans made few gains in the South. They lost the governorship in Arkansas and Florida and were unable to win any other statewide offices in the region. Most Democratic candidates opposed busing and identified themselves with the social conservatism of their white constituents. Nixon was somewhat ambivalent in campaigning against southern Democrats, since he coveted their votes in his bid for reelection and their support in Congress, where southern Democratic dissidence was as conspicuous as ever and where southerners still dominated the committee structure.

Even though the Nixon administration adopted an outspoken antibusing position in 1971 and 1972, it was unable to undermine George Wallace's political strength in the South. Many Wallace supporters had returned to the Democratic ranks in 1970. Following his narrow victory in the Alabama gubernatorial election of 1970, Wallace consolidated his political base in his home state and became a candidate for the Democratic presidential nomination in 1972. He called himself a national candidate, made plans to enter presidential primaries in and out of the South, and criticized both President Nixon and Democratic aspirants like Edmund S. Muskie, Hubert H. Humphrey, and George S. McGovern. In March 1972 Governor Wallace won a surprising victory in the Florida primary, an achievement that concerned Republican leaders and led them to intensify their own efforts in the southern states. Wallace moved on to win Democratic primaries in Tennessee, North Carolina, Michigan, and Maryland, while demonstrating impressive strength in the Wisconsin, Pennsylvania, and Indiana primaries. At that point fate intervened: the Alabama governor was shot by a would-be assassin on May 15 while campaigning in Maryland. Left paralyzed from the waist down, Wallace was forced to abandon his presidential campaign in 1972.

The Democratic party's reform of its delegate-selection process, which favored minority and liberal elements, helped Sen. George McGovern win the party's presidential nomination in 1972. The new selection procedures, as well as McGovern's liberalism, endorsement of civil rights and school busing, and forthright opposition to the war in Vietnam, alienated many conservative Democrats, particularly in the South. Few Democratic leaders in the region campaigned for the South Dakota senator, and a number of southern Democrats, including former governors John Connally of Texas and Mills Godwin of Virginia, worked actively for Nixon's election. Sam Nunn, the Democratic nominee for a vacant Senate seat in Georgia, openly declared his intention of voting for President Nixon. The latter, meanwhile, tried hard to appeal to white segregationist sentiment in the southern states. He made effective use of the highly emotional issue of busing. The controversy over "forced busing" offered Republicans a means of exploiting regional divisions within the Democratic party while drawing a distinction between busing and legal segregation. Nixon was careful not to antagonize powerful Democrats in the South and made clear his support of Senator Eastland's reelection in Mississippi.

Republican hopes were overwhelmingly realized in the South—and throughout the nation. Nixon and Agnew carried every southern

Republican Vote in Presidential and Congressional Elections,
1948–1984

Percent
Republican

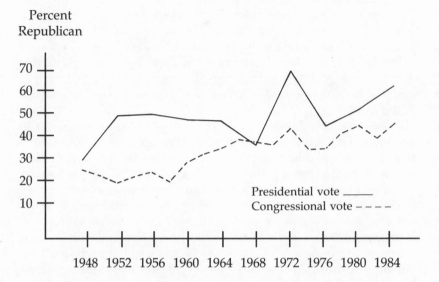

1948 1952 1956 1960 1964 1968 1972 1976 1980 1984

SOURCE: *Congressional Directory* (Washington: GPO, 1948–52), 81st
Cong., 1st sess.; 82d Cong., 1st sess.; 83d Cong., 1st sess.; Richard M.
Scammon, *America Votes* (Washington: *Congressional Quarterly*, 1956–85).

NOTE: These statistics refer to the eleven ex-Confederate states plus
Kentucky and Oklahoma. Beginning in 1978, election statistics from
Louisiana are excluded; in that state, under the provisions of a nonparty
election law, candidates in an open primary receiving a majority of votes
are declared elected and no general election is held.

state, winning more than 70 percent (as compared to 61 percent in
the United States as a whole) of the popular vote in the ex-Confederate
states. McGovern received only 28.9 percent of the region's popular
votes. Seldom had the color line been more visible in southern politics.
A great majority of the South's white voters supported Nixon, while
most of its black electorate voted for McGovern. The major difference
between the elections of 1968 and 1972 in the South was the absence
of the Wallace alternative in the latter contest. Had Wallace continued
as a candidate, he would probably have carried most of the southern
states. As it was, a great majority of those southerners who voted for
Wallace in 1968 cast their ballots for Nixon four years later. Survey
data suggests that three out of four such voters followed that course.
Nixon had apparently created a southern coalition based on white
disgruntlement over civil rights and a preference for state rights and
fiscal conservatism.

While the GOP sweep of the South did not extend below the presidential level in 1972, the party did make modest gains in other races. Republicans won six of twelve Senate elections in the southern states and increased their number of seats in the House of Representatives by seven, giving them about a third of the region's membership in the two houses of Congress. They were less successful in gubernatorial elections and despite some gains held only about 16 percent of the legislative seats in the eleven Old South states following the election. The Republican party was most successful in Virginia and North Carolina. In the Old Dominion, William L. Scott, a conservative, defeated the Democratic incumbent, the moderate William B. Spong, for a U.S. Senate seat. A year later Mills Godwin, a former Democratic governor, won the governorship as a Republican, with the help of a great many conservative Democrats. In 1972 North Carolina Republicans captured the governorship, a U.S. Senate seat, and four of the eleven seats in the House of Representatives. The new Republican governor was a moderate named James E. Holshouser. The newly elected Republican senator was Jesse A. Helms, an extreme conservative who defeated the liberal Democrat Nick Galifianakis.

Despite the disastrous setback in the presidential election of 1972, Democratic prospects in the South began to brighten in 1970. From the wreckage of the late 1960s and early 1970s, Democratic leaders moved to contain the protest politics of George Wallace and to meet the challenge of Republican growth. The consensus on racial segregation among southern politicians had begun to fall apart in the 1960s, and by the early years of that decade most office seekers in the peripheral South "no longer conformed to the traditional model of the segregationist white candidate."[5] By the early 1970s, segregationist campaign rhetoric had declined sharply even in the deep South. Alexander P. Lamis has described the political scene. "The racial tension that had alienated traditionally Democratic white voters lessened, and at the same time large numbers of blacks carrying strong Democratic party leanings entered the electorate. The potential flowing from this new situation was not lost on a host of Democratic office seekers, who put together potent black-white coalitions in the early 1970s."[6] As racial tensions declined in the 1970s and as the political participation of blacks—and whites—increased in the wake of suffrage reform and reapportionment, moderate Democrats began to attract many Wallace supporters. Wallace himself, who was reelected to a third term as governor in 1974, moved toward the center of the political spectrum. The nature of the Democratic party was clearly changing in the southern states, stimulated by the weakening vitality of the Dixiecrat mentality among Democrats, by Republican successes, and by the emergence of new Democratic leaders. This new Democratic leadership tried to avoid the label "liberal," did not ordinarily endorse "integrationist" policies, and made use of subtly differentiated appeals to diverse elements in the electorate.

In the short run, moreover, the frustration and collapse of the second Nixon administration worked to the advantage of Democrats in the South. Although white southerners tended to support Nixon's policies in continuing the war in Vietnam and were slow to condemn his behavior in the Watergate scandal, many of them were disillusioned and discouraged by the president's downfall. The leading roles assumed by Democrat Sam J. Ervin and Republican Howard H. Baker in the Senate investigation of Watergate also encouraged southern disaffection with Nixonian Republicanism. More generally, the 1970s witnessed what one journalist described, with some exaggeration, as a "new breed" of southern congressmen—"more independent and tolerant and more national in their outlook than their counterparts of previous decades."[7]

One manifestation of Democratic resurgence in the South was the election of a group of moderate governors during the 1970s. These governors sought to construct majority coalitions that included working-class whites and blacks as well as middle-class and professional people. Having been largely emancipated from the burden of the racial issue, they emphasized economic development and opportunity. Programmatic and goal-oriented, they tried to modernize their state governments and to extend public services. They represented a larger group of new activists who hoped to rehabilitate the Democratic party in the South and to strengthen its popular support. In their ranks were the likes of Reubin O. Askew of Florida, Dale Bumpers of Arkansas, James Earl "Jimmy" Carter, Jr., of Georgia, Edwin W. Edwards of Louisiana, James B. Hunt, Jr., of North Carolina, and John C. West of South Carolina.

The Democratic party's renewed vitality in the South was especially evident in four of the gubernatorial campaigns of 1970. One of those campaigns took place in Florida, where Reubin Askew defeated the Republican incumbent, Claude R. Kirk, Jr., on the basis of a broad reform coalition. Lawton Chiles, a young Democrat in the same mold, won a Senate seat that year. As governor, Askew boldly took the lead in the enactment of a tax on corporation profits and in securing other important reforms. He was reelected in 1974 and was succeeded four years later by Robert Graham, another representative of the new breed of southern governors. In Arkansas the party of Orval Faubus and James D. Johnson was pointed in a new direction by Dale Bumpers, a well-spoken moderate who defeated Faubus in the Democratic gubernatorial primary of 1970 and then won the general election against Gov. Winthrop Rockefeller. Bumpers was reelected in 1972 and was succeeded two years later by another moderate reformer, former U.S. representative David Pryor, who had narrowly lost a race against Sen. John L. McClellan in 1972. After Pryor was reelected in 1976, William "Bill" Clinton, a third Democratic moderate, won the governorship in 1978. Starting with Rockefeller's defeat in 1970, one political scientist observes, "attractive, skillful moderate Democratic leaders capitalized on strong white-voter allegiance to the Democratic party coupled with black support, which became solidly Democratic in the post-Rockefeller era, to reduce statewide Republican challenges from 1972 through 1978 to no more than nominal contests."[8]

Democratic moderation and broad-based campaign coalitions in South Carolina were continued with the election of Lt. Gov. John C. West as governor in 1970. West attracted most of the black votes and defeated Albert W. Watson, a former Democratic congressman, who waged a racist campaign that came close to succeeding. Racial issues began to lose strength after 1970, however, and even Sen. Strom Thurmond began to appeal for black support. South Carolina Democrats suffered a setback in 1974, when their nominee for governor, a liberal named Charles D. "Pug" Ravenel, was declared ineligible because he failed to meet the five-year residency requirement. James B. Edwards, the Republican nominee, was elected. But the Democrats carried the state for Jimmy Carter in 1976, and two years later their gubernatorial nominee, Richard W. Riley, was elected.

The reorientation of Democratic leadership in Georgia was more complicated and took longer. In the late 1960s, the Democratic party seemed to be disintegrating in the Empire State of the South. Lester Maddox had won the governorship in 1966 with a racist and reactionary campaign, and in 1968 the Democratic presidential ticket had come in third behind George Wallace and Richard Nixon. A new state leader emerged in 1970, however, when Jimmy Carter defeated former governor Carl Sanders for the Democratic gubernatorial nomination and then won the general election. Carter, who opposed busing and appealed to the social conservatism of rural and small-town Georgians, attracted much of the Talmadge-Maddox-Wallace following in his campaign against the racially moderate and urban-oriented Sanders. Yet, as governor, Carter expressed liberal racial views, set about reorganizing the state government, and began to fashion a coalition that included blacks and rural and small-town workers. His tenure as governor, Numan V. Bartley suggests, seemed to confirm "the triumph of a metropolitan ideology that stressed economic expansion, businesslike administration, and free market individualism."[9] The same kind of coalition helped elect George Busbee, another Democratic moderate, in 1974. Busbee was reelected in 1978.

Louisiana and Mississippi also showed signs in the early 1970s of moving away from an obsession with racial issues in state politics. Candidates in those states, as in other parts of the deep South, began to frame issues in terms of economic and class rather than social appeals. In 1971–72 Edwin W. Edwards, a congressman of Cajun background, won the governorship of Louisiana. As Edwards recalled in 1973, "I was elected by a coalition of blacks, farmers, [and] people from South Louisiana of French Cajun descent."[10] Edwards was re-elected in 1976, and Louisiana Democrats were able to carry the state for Carter in a close election that year. William Winter, who won the Mississippi governorship in 1971, began to bring blacks into the state's politics and government, and Charles "Cliff" Finch, who was elected as his successor in 1975, went further in creating a black-white Democratic coalition. Having acquired greater unity than they had possessed in a generation, Mississippi Democrats managed to deliver the state to Jimmy Carter in 1976. It was the first time Mississippi had voted Democratic in a presidential election since 1956.

The new-style Democrats were not immediately successful in the other southern states. In Tennessee Rep. Ray Blanton reclaimed the governorship for the Democrats in 1974, aided by Watergate and his success in attracting Wallace supporters back to the party. But Lamar Alexander, the Republican nominee, won the office in 1978 when the Democrats nominated a rich banker and controversy surrounded the Blanton administration. Tennessee Democrats could take some satisfaction in the election of James R. Sasser, a middle-of-the-road liberal, to the Senate in 1976 and in the fact that Jimmy Carter carried the state that year. Despite the North Carolina Republicans' success in 1972, Democratic moderates were able to control most of the state offices during the 1970s. Attorney General Robert B. Morgan was elected to the Senate in 1974, Lt. Gov. James B. Hunt, Jr., won the governorship in 1976, and Jimmy Carter carried the Tarheel State in the same year. Bitter factionalism among Virginia Democrats following the demise of the Byrd organization left the party there polarized and enervated, with a weak and diffused center, throughout the 1970s. Republicans controlled the governorship for twelve straight years after 1969, and after 1982 they held both U.S. Senate seats. Democrats presided over the state government of Texas until 1978, when Republican William P. Clements, Jr., was elected governor. The conservative faction of the Democratic party had long held the upper hand in Texas politics. Sen. Ralph Yarborough, the leading Democratic liberal in the state, was defeated by a conservative Democrat in 1970.

A stronger Democratic party in the South in the 1970s, along with the debilitating effects of Watergate on the Republican party, set the stage for the extraordinary rise of Jimmy Carter and his accession to the presidency. In 1972, while in the middle of his term as governor, Carter decided to run for president. The governor and his advisers decided to employ the strategy they had won with in Georgia—building on Carter's political base in the southwestern part of the state and putting together a broad coalition through a diversified platform and intensive campaigning—in the national arena. Beginning with Georgia, they set out to commit the rest of the South to Carter's candidacy, while entering a large number of presidential primaries both in and out of the southern region. Meanwhile, the Georgian traveled extensively throughout the United States in preparation for the preconvention campaign of 1976. He emphasized the innovative character of his governorship and his commitment to a new approach in race relations. In his inaugural address, he had declared that "the time for racial discrimination is over. Our people have already made this major and difficult decision. No poor, rural, weak, or black person should ever have to bear the additional burden of being deprived of the opportunity for an education, a job, or simple justice."[11]

Carter faced a major obstacle in the person of George Wallace, who was once again prepared to seek the Democratic presidential nomination by conducting a grass-roots campaign. Opinion polls in the spring of 1975 showed the Alabama governor to be the leading candidate among the Democratic leaders who were actively working for the nomination. But the political situation had changed since 1972, and in Carter, Wallace was confronted with a formidable opponent. Carter presented himself as a moderate, New South alternative to Wallace. To the surprise of many observers, the Georgian won a decisive victory over Wallace in the Florida preferential primary on March 9, and he went on to defeat the Alabamian in North Carolina, Georgia, Arkansas, Kentucky, and Tennessee. Carter's national strategy was also working. He won the New Hampshire primary in late February and proceeded to capture the delegates of ten other nonsouthern states in presidential primaries. When the Democratic national convention convened, the one-term governor from Georgia was nominated on the first ballot. Carter obviously benefited from the aftereffects of the Watergate scandal, and he was widely perceived as an antiestablishment candidate running against the "mess in Washington." He thus appealed both to the reaction against Richard Nixon and to the alienation and distrust felt by many of Wallace's supporters.

The Democratic presidential nominee had a broader appeal, however. He attracted widespread support in other regions as well as the South, and at the outset of the fall campaign he and his running mate, Sen. Walter F. Mondale of Minnesota, enjoyed a substantial lead in the polls over Pres. Gerald R. Ford and Sen. Robert Dole. Even so, the election was close, and the Democrats won with a bare majority of the popular vote and a majority of only 297 to 241 electoral votes. Carter and Mondale made their best showing in the South, winning eleven of the thirteen southern states and receiving 54 percent of the popular votes cast in the region. The Democrats lost Virginia and Oklahoma by extremely narrow margins. While the Democratic ticket, with strong support from Congressman Andrew Young and other Afro-American leaders, captured over 90 percent of the southern black votes, the Republicans had a lead of 53 to 46 percent among the South's white voters. Carter's strength in the South, his success in appealing to anti-Washington sentiment, and the image of honesty, sincerity, and trust that he projected were not alone responsible for his election. He was also able to mobilize a considerable part of the traditional New Deal coalition—religious and ethnic groups, racial minorities, and organized labor. "Fundamentally," one scholar concludes, "Carter won because he was a Democrat in a nation where Democrats outnumbered Republicans by approximately a two-to-one margin, and Republican Gerald R. Ford ran a close race because he was the incumbent."[12]

Millions of southerners felt a sense of pride and triumph in the election of a president from the heart of their region. Humbled, isolated, and bereft of a positive role in national affairs for generations, they savored a moment of vindication. "Whatever else he may do," the liberal journalist Tom Wicker wrote, "Jimmy Carter has removed the last great cause for Southern isolation; and even in the remote little farm towns that dot the Southern countryside, it is already possible to sense that Southerners are coming to believe that they finally belong to something larger than the South."[13] Still, the presidency of Jimmy Carter did little to clarify the ambiguity that had come to characterize southern politics. One reason may have been that Carter came to the presidency after waging a highly personalized campaign, which left him without a clear policy mandate and without the loyalty of established Democratic leaders. Entering the White House as an outsider, the Georgian had trouble with Congress, including the members of his own party. Had his administration been more successful, the president from Georgia might have had a more enduring influence on southern politics. But that is problematic. As it was, the Carter administration became increasingly vulnerable to Republican attacks. Despite the president's good intentions and some notable accomplishments, particularly in foreign affairs, he was eventually frustrated by intractable problems, a resurgent Congress, and a divided Democratic party. Ironically, the leadership of this southern president opened the door wider to Republican advances in the South.

Carter's renomination in 1980 was contested by Sen. Edward M. Kennedy of Massachusetts, who portrayed Carter as a weak and ineffectual leader who had abandoned the Democratic party's tradition of domestic reformism and was unable to forge a successful foreign policy. In the end, Carter won a series of preferential primaries and turned back the Kennedy challenge. The Democratic national convention then renominated Carter and Mondale. The Republicans, sensing victory, turned to Ronald Reagan, an ex-governor of California who had come close to winning the GOP nomination in 1976. The conservative Reagan provided a sharp contrast to Carter. He urged a reduction of federal spending and promised to "take government off the backs of the people." He blamed the Carter administration for the nation's economic doldrums and accused it of weakening the national defense and allowing the Soviet Union to achieve an advantage in strategic striking power. Carter fought back, but he remained on the defensive throughout the campaign, buffeted by a faltering economy, deteriorating relations with the Russians, and a humiliating crisis precipitated by the holding of American diplomats as hostages in Iran, which seemed to symbolize the bankruptcy of the president's leadership. Economic setbacks, including a sluggish growth rate, mounting deficits, and galloping inflation, undermined public confidence in the Carter administration. The Republicans, moreover, conducted a unified and well-organized campaign, in contrast to the Democrats' loosely organized and poorly integrated efforts.

In an election that brought the lowest U.S. turnout in the twentieth century, Reagan received 43.9 million popular votes (51 percent) to 35.5 million (41 percent) for Carter. Rep. John B. Anderson, an independent candidate, obtained 5.7 million votes. The Republicans had an overwhelming electoral margin of 489 to 49. Carter and Mondale carried only six states, including Carter's home state of Georgia. The Republican ticket won the other twelve southern states, but the outcome was very close in six of those commonwealths. The GOP majorities in Virginia, Florida, Texas, and Oklahoma were much larger. Whereas Carter captured 93 percent of the black ballots in the eleven ex-Confederate states, he received only 35 percent of the region's white votes. Among southern whites, he did best with older, low-income, and less well-educated voters. The Republicans also made gains below the presidential level in the South. They won new Senate seats in North Carolina, Georgia, Florida, and Alabama. They gained nine seats in the House of Representatives and also won the governorship of Arkansas.

By the 1980s the South's once-powerful Democratic delegations were becoming less formidable. For one thing, the number of Republican members of Congress from the South had steadily risen. Unlike the situation a few years earlier when the Democratic ascendancy was so overwhelming that the Republicans left many congressional seats uncontested, the minority party had begun to field candidates for most House and Senate seats. The 1970s brought "a core of right-wing Republican strength [from the South] in Congress."[14] After the 1980 elections, Republicans held eleven of the region's twenty-six Senate seats[15] and one-third of the House seats. Republican congressional strength was most impressive in Virginia, where the party held nine of the state's ten House seats following the elections of 1980 and both Senate seats after 1982. When the Republicans won control of the Senate in 1980, southern senators assumed an influential role. Howard Baker became the new majority leader, while Strom Thurmond, John G. Tower, and Jesse Helms took over the chairmanships of important Senate committees. Although the Democrats retained control of the House of Representatives, southerners no longer dominated the committee structure and leadership positions of the lower house as they once had. Only a decade before, southerners had headed almost half of the standing committees in the two houses. But deaths, resignations, and increasing competition had diluted the dominance formerly exercised by southern Democrats in both houses of Congress. The powerful figures of an earlier day—Richard B. Russell, Harry Flood Byrd, John L. McClellan, James O. Eastland, Howard W. Smith, and Wilbur Mills—had disappeared from the scene. New rules in the House of Representatives had diminished southern power, and in the mid-1970s a revolt of young liberals in that body was instrumental in the removal of two southern Democrats from important chairmanships. With the decline of civil rights as a major issue, southern Democratic unity in Congress fell somewhat. Significantly, a majority of the Democratic members from the South voted for an extension of the Voting Rights Act in 1975 and 1982.

Meanwhile, the Republican presence in the South was enhanced because the party's southern leaders included persons of influence and power. Senator Baker, for example, became a serious candidate for the presidency in the 1980s. Southern Republicanism was also encouraged by the Reagan administration, which showed its solicitude for the South in ways that were both tangible and symbolic. "Reagan's popularity," the columnist David Broder observes, "has created a real opportunity for political realignment of the region, down to the courthouse level."[16] One reason President Reagan and other GOP leaders looked to the South was the region's conservative tradition, and the reservoir of conservatism below the Potomac was recurrently replenished by white southerners' deep-seated views on economic and moral issues. Reagan's policies at home and abroad were popular among these southerners and received considerable support from the region's Democrats in Congress. This regional re-

Table 5. Percentage of Republican Victories for Selected Federal
Offices, 1965–1985

	President	Senator	Governor	State Legislator
South	69	33	24	14
Deep South	60	22	8	8
Peripheral South	77	43	34	21

SOURCE: Adapted from Earl Black and Merle Black, *Politics and Society in
the South* (Cambridge: Harvard Univ. Press, 1987), p. 311, by permission.

NOTE: These statistics refer to the eleven ex-Confederate states only.
The "deep South" states include South Carolina, Georgia, Alabama,
Mississippi, and Louisiana. The "peripheral South" states include Florida,
North Carolina, Tennessee, Virginia, Arkansas, and Texas.

sponse involved more than racial considerations. White southerners
generally liked the fortieth president's emphasis on lower taxes, economic growth, reduction of federal regulatory activities, resistance to
redistributive welfare programs, strong opposition to a "predatory"
Soviet Union, and the need to restore patriotism and renew traditional
values and institutions. Republican growth in the South, especially
in national and statewide election campaigns, was stimulated as well
by the disarray in the Democratic party and the lack of purposeful
and compelling leadership at the national level.

On the surface, at least, the presidential election of 1984 gave
Republicans in the South, as in other parts of the country, further
cause to be optimistic about their party's continued growth. The times
were propitious for the Grand Old Party. Economic recovery was in
full swing following the recession of 1981–82, foreign affairs had assumed a less hazardous outlook, and the president's popularity remained gratifyingly high. Reagan dominated the Republican party,
which was strongly united in support of his reelection. Democratic
prospects, on the other hand, were never very bright. The party went
through a long and bruising preconvention struggle before nominating former vice-president Walter Mondale and Rep. Geraldine A. Fer-
raro. The Democrats waged a forceful and energetic campaign, but
they were no match for the confident and united Republicans. Reagan
and his running mate, George Bush of Texas, won by a landslide,
receiving 54.5 million votes (59 percent) to 37.6 (41 percent) for the
Democratic ticket. The electoral vote was an overwhelming 525 to 13,
with the Republicans carrying every state except Mondale's Minnesota and the District of Columbia.

While Ronald Reagan demonstrated his own extraordinary political appeal in the election of 1984, the results of that contest were less certain in other respects. It was not clear whether Reagan's victories in 1980 and 1984 were part of a realignment of the political parties—a fundamental shift in voter affiliation that would last through several elections. Although the Republicans had captured the Senate as well as the White House, the Democrats remained in control of the House of Representatives and continued to dominate the governorships and state legislatures. Despite the decline in party identification and the growth of independentism, the Democrats were still ahead in terms of party preference and registration. Much would depend on whether Reagan succeeded in rebuilding the national government along conservative lines. The venerable Roosevelt coalition seemed to be disintegrating, and the Republicans were enjoying great success in presidential elections, having won six of the nine contests since 1952 and four out of the last five. Perhaps, as some scholars suggested, there were two separate constituencies in contemporary American politics—one for the presidency and one for Congress and state and local offices.

What these national trends meant for the South was uncertain, although it was increasingly apparent that the region's political future would be closely involved in whatever configuration the nation's politics might assume and that it would likely help establish that pattern. Unlike 1980, Reagan and Bush carried every southern state by a substantial majority in 1984. In other races, however, GOP gains in the southern states were limited. Notwithstanding the party's heavy majority at the presidential level, it barely held its own in congressional races, winning one additional House seat but losing a Senate seat in Tennessee. Following the 1984 elections, the southern Democrats had a majority of 15 to 11 Senate seats and 90 to 39 House seats. The Republicans did gain a governorship in North Carolina, but that left them with only two such positions in the thirteen southern states. In the elections of 1986, they lost five Senate and three House seats in the South, while winning four additional governorships.

For all their internal conflict and tumultuous experience in the recent past, Democrats in the South remained the dominant party in state and local politics. When South Carolinians voted Republican in presidential elections, Senator Thurmond once remarked, "They feel that's way out yonder and if they vote Republican there won't be any stigma. But in state elections, especially among the less enlightened people, there's still that stigma against Republicans that goes back to the military rule of 1866 to 1876."[17] Many southerners still felt a lingering attachment to the party of Bryan, Wilson, and Roosevelt. Southern Republicans were not unfamiliar with the stubborn reality of Democratic dominance at the local level. In their study of recent southern politics, Jack Bass and Walter DeVries speak of "the conservative Dixie Democrat who gets black votes by being a Democrat and white votes by voting conservative."[18] Robert Shaw, chairman of the Republican state committee in Georgia, explained the problem his party faced. "So what catches us is that you find the conservative rural vote going in voting the straight party ticket, and by the same token you find the urban blacks voting the straight party ticket. . . . they're voting hand in hand, and when they do, they're squeezing the lives out of us."[19] The Democrats had still another advantage. They were able in most southern states to "protect" the governorships from the direct impact of presidential campaigns by shifting gubernatorial elections to off-presidential years. Since the Democrats usually controlled the machinery of government at the local and state levels, aspiring politicians saw their best chance to be elected as Democrats, not as Republicans. This was graphically illustrated in the party's preponderance of legislative seats in the South: in 1984 the Democratic margin in senate seats was 441 to 99 and in house seats 1,162 to 355. The best Republican showing was in Tennessee with about 36 percent of the combined legislative seats.

Nevertheless, no aspect of the transformation of southern politics since World War II is more remarkable than the development of interparty competition. By the 1980s the Republican party had apparently become the majority party in presidential elections, and it was no longer a rarity to find Republican officeholders in congressional and statewide positions. The party was organized in every southern state, and it had begun to contest all statewide and congressional offices and an increasing number of local elections. As the Republican party grew stronger and became more competitive, it attracted a steady stream of conservative Democrats. Many of these Democratic defectors began to think of themselves as Republicans or independents. Republican growth in the South was related to the changing nature of the Democratic party: to the liberalization of the national party during the New Deal and after and to the recomposition of the party in the southern states.

A dramatic change in the party loyalties of white southerners had occurred, at least in national politics. A process of "dealignment" seemed to be dissolving the once-powerful Democratic coalition in the South without a new coalition being formed to replace it. The party system had splintered into minorities of Democrats, Republicans, and independents. Whereas Democrats in the South had outnumbered Republicans almost eight to one in the early 1950s, their advantage in party identification in presidential elections had disappeared by the 1980s. Polling data indicated that the percentage of

southern whites favorably disposed toward the Republican party
nearly doubled between 1976 and 1984. Political scientists estimate
that the Democrats suffered a net loss of 25 percent between the 1950s
and the 1980s, while the Republicans enjoyed a net gain of 20 percent
during that period. Meanwhile, a sharp drop occurred in the percentage of white southerners who considered themselves *strong*
Democrats. The GOP attraction was especially notable among conservatives, the college-educated, and the younger generation. A substantial majority of the South's white residents identified themselves
as conservatives, and in many respects the political outlook of the
white working class was quite similar to that of the white middle
class. Organized labor's lack of influence enhanced the political
strength of conservatives. The failure of southern liberalism, Earl
Black and Merle Black suggest, resulted from the fact that "too many
white voters welcome conservative positions and candidates and re-
ject the symbols, policies, and beneficiaries of contemporary liberalism."[20]

The most striking feature of the new Democratic party in the South
was the support it received from black politicians and black voters,
who registered in large numbers in the years after 1965 and entered
the Democratic party almost en masse. Blacks became the strongest
liberal element in the southern Democracy. While this phenomenon
encouraged many Democratic candidates to broaden their appeal to
include blacks, it also led thousands of white Democrats to leave their
traditional party. The number of blacks registered in the eleven states
of the Old South increased from 1.5 million in 1960 to 5.6 million (as
compared with 28 million whites) in 1984. By the latter year, the
registered percentage of the black voting-age population had almost
reached that of the white—66.2 to 75.3. In the meantime, the number
of black elected officials in the region rose rapidly, increasing from
fewer than a hundred in 1965 to about 3,500 in 1984. Most of these
officials were members of city councils, county commissions, school
boards, and law enforcement agencies. In Mississippi the number rose
from zero in 1965 to 521 in 1986, making that state the leader in black
elected officeholders. By 1980 there were 106 black mayors in the
region, mostly in small towns but including Richmond, Raleigh, Atlanta, Birmingham, and New Orleans. The number of blacks in southern legislatures also increased, reaching a total of 178 in both houses
by 1985. Virginia elected L. Douglas Wilder as lieutenant governor in
1985, making him the first black to hold a statewide office in the Old
Dominion, and Mississippi elected its first black Democratic member
of Congress in 1986.

It did not take long for the expanding black electorate to have an
effect on southern politics, particularly on Democratic leaders. Evi-

dence of changing attitudes and practices could be found throughout the South. In George Wallace's Alabama, for instance, the state Democratic party in 1966 removed the party emblem—"White Supremacy—For the Right"—from the ballot. Ernest F. Hollings of South Carolina, the first U.S. senator from the South to be elected after passage of the Voting Rights Act of 1965, illustrates the transitional response of many politicians to the new political environment. In 1969 Hollings, who had earlier defended the traditional racial order in his state, led a successful Senate battle to expand federal food stamps and other programs to combat hunger and malnutrition, an effort that would be especially helpful to blacks. A broader and more significant change occurred in the character of the southern black belts, which historically had been the bulwark of regional conservatism and solidarity. As Afro-American men and women began to register and vote in large numbers, the black belts began to shed their traditional conservatism and to express a more moderate and even liberal position on political issues. In South Carolina Hubert H. Humphrey won thirteen of the fifteen counties with black majorities in 1968. Only one of those counties had voted Democratic in 1964. In 1976 twelve of the state's black belt counties cast 64.9 percent of their ballots for Jimmy Carter—almost 10 percent higher than the other counties. "In general," one authority observes with respect to senatorial and gubernatorial elections, " . . . Republicans must draw in the area of 65 percent of the non-black vote to win in any of the heavily black Southern states."[21]

Southern efforts to dilute the black vote continued even after the Voting Rights Act went into effect. Particularly in the deep South, blacks were often subjected to voter reidentification, harassment at the polls, and economic threats. Black officeholding was minimized through the use of at-large elections for municipal and county offices, multimember districts, racial gerrymandering, and other forms of electoral discrimination. Southern whites did not often vote for black candidates in large numbers. When the Mississippi courts finally ordered a shift to single-member legislative seats in 1979, black leaders had high expectations in thirty districts with large Negro populations. But black candidates were successful in only fifteen house and two senate races. In 1982 state representative Robert Clark became the first black candidate in Mississippi to win Democratic nomination for Congress—with 57 percent of the primary vote. Yet he lost in the general election when many whites defected and voted for his Republican opponent. In 1986 another black candidate, Mike Espy, won the Democratic nomination for the same seat. He won a narrow victory. Richard Arrington, Jr., a black professor and member of the Birmingham city council, was elected mayor of that city in 1979; he won by carrying 98 percent of the black votes and only 12 percent of the white ballots. He was reelected in 1983. In 1980 blacks held only 4 percent of the elective county offices and 3 percent of the elective municipal offices in the South.

Southern blacks were still less active politically than were whites. Even after registering, their voting percentages tended to be poor. Black leaders in office, being human, found it difficult to live up to the expectations of their constituents. Writing in the mid-1960s, Donald R. Matthews and James W. Prothro suggested that "the concrete, measurable payoffs from Negro voting in the South will *not* be revolutionary."[22] They were right. The Democratic governors of the 1970s were unable or unwilling to undertake substantial programs for the benefit of blacks. "None of the new leaders," wrote Roy Reed, the *New York Times* southern correspondent, "has made real headway in providing industrial jobs for the multitudes of poor people who still live in the black belts. None has found the answers to newer problems such as urban blight and the growing concentration of economic power in fewer hands."[23] Despite their new role in politics, the political influence of southern blacks was limited. For one thing, they were a minority in most parts of the region. In 1920 blacks made up 32 percent of the population in the ex-Confederate states; by 1980 that proportion had declined to 20 percent (29 percent in the deep South and 15 percent in the peripheral South). In the 1980s black majorities existed in only eighty-six rural counties. While the black voter registration rate had risen almost to the level of whites in the South, Afro-Americans constituted less than one-fifth of the southern electorate. Furthermore, blacks were poorer, less well educated, and subjected to far worse living conditions than were whites. These disparities contributed to marked differences on such political issues as the government's responsibility for jobs, expenditures for welfare programs, and the relative importance of dealing with unemployment and inflation.

If southern politics had become more competitive, it had also become more democratic. This resulted in part from court decisions that forced the redistricting of congressional and legislative seats, from the invalidation of the poll tax and disfranchising devices, and from the effects of the Voting Rights Act of 1965 and hundreds of registration drives. It also stemmed from increasing registration of southern whites, often in response to the enfranchisement of blacks. In 1948 the political scientist Herman Clarence Nixon described the typical southern legislature as "chiefly a body of Democratic, small-town or rural, white men, a majority of whom represent a minority of the population of the state, not to mention the restricted suffrage by which the members were chosen in a party primary."[24] Thirty years later the composition of the region's legislatures had undergone a decided change. By the 1970s they were much more urban-oriented, and their members included increasing numbers of blacks, women, and Republicans. Competition for legislative seats had become keener. In some respects, politics had become more accessible and more meaningful to southerners than at any time since the late nineteenth century. Many of the disparities that differentiated political affairs in the South from other parts of the country had disappeared. The turnout of southern voters, particularly in presidential and statewide elections, increased dramatically after 1960. By 1980 the percentage of the voting-age population in the South casting ballots in the presidential election had risen to 47.4; the national percentage was 52.6. Meanwhile, more southern voters were attracted to general elections than to Democratic primaries, telling evidence of the arrival of two-party competition below the Potomac.

The new southern electorate was clearly influenced by the massive restructuring of the South's economy and society: the dynamic growth of industry, business, and finance; rapid urbanization and the prevalence of suburban affluence; the swelling middle class and the in-migration of corporate executives and business managers. These developments affected the entire region, but in states such as Texas, Florida, and Virginia, the results were spectacular. The Sunbelt mentality blossomed. The growth of urbanization approached national rates, led by Florida with 84 percent and Texas with 80 percent in 1980. Southern cities spawned their own ghettos, the farm population was greatly diminished, and the mass of industrial workers and white-collar employees showed little interest in organized labor. By 1980 migrants from other parts of the country accounted for 20 percent of the South's white inhabitants. In many respects, the region seemed to be experiencing the fruition of the New South dream. This New South looked more promising to Republicans than to Democrats. The more affluent elements and the growing middle class were disposed to acquiesce in a measure of social change, including racial readjustment, but they had strong conservative predilections on economic questions and cultural issues.

Political change was in considerable part a consequence of the region's profound economic and social transformation. Thus, the South's dynamic involvement in the emergence of a national, integrated economy was a significant factor in the acceptance of black enfranchisement and a new political system. "In every southern state," a recent study notes, "industrialization has multiplied and diversified the number of institutions—banks, insurance companies, utilities, construction firms, real estate interests, transportation companies, communications businesses, leading law firms—that make up state power structures, while simultaneously augmenting the collective resources at the disposal of state 'establishments.' "[25] The political effects of urbanization were also striking; they included the decline of the rural South as a source of political leadership and power and the rise of influential urban leaders and interests. The large metropolitan and medium-urban sector provided 70 percent of the southern vote in the presidential election of 1980. The new middle class, in which white women constituted a notable part, was at the very heart of political change in the South. As two analysts write, "Middle-class southerners occupy most of the region's political offices, dominate its key decisionmaking institutions in the private sector, and control most of its communications and mass media."[26]

While the individual states responded in uniquely different ways in adapting their politics to the pressures of change, they were generally affected by the region's economic and social transformation: the decline of agriculture, increasing economic diversification, urbanization and suburbanization, and extensive migration within and between states. Reapportionment affected the entire region, hastening the decline of rural influence and the transfer of political power to metropolitan and urban areas. All thirteen states were involved in the disruption of the Solid South: in the revolt against the region's historic bulwark—the Democratic party—and in the growth of Republicanism. In every state politics became more competitive, and the emergence of an effective Republican opposition, along with the challenge of George Wallace and other insurgents, stimulated renewed Democratic efforts in state and local contests. These developments were related to the expansion of the southern electorate—to the enfranchisement of the black masses, to the dramatic increase in the registration of whites, and to the marked rise in voter turnout. Women became an important part of the new electorate, and their turnout in the presidential election of 1980 was higher than that of southern men. Although southern women took the lead in organizing a regional suffrage movement early in the century, played a vital role in many reform campaigns, and gradually found new opportunities for public service, they were not prominently involved in electoral politics, seeing that as a male sphere. But that has changed, and they have become more active, not only as voters, but also as party workers, candidates, and officeholders, particularly in local and municipal politics.

In the South, as elsewhere, old-style personal politics and other traditional forms of campaigning gave way to expensive and high-powered media appeals to the mass of voters and to a diminished role for the political party. The changing technology of mass communications hastened the adoption of new techniques of campaigning based on telephone polling and television advertising. Meanwhile, the South was undergoing what two political scientists describe as "a grand secular transition from a politics of faction to a politics of faction and party."[27] Durable factions in the region's one-party politics largely disappeared, replaced by transient factions in multifactional primaries. Gubernatorial tenure grew longer in most states, and governors became more important as party leaders. While few of these governors were neo-Populists, most of them were willing to spend money for public services, especially education. Segregationist-type leaders virtually passed from the political scene. Every southern state could boast an increasingly competitive two-party politics. Another common theme was the concentration of political power in the hands of powerful elites. If southern politics had became more open, more democratic, and more competitive in certain respects, it was nonetheless true that disproportionate power was exercised by large, well-organized, and well-financed interest groups along the entire range of the political process. Special interests were also effective in shaping public policy. During the 1984 session of the general assembly in Virginia, for example, no fewer than 401 groups employed lobbyists who were officially registered, representing business, occupations and professions, agriculture, labor, education, and so on. The business community, one scholar writes, "remains the dominant set of interests represented at the Capitol and in particular, such long established business interests as the railroads, banks, truckers, manufacturers, retailers, utilities and homebuilders retain a strong presence, adapting to the changing landscape."[28]

Early in the twentieth century, and even as late as the 1930s, it made sense to divide the South into three political subregions: the states of the upper South, the lower South, and the trans-Mississippi Southwest. Over the years since World War II, these classifications have become progressively less distinctive. Insofar as a meaningful typology for contemporary southern politics is concerned, the best approach may be simply to divide the political South into two categories of states: those states that comprise the peripheral or outer South and those that make up the inner or deep South. Although these divisions are somewhat arbitrary, they reflect genuine differences in condition and behavior, and they may offer a useful framework in which to consider the distinguishing features of the state political systems.

In general, the states of the peripheral South were historically more diversified economically, had closer ties with the North, were more divided over secession, had fewer blacks, and were less obsessed with the politics of race than was the deep South. Several of these states retained a hardy but minority brand of mountain Republicanism, and since World War II they have made the greatest progress toward two-party politics. Some of them have undergone such dramatic change that they no longer appear to be peculiarly "southern." The inner South, on the other hand, which was more closely identified with the plantation system and was more united in its support of secession and the Democratic party, retains much of its traditional culture. Having the largest percentage of blacks, the states of the deep South were more preoccupied with the "race question" than was the upper South. This preoccupation continued in the post–World War II period, and it was a major consideration in the rebellion against the national Democratic party and in the political extremism manifested in the overwhelming support of Goldwater and Wallace. While Republicans have gained strength and respectability and while Democrats have broadened their appeal to include black voters, the politics of these states is still in flux, characterized by instability and unpredictability.

Perhaps none of the southern states has experienced greater political change since mid-century nor witnessed a more spectacular Republican breakthrough than Virginia. The most important aspect of politics in the Old Dominion was the Byrd machine's long domination, which was perpetuated through low voter participation and tight control over the counties. But with the demise of the machine in the mid-1960s and the splintering of the Democratic party, the Republicans won the governorship and a U.S. Senate seat. They dominated statewide and congressional elections in the 1970s, until a moderate and reorganized Democratic party regained the governorship under the leadership of Charles S. Robb in 1981. Robb was followed by another centrist Democrat. Interparty competition had unmistakably come to Virginia. Meanwhile, urban growth and economic development had changed the political setting, the electorate had greatly increased in size, and the weight of the urban voters had altered the nature of statewide elections and the process of political decision making. With the decline of the political oligarchy, the old values of a restricted electorate, rule by the "better sort," and limited social services were largely repudiated.

In two other upper South states—Tennessee and North Carolina—the Democrats lost their monopoly of statewide offices, and competition between the parties became more intense. The Democratic structure that resulted from the powerful role of Edward H. Crump's Memphis organization came to an end in the early 1950s, and for about a decade thereafter a vague dual factionalism revolving around Senators Estes Kefauver and Albert Gore, on the one hand, and Governors Frank G. Clement and Buford Ellington, on the other, characterized the Democratic party. As these leaders passed from the scene in the 1960s, the party fell into disarray, setting the stage for Republican victories in 1966 and 1970. The Republicans benefited from strong leadership, notably that of Senator Baker in national politics and Lamar Alexander, who served as governor from 1979 to 1987. The Democrats remained strong, however, and following the elections of 1986, they controlled the governorship, both U.S. Senate seats, and six of the state's nine congressional seats. Still, the Republican party was a genuine competitive force. Building on its traditional strength in East Tennessee, Republican influence grew in the cities and in West Tennessee, a conservative area once dominated by the Democrats.

In similar fashion, North Carolina Republicanism spread eastward from its historic base in the mountains, picking up adherents in the dynamic Piedmont crescent and eventually attracting conservative white support in the traditionally Democratic farm country of the east. There were competing factions in both parties, but by the late 1970s the most powerful Republican voice was that of the ultraconservative Sen. Jesse Helms, while the spokesman for Democrats was a moderate and successful coalition builder, Gov. James B. Hunt, Jr.[29] During the first half of the 1980s, the Republicans controlled both U.S. Senate seats, and in 1984 they won the governorship again. In 1986 the Democrats regained one of the Senate places and won two additional congressional seats. North Carolina, like Tennessee and Virginia, had become an intensely contested battleground between Republicans and Democrats in presidential, congressional, and statewide elections.

Political change in Florida and Texas, while quite remarkable, lagged behind the extraordinary economic and social transformation of those states in the postwar period. Florida's rate of population growth, magnitude of urbanization, and increase in per capita income led the South. Its population more than tripled between 1940 and 1980, and an influx of outsiders, many of whom were northerners, poured into the state. These conditions provided fertile ground for Republicanism. Beginning in 1952, Florida Republicans won seven of the next nine presidential elections, and in 1966 they captured the governorship and a Senate seat. New leaders such as Reubin Askew and Lawton Chiles soon rejuvenated the Democratic party on the basis of an expanded constituency and a progressive agenda. Reapportionment, the approval of a new constitution in 1968, and a sharp increase in voter registration and turnout strengthened the political role of the cities and enhanced the influence of Republicans, blacks, and other minorities. Although the state's politics was affected by the geographic cleavage between the conservative, Old South region to the north and the booming, urban-centered areas of central and south Florida, the atomized one-party system described by V.O. Key in 1949 was replaced by a competitive and increasingly stable biparty system throughout the state.

The advance toward two-partyism in Texas was slower and more inchoate. The state's dynamic economy and new wealth created by industrial and commercial expansion generated powerful conservative forces in politics. Republicans profited from these forces, but so did the Democrats. The latter were also strengthened by the potent leadership of Lyndon Johnson and Sam Rayburn in national politics and by effective state leaders such as Price Daniel and John B. Connally. While the liberal-conservative factionalism that characterized the Democratic party in the 1930s and 1940s continued after mid-century, conservatives won most of the statewide contests. Nevertheless, the Republicans made gains, and the liberal policies promulgated by the national Democratic party caused many conservative Democrats to identify with the minority party, including former governor Connally in 1973. Republican growth might be accelerated if Texas liberals were ever able to bring together Mexican-Americans (21 percent of the population in 1980), blacks, organized labor, and other dissatisfied elements. Meantime, Texas gave the appearance of being a three- rather than a two-party state, with conservative and liberal Democrats and Republicans.

Kentucky and Oklahoma, two other states of the peripheral South, were also traditionally Democratic. The Republicans made significant gains in Kentucky in the 1940s and 1950s, but their major advances in Oklahoma did not come until the 1960s and 1970s. As was true throughout the South, politics in both states retained a strong Democratic flavor below the state level. Kentucky Democrats tended to be moderate and to be more in line with the policies of the national party than Democrats in many other southern states. Despite the Republican challenge, the Democrats controlled the governorship for forty years after 1946, except for the four-year term of Louie B. Nunn. Kentucky Republicans were more competitive in Congress, holding three of the state's seven seats in the House during the 1980s and capturing one of the Senate seats in 1984. In Oklahoma a bipartisan, conservative consensus reflected the widespread conviction in the state that minimal taxes were essential to economic growth. Though less fragmented than in prewar years, the Democratic party remained amorphous, and personal rivalries flourished. The rural exodus from the counties south of the Canadian River hurt the Democrats, while migration from the North and the state's increasing urbanization aided the Republicans. Despite the growing two-party competition, observers noted an increasing public mood of independence, if not indifference, toward both parties. As two historians remark: "The old armies of 'yellow-dog' Democrats and 'rock-ribbed' Republicans have passed. In their places are a decisive bloc of voters unattached to either party."[30]

Geographically, Arkansas belongs to the peripheral South, but in some respects its politics is more like that of the inner than the outer South. The state held on to the poll tax until the very end, and it waited until the 1960s to adopt a genuine registration system. Traditional Democratic loyalties remained strong among whites. Arkansas was also the scene of an obsessive racism orchestrated by Orval Faubus that overcame the amorphousness of the Democratic party. This was followed by the success of Winthrop Rockefeller's moderate Republicanism, which in turn was superseded by the governorship of Dale Bumpers and other new-style Democrats. The success of both Rockefeller and Bumpers reflected the growing importance of black voters in Arkansas politics. Republicans won the governorship again in 1980, and the party controlled two of the state's four House seats in the early 1980s. The state's old-time sectionalism had become less important, party organization on a statewide basis was being attempted, and a two-party politics appeared to be emerging.

South Carolina seemed to be following a similar path. The state's basic conservatism was at least partly offset by the enfranchisement of its large black population. The Republicans, given a momentous boost by the party switch of Senator Thurmond and the white backlash in the 1960s, grew steadily stronger. They made notable gains in the urban sector of the upcountry Piedmont. They elected a governor in 1974 and again in 1986, and in the early 1980s, the minority party controlled half the state's seats in the House of Representatives. Meanwhile, however, the Democrats successfully pursued a politics of moderation and the cultivation of black-white coalitions.

Two other deep South states—Georgia and Louisiana—experienced great political turmoil and change but made only limited progress toward two-party politics. The bifactionalism that characterized the dominant Democratic party in both states disappeared after midcentury, wiped out by the rise of Herman Talmadge in Georgia and by the pressure of massive resistance in Louisiana. The politics of race preoccupied both states in the late 1950s and early 1960s. Disarray among the Democrats, heightened by the civil rights movement and Lyndon Johnson's Great Society, promoted Republican growth in the two states. Both Georgia and Louisiana voted for Goldwater in 1964 and Wallace in 1968. Nevertheless, following the civil rights era, a more moderate Democratic leadership asserted itself in the two commonwealths. In Georgia, two scholars have written, the new Democratic coalition "consists of blacks, courthouse Democrats who have learned the benefits of black allegiance to the Democratic party, a developing role for organized labor, rural whites with a Democratic heritage who remain suspicious of urban Republicans and their country club image, a few white urban liberals, and the top echelon of the business and financial community, who tend to view Georgia Republicans as somewhat unstable political amateurs."[31] Although the "ticketing system," in which one faction's candidates for various offices ran on the same ticket, is no longer used in Louisiana, the class basis of Longism has not entirely disappeared. The continuation of geographical, ethnic, and religious conflicts has no doubt slowed the development of a more rational and stable party system in that state. In Georgia, on the other hand, the abolition of the county-unit system and the effects of legislative reapportionment have led to a new emphasis on the popular vote in statewide campaigns and also to dominance of the urban over the rural and small-town areas.

Mississippi and Alabama, the other states of the deep South, continued to be the most "southern" commonwealths in the region. In the post–World War II period, Mississippi retained its distinction as the poorest and most rural state in the Union. It also had the highest percentage of blacks. The economic and ideological differences reflected in the historic conflict between the hills and the delta became less salient after the war, surrendering to the racist politics of Bilbo, Eastland, and Barnett. As one analysis suggested in 1972, the nature of the division in Mississippi politics changed after 1948. "Basically, the new cleavage results from a new direction of the political issues of the state. In general, the conservative forces have won the upper hand over the neopopulist elements, as a result of the developing industrialization and urbanization and the emergence of race as the most dominant issue in Mississippi elections."[32] The race issue could, in fact, explain the most significant developments in the state's tortured political course since World War II: the revolt against the national Democratic party, the growth of Republicanism, and the effort of moderate Democratic leaders to assimilate black voters and politicians into winning coalitions. While this was happening, Republican prospects improved, with presidential victories in 1980 and 1984, the capture of a Senate seat in 1978, and control of two of the state's five House seats in the 1980s.

In Alabama the longtime political division between the black belt planters and business "big mules," on the one hand, and the northern hill country and southeastern Wiregrass, on the other, did not immediately disappear following the war. Liberals such as Senators Hill and Sparkman and Governor Folsom headed a New Deal, loyalist faction against the conservative States' Righters. But the rise of massive resistance eroded these divisions and paved the way for the remarkable career of George Wallace, who dominated Alabama politics in the 1960s and 1970s. Wallace's hegemony delayed the development of the Republican party in the state as well as the reorganization of the Democratic party along more moderate and pluralistic lines. Yet notable changes came even in Alabama. Legislative reapportionment broke the hold of white conservatives on the black belt. The rising tide of black voters began to influence statewide campaigns and to elect Negroes to local offices. In the post–civil rights era, Wallace himself moderated his racial position and sought the support of black Alabamians. And the Republican party gained strength, first by winning presidential elections and then by gaining a Senate seat and three of the state's seven House seats in 1980. Taking advantage of a fierce factional struggle in the Democratic party, the Republicans captured the governorship in 1986.

Although southern politics retained a strong conservative flavor, the political scene in the 1980s was almost unbelievably different from that of the 1930s. The Solid South had been shattered. Disfranchisement, malapportionment, and the one-party system had largely disappeared. Rural domination of state government had ended, and the political leverage of the old county-seat governing class had declined drastically. Urban voters, now making up a majority of the electorate, had begun to carry much greater weight in election campaigns and in policy outcomes. Blacks had become a significant factor in the region's politics. The Republican party had become respectable and competitive. The southern electorate had expanded dramatically, and the turnout for elections had risen proportionately. During the 1970s and 1980s, state governments throughout the South were modernized in an effort to make them more effective in carrying out their enlarged governing mission. The situation had also changed in Washington. Southern congressional delegations now included a substantial number of Republicans, and by the mid-1970s southern Democrats had yielded their domination of the congressional committee system. There appeared to be greater agreement and less friction, in and out of Congress, between the southern and nonsouthern wings of the Democratic party. But if the old order was passing away, it was not clear how fundamental the changes were that ushered in the new order. The rules of the political game had changed, the number of players had increased and become more diversified, the expectations of constituents had risen, and politics seemed to have become more responsive to public pressure and public needs. Yet the acquisition of power within the political system was limited, a distinct racial cleavage characterized electoral politics, particularly in presidential contests, and the white middle class was the major beneficiary of the new southern politics.[33]

Epilogue

Politics in the South, as in other parts of the United States, reflected and helped rationalize economic and social changes in the society. For a long time after the Civil War, the southern economy was depressed, underdeveloped, and concentrated along agricultural and extractive lines. It was a colonial economy. Political power in such a milieu gravitated into the hands of planters and businessmen. New credit and land tenure arrangements, as well as the increasingly capitalist nature of the agricultural economy, weakened the economic and political independence of yeomen and tenant farmers. The southern masses suffered from endemic poverty and growing dependency. Meanwhile, the controlling voices in rural areas and small communities throughout the region were those of the county-seat elites. These developments contributed to the agrarian uprising of the late 1880s and the Populist insurgency of the early 1890s, a political upheaval that coincided with and was partly responsible for a major realignment in the American party system. Whatever their proportional influence, planters, commercial groups, and industrialists assumed a dominant role in Democratic politics and state government in the South. By the turn of the century, most black men and perhaps a third of the white men had been removed from any part in the political process.

The one-party system was consolidated early in the twentieth century. Far-reaching structural changes were put into place: stringent voter qualifications to reduce and alter the composition of the electorate, malapportioned legislatures that overrepresented the black belts, constitutional limitations on the imposition of taxes, and provisions designed to restrict formal decision making in politics to routine matters. The result was a politics dominated to a great extent by black belt planters, commercial and industrial interests, and the local governing class. Even so, the system was flexible enough to allow for some redistribution of political power and an expansion of governmental functions. While disfranchisement and the new ballot laws contributed to the widespread deprivation and apathy in southern politics, the introduction of primary elections, the growth and diversity of new interest groups, and the reform campaigns of southern progressives opened up the political system of the individual states and made politicians responsive to a wider array of constituents and organizations. The major beneficiaries of this shift were the emerging middle-class and professional people in the growing cities and towns. These groups were instrumental in the reform movements to make state and municipal governments honest, efficient, and capable of providing public services. They filled the ranks of numerous civic, commercial, and professional organizations. By the 1920s they were coming into their own.

Having become institutionalized in the early 1900s, the one-party system dominated the region's political life, gave southern Democrats an influential voice in the national councils of their party and in Washington, and enabled white southerners to safeguard their most prized interests, including racial segregation and a large measure of autonomy in the conduct of state and local politics. The administrations of two Democratic presidents and the exigencies of two world wars brought new challenges and opportunities to southern political leaders, but those developments failed to introduce significant changes in the formal structure of southern politics or to alter the one-party system appreciably. Nevertheless, the party realignment of the 1930s, the enormous popularity of Franklin D. Roosevelt, and the creation of the New Deal coalition transformed the position of the South in the Democratic party and began in various ways to undermine the region's traditional politics. However undemocratic and conservative their politics may have been, the southern states made some progress in their efforts to cope with the realities of modern industrial life.

The Great Depression and the New Deal marked a decisive turning point in the economic and political history of the South. The long-term effects of these events were not always evident at the time. Thus, a recent study of North Carolina and the New Deal found that "conservative individualism" persisted in that state, along with what George B. Tindall has called "the vision of an organic traditional community with its personal relationships, its class distinctions, its habits of deference to the squirearchy."[1] But the depression and the New Deal brought about massive changes in southern life, including the breakdown and transformation of plantation agriculture, the vast migration off the land, and the disruption of such elements of the social order as the "network of dependency relationships" so basic to the region's labor system.[2] The developments of the 1930s slowly began to reorganize the workplace of the industrial South. By the latter part of the decade, the New Deal, having helped make the South a national problem, was moving to nationalize it. The war encouraged the integration of the South into the national economy, bringing the region an outpouring of federal expenditures and an infusion of new industry. Yet those years also confronted southerners with the reality of growing federal intrusion and the specter of outside interference in their long-established pattern of race relations. Meanwhile, beginning with the New Deal, the South demonstrated a growing fiscal dependency on federal disbursements.[3]

In 1948 the pressure of these events and the political sensibility of a new national administration precipitated a dramatic break in the South's longtime party loyalty. That break marked the beginning of a process that disrupted the Solid South, first in presidential elections and then more slowly in the electoral politics at lower levels. The South's open rebellion against the national Democratic party in 1948, its resort to massive resistance in an effort to preserve white unity in the face of federally mandated desegregation of the public schools, and the guerrilla warfare many southern Democrats waged against the liberal leaders and policies of their national party produced a period of great turbulence and uncertainty in the region's politics during the 1950s and 1960s, particularly in the deep South. And the collapse of massive resistance was followed by a time of painful accommodation for many white southerners and increasing evidence of Republican strength in Dixie. A significant feature of this troubled landscape was the appearance of a group of new "Whigs," who have been described as "southern politicians who numbered economic development as their first priority and who looked to the federal government to underwrite the effort."[4] These politicians were sensitive barometers of the vast economic and social changes that were transforming their region after World War II.

The metamorphosis of the South in the postwar period—the growth of advanced industrial production and modern marketing networks, the formation of new capital from internal and external sources, the continued out-migration of blacks, the in-migration of industrial entrepreneurs, businessmen, and professional people, the rapid rise of urban and suburban life, and the heightened attractiveness of the southern region in terms of economic opportunity, tourism, and permanent residency—has begun to have important consequences for southern politics. This regional transformation is related to a larger nationalizing process that is evident in such trends as the growing homogeneity of working conditions and consumer goods across the country, the development of national "labor markets" for many skilled trades and professions, and the increasing number of state and local government programs that receive funds and performance standards from federal agencies. These tendencies

have helped make the political system in the various southern states
more open and accessible, more pluralistic, and more urban centered.
At the same time, the expansion of the electorate, the increase in voter
turnout, and the unaccustomed competition between political parties
have given the politics of the southern states the kind of broad base
it has not had since the late nineteenth century. In short, the South
has experienced a political revolution during the last four decades. It
is not yet clear what structure the South's politics will assume in the
years ahead. The historian can only surmise that the southern states
are still in a period of political transition and that a more stable pattern
of politics will eventually assert itself.

For all its eccentricities, southern politics has been a national as
well as a sectional institution. It has been part of a national system,
and it has served national purposes. At one level the South functioned
as an economic, ethnocultural, and political antipode for the North.
The two regions, C. Vann Woodward writes, historically served each
other as inexhaustible scapegoats in "the old game of regional polem-
ics." "Back and forth the dialogue has gone, sometimes at shrill pitch
and sometimes in low key, depending on the temper of the times and
the moods and needs of the participants."[5] The South has also played
an essential part in the American party system and in the realignment
of parties within the system. Southern Democrats and northern Republicans maintained a sort of symbiotic relationship during the first
part of the twentieth century; they had reached a modus vivendi on
the treatment of blacks, and each party was dominant in its own
sphere. With the coming of the New Deal and the political transformation of the 1930s, a more active collaboration developed between
the two regional groups, first in the form of the conservative coalition
and later in the growth of Republicanism in the South, usually with
the help of southern Democrats. In a sense, the emergence of a strong
Republican party in the southern states represents another albeit delayed stage in the partisan realignment that began in the 1930s.

There is a reverse side to the South's experience in national politics. That is the way in which the pressure of national politics and
policies has shaped southern politics. One need only cite the far-
reaching decisions of the federal courts since 1944 or the momentous
effects of the civil rights laws of the 1960s to be convinced of this
point. Southern politics has also responded to the constraints of the
national party system. Although the South was able for decades to
benefit from its majority position in the Democratic party, it was
forced to make concessions to other regions, as in the 1920s, and
following the realignment of the 1930s, its role in the party was lessened. Ultimately, the Democratic party was no longer widely perceived by white southerners as a dependable bulwark against

unwanted intrusion from the outside. By that time, southerners could no longer agree upon the South's most vital political interests. The disruption of the Solid South began a process of nationalizing voting alignments in the region. One scholar has even asserted that George Wallace's third-party movement "corresponds not only to a nationalizing of southern politics, but a southernizing of national politics."[6] Meanwhile, the gradual development of two-party competition seems to have strengthened the discipline of national parties in the South and to have enhanced the region's role in national politics.

After a long life, the Solid South is dead! Born in the divisive and unsettled years of the late nineteenth century, it entered upon an extended period of political dominance, stability, and vitality. Then, as it grew older, the one-party system began to show signs of weakness; it became increasingly anachronistic, crotchety, and vulnerable to internal changes and outside pressures. Its final years were crisis-ridden and unhappy, marked by struggle to the very end.

Throughout its life, the Solid South was sustained by the region's distinctive political culture. The political culture says something about the character of political leadership in the South, the stress on personality in politics, and the role of the demagogue in southern affairs. Like so many other ideas and institutions associated with the origins of the New South, the culture of southern politics owed a great deal to the leadership of the Redeemers, whose rhetoric emphasized such values as white superiority and fraternity and community integrity. The ideal of the organic community was an important source of the conservatism in southern politics—of the southerner's defensiveness, suspicion of change, and adherence to traditional values. Other elements in this complex of political traditions included the heritage of social paternalism from the Old South, the personalism that suffused the folk culture, the emphasis of southern Protestantism on localism and the standards of personal morality, and the mythology of the Lost Cause and Reconstruction. These cultural distinctions have not entirely disappeared. While the Solid South has passed from the scene, many of its essential elements and much of the political culture in which it once flourished are still significant determinants of southern politics. Ironically, these very elements and this very culture played an important role in the death as well as the life of the Solid South.

Notes

Preface

1. V.O. Key, Jr., with the assistance of Alexander Heard, *Southern Politics in State and Nation* (New York, 1949), p. 315.
2. See, for example, Alexander P. Lamis, *The Two-Party South* (New York, 1984).
3. Walter Dean Burnham, "Party Systems and the Political Process," in William Nisbet Chambers and Walter Dean Burnham, eds., *The American Party Systems: Stages of Political Development* (New York, 1967), p. 284.
4. Fred Hobson, *Tell About the South: The Southern Rage to Explain* (Baton Rouge, 1983), p. 15.

1. Forging the Solid South

1. W.J. Cash, *The Mind of the South* (New York, 1941), p. 111.
2. Roy F. Nichols, "The Operation of American Democracy, 1861–1865: Some Questions," *Journal of Southern History* 25 (Feb. 1959): 43.
3. Robert Penn Warren, *The Legacy of the Civil War: Meditations on the Centennial* (New York, 1961), p. 14.
4. Quoted in C. Vann Woodward, *Origins of the New South, 1877–1913* (Baton Rouge, 1951), p. 100.
5. Joseph E. Brown to Rufus B. Bullock, Dec. 3, 1868, quoted in Numan V. Bartley, *The Creation of Modern Georgia* (Athens, 1983), p. 67.
6. Cash, *Mind of the South*, p. 111.
7. David M. Potter, *The Impending Crisis, 1848–1861* (New York, 1976), p. 469.
8. See Charles Reagan Wilson, *Baptized in Blood: The Religion of the Lost Cause, 1865–1920* (Athens, Ga., 1980), for an illuminating treatment of this theme.
9. Hilary A. Herbert et al., *Why the Solid South? Or, Reconstruction and Its Results* (Baltimore, 1890), p. 430.
10. Charles Chilton Pearson, *The Readjuster Movement in Virginia* (New Haven, 1917), p. 175.
11. James Tice Moore, "Redeemers Reconsidered: Change and Continuity in the Democratic South, 1870–1900," *Journal of Southern History* 44 (Aug. 1978): 362.
12. Woodward, *Origins of the New South*, p. 20.
13. Judson Clements Ward, Jr., "Georgia under the Bourbon Democracy, 1872–1890" (Ph.D. diss., University of North Carolina, 1947), p. iv.
14. Albert D. Kirwan, *Revolt of the Rednecks: Mississippi Politics, 1876–1925* (Lexington, Ky., 1951), p. 308.
15. I.A. Newby, *The South: A History* (New York, 1978), p. 302.
16. Gordon B. McKinney, "Southern Mountain Republicans and the Negro, 1865–1900," *Journal of Southern History* 41 (Nov. 1975): 493–94.
17. John Sherman to Robert O. Hebert, June 19, 1879, quoted in Vincent P. De Santis, "President Hayes's Southern Policy," *Journal of Southern History* 21 (Nov. 1955): 485.

18. Knoxville *Journal and Tribune*, quoted in Verton M. Queener, "The East Tennessee Republicans in State and Nation, 1870–1900," *Tennessee Historical Quarterly* 2 (June 1943): 111.

19. Edward C. Williamson, *Florida Politics in the Gilded Age, 1877–1893* (Gainesville, Fla., 1976), p. 45.

20. Quoted in Curtis Carroll Davis, "Very Well-Rounded Republican: The Several Lives of John S. Wise," *Virginia Magazine of History and Biography* 71 (Oct. 1963): 472.

21. The source of these calculations is J. Morgan Kousser, *The Shaping of Southern Politics: Suffrage Restriction and the Establishment of the One-Party South, 1880–1910* (New Haven, 1974), p. 27.

22. Woodward, *Origins of the New South*, p. 80.

23. Paul D. Escott, *Many Excellent People: Power and Privilege in North Carolina, 1850–1900* (Chapel Hill, 1985), p. 31.

24. Robert C. McMath, Jr., *Populist Vanguard: A History of the Southern Farmers' Alliance* (Chapel Hill 1975), p. 152.

25. Theodore Saloutos, *Farmer Movements in the South, 1865–1933* (Berkeley, Calif., 1960), p. 75 (first quotation); Cecil Johnson, ed., "A Letter from John Sharp Williams," *Journal of Mississippi History* 23 (Oct. 1961): 230 (second quotation).

26. Bartley, *Creation of Modern Georgia*, p. 95.

27. Sheldon Hackney, *Populism to Progressivism in Alabama* (Princeton, 1969), pp. 30–31.

28. Escott, *Many Excellent People*, p. 241.

29. Key, *Southern Politics*, p. 8.

30. Quoted in Vincent P. De Santis, *Republicans Face the Southern Question—The New Departure Years, 1877–1897* (Baltimore, 1959), p. 233.

31. C. Vann Woodward, *The Burden of Southern History* (Baton Rouge, 1960), p. 150.

32. James H. "Cyclone" Davis, quoted in Roscoe C. Martin, *The People's Party in Texas: A Study in Third Party Politics* (Austin, 1933), p. 184.

33. Kousser, *Shaping of Southern Politics*, pp. 11, 238.

2. The One-Party System

1. William A. Anderson, quoted in Raymond H. Pulley, *Old Virginia Restored: An Interpretation of the Progressive Impulse, 1870–1930* (Charlottesville, Va., 1968), p. 128.

2. Key, *Southern Politics*, p. 425.

3. Ibid., pp. 416–17.

4. Quoted in "The Progress of the 'Direct Primary' Reform," *World's Work* 6 (Aug. 1903): 3715–16.

5. Quoted in L.M. Holland, *The Direct Primary in Georgia* (Urbana, 1949), p. 55.

6. George Brown Tindall, *The Emergence of the New South, 1913–1945* (Baton Rouge, 1967), pp. 20–21.

7. Cortez A.M. Ewing, *Primary Elections in the South: A Study in Uniparty Politics* (Norman, Okla., 1953), p. 56.

8. The following discussion of the pattern of state politics in the early twentieth-century South, as well as the treatment of national politics in the next chapter, relies heavily upon the author's *Southern Progressivism: The Reconciliation of Progress and Tradition* (Knoxville, 1983), pp. 36–107.

9. Hackney, *Populism to Progressivism in Alabama*, p. 254.

10. In 1903 Leo Frank was indicted and tried for allegedly assaulting and murdering thirteen-year-old Mary Phagan, an employee of his Atlanta pencil factory. Tom Watson led the outcry against Frank, whom he described as a "typical young libertine

Jew." Watson's virulent charges probably contributed to the public clamor against Frank and to his conviction and subsequent lynching at the hands of a mob in 1915.

11. The outcome in statewide primaries was determined not by direct popular vote but by a majority of county-unit votes. The candidate with a plurality of votes in each county received that county's unit votes. In 1910 Georgia had 147 counties, each of which was allotted at least two unit votes. The relatively few large counties received four or six unit votes, depending on the size of their population. This system was strongly biased against the state's cities and larger counties.

12. James C. Derieux, "Crawling toward the Promised Land," *Survey* 48 (April 29, 1922): 178.

13. David L. Carlton, *Mill and Town in South Carolina, 1880-1920* (Baton Rouge, 1982), p. 221.

14. Key, *Southern Politics*, p. 103.

15. E. Merton Coulter, quoted in Joseph Frazier Wall, *Henry Watterson: Reconstructed Rebel* (New York, 1956), p. 76.

16. Lee A. Dew, " 'On a Slow Train through Arkansaw'—The Negative Image of Arkansas in the Early Twentieth Century," *Arkansas Historical Quarterly* 39 (Summer 1980): 125-35 (quotation on p. 126).

17. "The Gentleman from Arkansas," *Public Opinion* 40 (April 21, 1906): 488.

18. Rupert B. Vance, "A Karl Marx for Hill Billies: Portrait of a Southern Leader," *Social Forces* 9 (Dec. 1930): 180.

19. Raymond Arsenault, *The Wild Ass of the Ozarks: Jeff Davis and the Social Bases of Southern Politics* (Philadelphia, 1984), p. 118.

20. M.G. Cunniff, "Texas and the Texans," *World's Work* 11 (March 1906): 7270.

21. Worth Robert Miller, "Building a Progressive Coalition in Texas: The Populist-Reform Democrat Rapprochement, 1900-1907," *Journal of Southern History* 52 (May 1986): 163.

22. James R. Green, *Grass-Roots Socialism: Radical Movements in the Southwest, 1895-1943* (Baton Rouge, 1978), pp. xiv, xvii.

3. In the National Arena

1. Walter Dean Burnham, "The Changing Shape of the American Political Universe," *American Political Science Review* 59 (March 1965): 25.

2. Numan V. Bartley, "The South and Sectionalism in American Politics," *Journal of Politics* 38 (Aug. 1976): 254.

3. William Garrott Brown, "The South in National Politics," *South Atlantic Quarterly* 9 (April 1910): 106.

4. "Why Not Southern Democratic Leadership?" *World's Work* 4 (Aug. 1902): 2367.

5. John Sharp Williams to Woodrow Wilson, March 31, 1914, in Arthur S. Link and associates, eds., *The Papers of Woodrow Wilson*, vol. 29 (Princeton, 1979), p. 388.

6. James Calvin Hemphill, "The Conservatism of the South," quoted in ibid., vol. 16 (Princeton, 1973), p. 287.

7. Woodward, *Origins of the New South*, p. 469.

8. Henry D. Clayton to William Jennings Bryan, Jan. 22, 1908, Henry De Lamar Clayton Papers, University of Alabama Library.

9. Quoted in "A Southern Democratic Leader?" *Public Opinion* 40 (March 31, 1906): 393.

10. Ulrich B. Phillips, "Conservatism and Progress in the Cotton Belt," *South Atlantic Quarterly* 3 (Jan. 1904): 4.

11. "New Political Sentiment in the South," *World's Work* 1 (Dec. 1900): 134; "The

Sorrow of the South," ibid. 9 (Dec. 1904): 5563–64; "Sectional Self-Consciousness," ibid. 14 (Sept. 1907): 9277.

12. Henry A. Page to Walter Hines Page, Oct. 8, 1901, Walter Hines Page Papers, Houghton Library, Harvard University

13. Edwin Mims, "President Theodore Roosevelt," *South Atlantic Quarterly* 4 (Jan. 1905): 48–62; Alexander J. McKelway, "The Progressive South," unpublished manuscript (1914), Alexander J. McKelway Papers, Manuscripts Division, Library of Congress.

14. Walter Hines Page to William Howard Taft, Nov. 7, 1908, Jan. 5, 1909, Page Papers.

15. T.C. Carter to Jacob McGavock Dickinson, Feb. 24, 1909, Jacob McGavock Dickinson Papers, Tennessee State Library and Archives.

16. Richard Evelyn Byrd to Woodrow Wilson, Nov. 10, 1910, in Arthur S. Link and associates, eds., *The Papers of Woodrow Wilson*, vol. 22 (Princeton, 1976), p. 20.

17. Edwin A. Alderman, "A Virginia Democrat," *Harper's Weekly* 55 (May 6, 1911): 7.

18. Arthur S. Link, *Wilson: The Road to the White House* (Princeton, 1947), p. 171.

19. Benjamin F. Long to Walter Hines Page, March 15, 1913, Page Papers.

20. Cone Johnson to Woodrow Wilson, Dec. 17, 1912, in Arthur S. Link and associates, eds., *The Papers of Woodrow Wilson*, vol. 25 (Princeton, 1978), p. 603.

21. Arthur S. Link, "Woodrow Wilson and the Democratic Party," *Review of Politics* 18 (April 1956): 148.

22. Burton Ira Kaufman, "Virginia Politics and the Wilson Movement, 1910–1914," *Virginia Magazine of History and Biography* 77 (Jan. 1969): 16.

23. Morton Sosna, "The South in the Saddle: Racial Politics during the Wilson Years," *Wisconsin Magazine of History* 54 (Autumn 1970): 30. The key words in this conclusion are "the direct impact of race consciousness upon national politics." It should be noted that racist ideas were pervasive throughout the nation during this period.

24. Woodrow Wilson to Edith Bolling Galt, Aug. 13, 1915, in Arthur S. Link and associates, eds., *The Papers of Woodrow Wilson*, vol. 34 (Princeton, 1980), p. 180.

25. Tindall, *Emergence of the New South*, p. 40.

26. Richard L. Watson, Jr., "Principle, Party, and Constituency: The North Carolina Congressional Delegation, 1917–1919," *North Carolina Historical Review* 56 (July 1979): 323.

27. George B. Rose to A.H. Nichols, Dec. 22, 1920, George B. Rose Papers, Arkansas Historical Commission, Little Rock.

28. Quoted in Tindall, *Emergence of the New South*, p. 169.

29. Bartley, *Creation of Modern Georgia*, p. 169.

30. Claude Kitchin to E.S. Candler, Jr., Nov. 1, 1915, Claude Kitchin Papers, Southern Historical Collection, University of North Carolina Library.

31. Quoted in Richard L. Watson, Jr., "A Testing Time for Southern Congressional Leadership: The War Crisis of 1917–1918," *Journal of Southern History* 44 (Feb. 1978): 37.

32. Quoted in ibid., p. 8.

33. Quoted in David Burner, *The Politics of Provincialism: The Democratic Party in Transition, 1918–1932* (New York, 1967), p. 115.

34. Ibid., p. 224.

35. Tindall, *Emergence of the New South*, p. 247.

36. Quoted in Norman D. Brown, *Hood, Bonnet, and Little Brown Jug: Texas Politics, 1921–1928* (College Station, Tex., 1984), p. 416.

37. This was not true in the case of Louisiana, where religion seems to have been the primary issue. Although Smith carried the state handily, his strongest support came from the Catholic and antiprohibition parishes; he was weakest in the Protestant

parishes, some of which had black majorities. See Steven D. Zink, "Cultural Conflict and the 1928 Presidential Campaign in Louisiana," *Southern Studies* 17 (Summer 1978): 175-97.

38. Quoted in Brown, *Hood, Bonnet, and Little Brown Jug*, p. 409.

39. Seth Shepard McKay, *Texas Politics, 1906-1944: With Special Reference to the German Counties* (Lubbock, Tex., 1952), pp. 178-79.

4. The Classic Period of Southern Politics

1. Tindall, *Emergence of the New South*, p. 219.

2. Daniel Joseph Singal, "Broadus Mitchell and the Persistence of New South Thought," *Journal of Southern History* 45 (Aug. 1979): 356.

3. Danney Goble, "Oklahoma Politics and the Sooner Electorate," in Anne Hodges Morgan and H. Wayne Morgan, eds., *Oklahoma: New Views of the Forty-Sixth State* (Norman, 1982), p. 150.

4. Reinhard H. Luthin, *American Demagogues: Twentieth Century* (Boston, 1954), p. 157.

5. Quoted in Brown, *Hood, Bonnet, and Little Brown Jug*, p. 97.

6. Luthin, *American Demagogues*, p. 164.

7. Quoted in Brown, *Hood, Bonnet, and Little Brown Jug*, p. 96.

8. Quoted in ibid., p. 345.

9. Quoted in Luthin, *American Demagogues*, p. 46.

10. Louis B. Wright, *Barefoot in Arcadia: Memories of a More Innocent Era* (Columbia, S.C., 1974), pp. 134-35.

11. Derieux, "Crawling toward the Promised Land," p. 175.

12. Key, *Southern Politics*, p. 160.

13. Cash, *Mind of the South*, p. 284.

14. T. Harry Williams, *Romance and Realism in Southern Politics* (Athens, Ga., 1961), p. 63.

15. Cash, *Mind of the South*, p. 285.

16. Arthur M. Schlesinger, Jr., *The Age of Roosevelt: The Politics of Upheaval* (Boston, 1960), p. 48.

17. Cash, *Mind of the South*, p. 284.

18. Hugh Davis Graham, ed., *Huey Long* (Englewood Cliffs, N.J., 1970), p. 2.

19. T. Harry Williams, "The Gentleman from Louisiana: Demagogue or Democrat," *Journal of Southern History* 26 (Feb. 1960): 17.

20. Key, *Southern Politics*, p. 70.

21. Ibid., p. 107.

22. Allan A. Michie and Frank Ryhlick, *Dixie Demagogues* (New York, 1939), p. 182.

23. Quoted in William Anderson, *The Wild Man from Sugar Creek: The Political Career of Eugene Talmadge* (Baton Rouge, 1975), p. 226.

24. Sarah McCulloh Lemmon, "Eugene Talmadge," in David C. Roller and Robert W. Twyman, eds., *The Encyclopedia of Southern History* (Baton Rouge, 1979), p. 1175.

25. Bartley, *Creation of Modern Georgia*, p. 175.

26. Alexander Heard, "Horseback Summary Statement of Political Power Arrangement within the Democratic Party in Alabama," Jan. 12, 1947, Southern Politics Collection, Vanderbilt University Library.

27. Tindall, *Emergence of the New South*, pp. 647-48.

28. Key, *Southern Politics*, p. 255.

29. David R. Colburn and Richard K. Scher, *Florida's Gubernatorial Politics in the Twentieth Century* (Tallahassee, 1980), p. 73.

5. The South and the New Deal

1. Frank Freidel, *F.D.R. and the South* (Baton Rouge, 1965), pp. 1–2.

2. David M. Potter, *The South and the Concurrent Majority* (Baton Rouge, 1972), p. 68.

3. Earl Black and Merle Black, *Politics and Society in the South* (Cambridge, Mass., 1987), p. 214.

4. H.C. Nixon, "The Changing Political Philosophy of the South," *Annals of the American Academy of Political and Social Science* 153 (Jan. 1931): 247.

5. Per capita federal expenditures by region during the years 1933–1939 were West $306, Midwest $224, Northeast $196, and South $189. See Gavin Wright, *Old South, New South: Revolutions in the Southern Economy since the Civil War* (New York, 1986), p. 260.

6. Tindall, *Emergence of the New South*, p. 609.

7. Travis M. Adams, "The Arkansas Congressional Delegation during the New Deal, 1933–1936" (M.A. thesis, Vanderbilt University, 1962).

8. Edward L. Schapsmeier and Frederick H. Schapsmeier, "Farm Policy from FDR to Eisenhower: Southern Democrats and the Politics of Agriculture," *Agricultural History* 53 (Jan. 1979): 354.

9. Turner Catledge, *My Life and "The Times"* (New York, 1971), pp. 67–68.

10. Quoted in Michie and Ryhlick, *Dixie Demagogues*, p. 184.

11. Max Freedman, ed., *Roosevelt and Frankfurter: Their Correspondence, 1928–1945* (Boston, 1967), pp. 282–83.

12. Walter White, *A Man Called White: The Autobiography of Walter White* (New York, 1948), pp. 169–70.

13. George Wolfskill and John A. Hudson, *All But the People: Franklin D. Roosevelt and His Critics, 1933–1939* (New York, 1964), p. 257.

14. John Robert Moore, "Senator Josiah W. Bailey and the 'Conservative Manifesto' of 1937," *Journal of Southern History* 31 (Feb. 1965): 21–39 (quotation on p. 34).

15. Quoted in James T. Patterson, "The Failure of Party Realignment in the South, 1937–1939," *Journal of Politics* 27 (Aug. 1965): 602–3.

16. Marian D. Irish, "The Southern One-Party System and National Politics," *Journal of Politics* 4 (Feb. 1942): 90.

17. Anthony J. Badger, *North Carolina and the New Deal* (Raleigh, 1981), p. 96.

18. George E. Mowry, *Another Look at the Twentieth-Century South* (Baton Rouge, 1973), p. 60.

19. Quoted in James A. Hodges, "The New Deal and the South: The Limits of Reform," paper presented at the annual meeting of the Southern Historical Association, Nov. 1972.

20. David S. Allen to James F. Byrnes, March 6, 1935, James F. Byrnes Papers, Clemson University Library.

21. Roger Biles, *Memphis in the Great Depression* (Knoxville, 1986), p. 86.

22. Alan Brinkley, "The New Deal and Southern Politics," in James C. Cobb and Michael V. Namorato, eds., *The New Deal and the South* (Jackson, Miss., 1984), p. 107.

23. Ibid., p. 111.

24. Cash, *Mind of the South*, p. 364.

25. Quoted in Ralph J. Bunche, *The Political Status of the Negro in the Age of FDR*, ed. Dewey W. Grantham (Chicago, 1973), p. 429.

26. See Numan V. Bartley, "The Era of the New Deal as a Turning Point in Southern History," in Cobb and Namorato, *New Deal and the South*, pp. 135–46, for a suggestive discussion of these points.

27. Quoted in Robert J. Bailey, "Theodore G. Bilbo and the Senatorial Election of 1934," *Southern Quarterly* 10 (Oct. 1971): 96.

28. Quoted in Roland Young, *Congressional Politics in the Second World War* (New York, 1956), p. 84.

29. Julius Turner, *Party and Constituency: Pressures on Congress* (Baltimore, 1951), pp. 134–36.

30. Ellis Gibbs Arnall, *The Shore Dimly Seen* (Philadelphia, 1946), p. 101.

31. Quoted in Fletcher M. Green, "Resurgent Southern Sectionalism, 1933–1955," *North Carolina Historical Review* 33 (April 1956): 225.

32. Quoted in Robert A. Garson, *The Democratic Party and the Politics of Sectionalism, 1941–1948* (Baton Rouge, 1974), p. 48.

33. Leon C. Phillips, "A Southern Democrat Renounces the New Deal Party," *Manufacturers' Record* 112 (Aug. 1943): 32–33.

34. Gessner T. McCorvey, "Democratic Party Regulations Explained," *Alabama Historical Quarterly* 6 (Spring 1944): 66.

35. Quoted in John Morton Blum, *V Was for Victory: Politics and American Culture during World War II* (New York, 1976), p. 193.

36. Quoted in Garson, *Democratic Party and the Politics of Sectionalism*, p. 12.

37. William D. Barnard, *Dixiecrats and Democrats: Alabama Politics, 1942–1950* (University, Ala., 1974), p. 20.

38. Garson, *Democratic Party and the Politics of Sectionalism*, p. 231.

39. Ibid., pp. xi, 316.

40. Robert J. Steamer, "Southern Disaffection with the National Democratic Party," in Allan P. Sindler, ed., *Change in the Contemporary South* (Durham, N.C., 1963), p. 170.

41. William C. Havard, Jr., "Southern Politics: Old and New Style," in Louis D. Rubin, Jr., ed., *The American South: Portrait of a Culture* (Baton Rouge, 1980), p. 38.

6. The Politics of Massive Resistance

1. Quoted in Numan V. Bartley, *The Rise of Massive Resistance: Race and Politics in the South during the 1950's* (Baton Rouge, 1969), p. 41.

2. Ibid., p. 46.

3. For the role of "entrepreneurial individualists," see Black and Black, *Politics and Society in the South*, pp. 27–34, 45–46.

4. Bartley, *Rise of Massive Resistance*, p. 42.

5. Numan V. Bartley and Hugh D. Graham, *Southern Politics and the Second Reconstruction* (Baltimore, 1975), p. 40.

6. Grover C. Hall, Jr., quoted in George E. Sims, *The Little Man's Big Friend: James E. Folsom in Alabama Politics, 1946–1958* (University, Ala., 1985), p. 140.

7. Key, *Southern Politics*, p. 255.

8. Bartley and Graham, *Southern Politics and the Second Reconstruction*, p. 46.

9. Key, *Southern Politics*, p. 252.

10. Goble, "Oklahoma Politics and the Sooner Electorate," p. 160.

11. John Ed Pearce, *Divide and Dissent: Kentucky Politics, 1930–1963* (Lexington, Ky., 1987), p. 60.

12. Charles P. Roland, *The Improbable Era: The South since World War II* (Lexington, Ky., 1975), p. 36; Robert Fredrick Burk, *The Eisenhower Administration and Black Civil Rights* (Knoxville, 1984), p. 143.

13. Thomas D. Clark, *The Emerging South*, 2d ed. (New York, 1968), p. 200.

14. Albert P. Blaustein and Clarence Clyde Ferguson, Jr., *Desegregation and the Law: The Meaning and Effect of the School Segregation Cases*, 2d ed. (New York, 1962), p. 212.

15. Bartley, *Rise of Massive Resistance*, p. 83.

16. Quoted in David R. Goldfield, *Promised Land: The South since 1945* (Arlington Heights, Ill., 1987), p. 79.

17. These laws provided for the individual assignment of pupils to schools and established prerequisites for the use of local administrators in making such placements. They also created a system of administrative remedies for parents dissatisfied with the results.

18. Bartley, *Rise of Massive Resistance*, pp. 109–10.

19. Ibid., p. 115.

20. Ibid., pp. 116–17.

21. William P. Cooper to Estes Kefauver, June 5, 1957, Estes Kefauver Papers, University of Tennessee Library.

22. Quoted in Bartley, *Rise of Massive Resistance*, p. 121.

23. Ibid., p. 213.

24. Ibid., pp. 17–20. Bartley describes the politicians and political activists who led the massive resistance campaign as "neo-bourbons." Their social, economic, and political outlook, he writes, was "in the tradition of nineteenth century bourbonism."

25. Anthony Lewis and the *New York Times, Portrait of a Decade: The Second American Revolution* (New York, 1964), p. 57.

7. The Second Reconstruction

1. Anniston (Ala.) *Star*, Feb. 28, 1960, quoted in Gary W. Reichard, "Democrats, Civil Rights, and Electoral Strategies in the 1950s," *Congress & the Presidency* 13 (Spring 1986): 71.

2. M. Lee Smith, "The Nixon Campaign in the South: A Chapter in the Rise of a Two-Party South" (Honors essay, Vanderbilt University, 1964), pp. 47–48.

3. Quoted in O. Douglas Weeks, *Texas in the 1960 Presidential Election* (Austin, 1961), p. 38.

4. Six of the eleven Alabama electors voted for Byrd. One Oklahoma elector also cast his ballot for the Virginian. A movement in several southern states to make use of a "free elector" scheme lost strength with Lyndon Johnson's nomination for vice-president.

5. Quoted in Reichard, "Democrats, Civil Rights, and Electoral Strategies," p. 73.

6. Richard B. Russell to Harvey J. Kennedy, Nov. 17, 1960, Richard B. Russell Papers, University of Georgia Library.

7. Richard B. Russell to James B. Burch, Nov. 9, 1960, Russell Papers.

8. Quoted in Carl M. Brauer, *John F. Kennedy and the Second Reconstruction* (New York, 1977), p. 62.

9. John Egerton, *A Mind to Stay Here: Profiles from the South* (New York, 1970), p. 32.

10. Meanwhile, the proportion of southern whites with pro-Democratic party images declined from 62 to 52 percent. See Donald R. Matthews and James W. Prothro, *Negroes and the New Southern Politics* (New York, 1966), pp. 385–86.

11. Quoted in Roman Heleniak, "Lyndon Johnson in New Orleans," *Louisiana History* 21 (Summer 1980): 274.

12. In 1962 Republicans won four new House seats in the South, one each in Florida, North Carolina, Tennessee, and Texas.

13. Although the insurgents refused this token recognition, they were able to tell their story to the nation during nationally televised credentials hearings. The credentials committee's recommendation, that in the future a state must ensure that "all voters, regardless of race, color, creed or national origin, will have the opportunity to participate fully in party affairs," was one of the antecedents of the delegate-selection-

reforms adopted at the Democratic national convention in 1972. See Jack Bass and Walter DeVries, *The Transformation of Southern Politics: Social Change and Political Consequence since 1945* (New York, 1976), pp. 204-5.

14. Heleniak, "Lyndon Johnson in New Orleans," p. 269.

15. Bernard Cosman, *Five States for Goldwater: Continuity and Change in Southern Voting Patterns* (University, Ala., 1966), p. 55.

16. Neil R. McMillen, "Black Enfranchisement in Missisippi: Federal Enforcement and Black Protest in the 1960s," *Journal of Southern History* 43 (Aug. 1977): 364.

17. Ibid., p. 367.

18. Quoted in Harvard Sitkoff, *The Struggle for Black Equality, 1954-1980* (New York, 1981), p. 188.

19. McMillen, "Black Enfranchisement in Mississippi," p. 371.

20. Black and Black, *Politics and Society in the South*, p. 136.

21. Matthews and Prothro, *Negroes and the New Southern Politics*, p. vii.

22. Charles Sallis and John Quincy Adams, "Desegregation in Jackson, Mississippi," in Elizabeth Jacoway and David R. Colburn, eds., *Southern Businessmen and Desegregation* (Baton Rouge, 1982), p. 247.

23. Kenneth E. Harrell, "Edward Thompson Breathitt, Jr.," in Lowell H. Harrison, ed., *Kentucky's Governors, 1792-1985* (Lexington, Ky., 1985), p. 171.

24. Bartley and Graham, *Southern Politics and the Second Reconstruction*, p. 117.

25. Perry H. Howard, "Louisiana: Resistance and Change," in William C. Havard, ed., *The Changing Politics of the South* (Baton Rouge, 1972), p. 562.

26. Bartley, *Creation of Modern Georgia*, p. 196.

27. Joseph L. Bernd, "Georgia: Static and Dynamic," in Havard, *Changing Politics of the South*, p. 344.

28. Marshall Frady, *Wallace* (New York, 1968), p. vii.

29. Jack Bass and Walter DeVries interview with Bill Baxley, July 9, 1974, Southern Historical Collection, University of North Carolina Library.

30. Frady, *Wallace*, p. 1.

31. Ibid., p. 9.

32. Jack Bass and Walter DeVries interview with George C. Wallace, July 15, 1974, Southern Historical Collection.

33. Donald S. Strong, "Alabama: Transition and Alienation," in Havard, *Changing Politics of the South*, p. 452.

34. Richard B. Russell to John H. Dillard, Oct. 30, 1968, Russell Papers.

35. Black and Black, *Politics and Society in the South*, p. 308.

8. Toward a Two-Party South

1. Charles N. Fortenberry and F. Glenn Abney, "Mississippi: Unreconstructed and Unredeemed," in Havard, *Changing Politics of the South*, p. 500; James R. Scales and Danney Goble, *Oklahoma Politics: A History* (Norman, 1982), p. 343.

2. Quoted in George Brown Tindall, *The Disruption of the Solid South* (Athens, Ga., 1972), p. 71.

3. The Senate rejected two of these nominations: Clement F. Haynsworth, Jr., of South Carolina and G. Harrold Carswell of Florida. It confirmed the nomination of Lewis F. Powell of Virginia.

4. Reg Murphy and Hal Gulliver, *The Southern Strategy* (New York, 1971), p. 3.

5. Earl Black, *Southern Governors and Civil Rights: Racial Segregation as a Campaign Issue in the Second Reconstruction* (Cambridge, Mass., 1976), p. 158.

6. Alexander P. Lamis, *The Two-Party South* (New York, 1984), p. 5.

7. Jack Nelson, "South from the Potomac," in Frank E. Smith, ed., *I'll Still Take My Stand* (Vicksburg, Miss., 1980), p. 9.

8. Lamis, *Two-Party South*, p. 120.

9. Bartley, *Creation of Modern Georgia* (Athens, 1983), p. 206.

10. Quoted in Lamis, *Two-Party South*, p. 111.

11. Quoted in Numan V. Bartley, "1940 to the Present," in Kenneth Coleman, ed., *A History of Georgia* (Athens, 1977), p. 402.

12. Numan V. Bartley, *Jimmy Carter and the Politics of the New South* (St. Louis, 1979), p. 11.

13. Nashville *Tennessean*, Dec. 26, 1976.

14. Jack Bass, "V.O. Key Revisited," *South Atlantic Urban Studies* 3 (1979): 267.

15. One of the other Senate seats was held by Harry F. Byrd, Jr., who classified himself as an independent but usually voted with the Republicans.

16. Charlotte *Observer*, Aug. 8, 1986.

17. Quoted in Lamis, *Two-Party South*, p. 70.

18. Bass and DeVries, *Transformation of Southern Politics*, p. 75.

19. Jack Bass and Walter DeVries interview with Robert Shaw, April 24, 1974, Southern Historical Collection.

20. Black and Black, *Politics and Society in the South*, p. 230.

21. John R. Petrocik, "Realignment: The South, New Party Coalitions and the Elections of 1984 and 1986," in *Where's the Party? An Assessment of Changes in Party Loyalty and Party Coalitions in the 1980s* (Washington, D.C., 1987), p. 52.

22. Matthews and Prothro, *Negroes and the New Southern Politics*, p. 481.

23. Quoted in Goldfield, *Promised Land*, p. 192.

24. H.C. Nixon, "The Southern Legislature and Legislation," in Taylor Cole and John H. Hallowell, eds., *The Southern Political Scene, 1938-1948* (Gainesville, Fla., 1948), p. 412.

25. Black and Black, *Politics and Society in the South*, p. 23.

26. Ibid., p. 58.

27. Earl Black and Merle Black, "The Partial Transformation of Southern Democracy: State Intraparty Politics, 1920-85," paper presented at the annual meeting of the American Political Science Association, Aug. 1986.

28. John Whelan, "Interest Groups in Virginia: A New Look for a 'Political Museum Piece,' " paper presented at the annual meeting of the Southern Political Science Association, Nov. 1986.

29. In the 1980s Helms, operating through a powerful North Carolina–based political action committee known as the National Congressional Club, became an active leader in a nationwide campaign to register conservative Americans, elect candidates of the "New Right," and support the policies of the so-called Moral Majority. This extreme factionalism led to a growing clash in various parts of the country between Republican "establishment" politicians and the "Religious Right."

30. Scales and Goble, *Oklahoma Politics*, p. 343.

31. Bass and DeVries, *Transformation of Southern Politics*, p. 150.

32. Fortenberry and Abney, "Mississippi: Unreconstructed and Unredeemed," p. 504.

33. In the early 1940s, Numan V. Bartley writes, "the principal purpose of state government in Georgia as elsewhere in the South was the protection and promotion of white supremacy and social stability; in the early 1970s its chief function was the protection and promotion of economic and industrial progress." Bartley, *Creation of Modern Georgia*, p. 179.

Epilogue

1. Badger, *North Carolina and the New Deal*, pp. 96–97; George Brown Tindall, *The Persistent Tradition in New South Politics* (Baton Rouge, 1975), p. 22.

2. See Bartley, "Era of the New Deal," pp. 138–41.

3. Bruce J. Schulman, " 'This Truly American Section': Federal Policy and the Nationalization of the South, 1938–1960," paper presented at the annual meeting of the American Historical Association, Dec. 1986.

4. Ibid., p. 12.

5. C. Vann Woodward, *American Counterpoint: Slavery and Racism in the North-South Dialogue* (Boston, 1971), pp. 6–7.

6. Walter Dean Burnham, *Critical Elections and the Mainsprings of American Politics* (New York, 1970), p. 189.

Bibliographical Essay

In considering the sources for a historical study of southern politics in the twentieth century, one quickly discovers two things of great importance. The first is the abundance and scope of such sources, ranging from a variety of primary materials to all manner of scholarly monographs and other secondary works. The second compelling aspect of the question is the dynamic character of the scholarship, especially during the last quarter-century. Those working in this field have asked new questions and emphasized new themes. Their contributions reflect more adequate research and stronger analysis than was true of earlier scholars. This literature is so extensive, particularly in the form of journal articles, that it is almost impossible to read it all. Contributors include not only historians but political scientists, sociologists, political journalists, and other writers. This book leans heavily on the work of these writers. Without their contributions this study could not have been written.

The commentary that follows is not a comprehensive evaluation of sources used in the writing of this book. It is intended, instead, to identify the major sources on which I have relied, to suggest the nature of the extensive monographic literature that bears on modern southern politics, and to comment on the most significant interpretations advanced by scholars and other interpreters. No attempt is made to evaluate the vast literature in scholarly journals. I hope the essay will introduce readers to the large and impressive body of books and monographs devoted to the southern political experience during the last hundred years.

Contemporary Sources

Although it was impossible for me to undertake a systematic examination of manuscript collections for this project, I have used a fairly representative group of personal and public papers. Earlier research led me to make a search in the various state archives for the letterbooks and official papers of southern governors during the progressive era. Among other manuscript collections consulted for this work were those of the following individuals:

Edwin A. Alderman, University of Virginia Library.
Josiah W. Bailey, Duke University Library.
William Watts Ball, Duke University Library.
John H. Bankhead, Alabama Department of Archives and History.
William D. Bankhead, Alabama Department of Archives and History.
Alben W. Barkley, University of Kentucky Library.
Allen Caperton Braxton, University of Virginia Library.
Charles Hillman Brough, University of Arkansas Library.
Napoleon B. Broward, University of Florida Library.
Edgar A. Brown, Clemson University Library.
William Garrott Brown, Duke University Library.
Albert Sidney Burleson, University of Texas Library.
James F. Byrnes, Clemson University Library.
Edward Ward Carmack, University of North Carolina Library.
Walter Clark, North Carolina Department of Archives and History.
Laura Clay, University of Kentucky Library.
Henry De Lamar Clayton, University of Alabama Library.
Grover Cleveland, Library of Congress.
Horace Chilton, University of Texas Library.
Oscar B. Colquitt, University of Texas Library.
Braxton B. Comer, University of North Carolina Library.
Henry Groves Connor, University of North Carolina Library.
John W. Daniel, University of Virginia Library.
Josephus Daniels, Library of Congress and University of North Carolina Library.
Jeff Davis, University of Arkansas Library.
Jacob McGavock Dickinson, Tennessee State Library and Archives.
J. Taylor Ellyson, University of Virginia Library.
Rebecca Latimer Felton, University of Georgia Library.
Henry D. Flood, Library of Congress.
Edward J. Gay, Louisiana State University Library.
Carter Glass, University of Virginia Library.
J. Bryan Grimes, University of North Carolina Library.
James Hay, University of Virginia Library.
James C. Hemphill, Duke University Library.
Richmond P. Hobson, Library of Congress.
James S. Hogg, University of Texas Library.
Cordell Hull, Library of Congress.
Estes Kefauver, University of Tennessee Library.
Claude Kitchin, University of North Carolina Library.
Ladislas Lazaro, Louisiana State University Library.
Ralph McGill, Emory University Library.
Alexander J. McKelway, Library of Congress.
Jeff: McLemore, University of Texas Library.
Thomas Nelson Page, Duke University Library.
Walter Hines Page, Harvard University Library.
John M. Parker, University of North Carolina Library.
Theodore Roosevelt, Library of Congress.

Richard B. Russell, University of Georgia Library.
Hoke Smith, University of Georgia Library.
Mendel L. Smith, University of South Carolina Library.
Augustus O. Stanley, University of Kentucky Library.
Oliver D. Street, University of Alabama Library.
Henry St. George Tucker, University of North Carolina Library.
Oscar W. Underwood, Alabama Department of Archives and History.
Oswald Garrison Villard, Harvard University Library.
Thomas E. Watson, University of North Carolina Library.
John Sharp Williams, Library of Congress.
Edgar S. Wilson, Mississippi Department of Archives and History.
Woodrow Wilson, Library of Congress.

Three extensive interviewing projects have contributed to my understanding of recent southern politics. The first of these are the transcripts of over 500 interviews conducted in 1947 and 1948 by Alexander Heard and Donald S. Strong for V.O. Key's *Southern Politics in State and Nation* (1949). These transcripts are located in the Vanderbilt University Library. Another set of interviews was carried out during the years 1973–75 by Jack Bass and Walter DeVries for their book, *The Transformation of Southern Politics: Social Change and Political Consequence since 1945* (1976). The transcripts of these interviews, numbering more than 300, are in the Southern Historical Collection, University of North Carolina. The third group is made up of interviews and observations made in the late 1950s and early 1960s by the journalist Benjamin Muse, who traveled through the South for the Southern Regional Council's Southern Leadership Project. This collection is housed in the Robert W. Woodruff Library of the Atlanta University Center. A valuable published collection of interviews can be found in Ralph J. Bunche, *The Political Status of the Negro in the Age of FDR*, ed. Dewey W. Grantham (Chicago: Univ. of Chicago Press, 1973). In preparing this working paper for Gunnar Myrdal's *An American Dilemma*, Bunche drew upon more than 500 interviews conducted by his assistants with black and white southerners in 1939 and 1940.

A number of southern states, including Kentucky and North Carolina, attempt to publish the public addresses and papers of their governors as soon as possible after they leave office. The *Public Papers of the Presidents of the United States* (Washington, D.C.: U.S. Government Printing Office, 1961–), beginning with the administration of Herbert Hoover but excluding that of Franklin D. Roosevelt, provide a source of considerable importance for the South in national politics. For other examples of useful published documents, see Elting E. Morison et al., eds., *The Letters of Theodore Roosevelt*, 8 vols. (Cambridge: Harvard Univ. Press, 1951–54); Charles Seymour, ed., *The Intimate Papers of Colonel House*, 4 vols. (Boston: Houghton Mifflin, 1926–28); Arthur S. Link and associates, eds., *The Papers of Woodrow Wilson*, vols. 1–58 (Princeton: Princeton Univ. Press, 1966–88); Samuel I. Rosenman, ed., *The Public Papers and Addresses of Franklin D. Roosevelt*, 13 vols. (New York: Random House, 1938–50); Aubrey Lee Brooks and Hugh Talmage Lefler, eds., *The Papers of Walter Clark*, 2 vols. (Chapel Hill: Univ. of North Carolina Press, 1948–50); and Robert C. Cotner, ed., *Addresses and State Papers of James Stephen Hogg* (Austin: Univ. of Texas Press, 1951).

Several regional and national newspapers were consulted for this study, but no effort was made to read the voluminous files of these journals in a systematic fashion. The author has relied more heavily on a number of specialized journals and news magazines, including the *Southern School News*, published by the Southern Education Reporting Service; *South Today* and *Southern Changes*, published by the Southern Regional Council; and *Southern Exposure*, published by the Institute for Southern Studies.

Presidential election returns can be found in W. Dean Burnham, ed., *Presidential Ballots, 1836–1892* (Baltimore: Johns Hopkins Univ. Press, 1955); Edgar E. Robinson, ed., *The Presidential Vote, 1896–1932* (Stanford: Stanford Univ. Press, 1934); and Richard M. Scammon, comp., *America at the Polls: A Handbook of American Presidential Statistics, 1920–1964* (Pittsburgh: Univ. of Pittsburgh Press, 1965). See also Richard M. Scammon, comp., *America at the Polls: A Handbook of Contemporary American Statistics*, 17 vols. (Washington, D.C.: Governmental Affairs Institute, 1956–87), which extends through the elections of 1986. Paul T. David, *Party Strength in the United States, 1872–1970* (Charlottesville: Univ. Press of Virginia, 1972), is a useful statistical study of the relative strength of the political parties in terms of presidential, congressional, and gubernatorial returns. Primary election returns are provided by Alexander Heard and Donald S. Strong, eds., *Southern Primaries and Elections, 1920–1949* (University, Ala.: Univ. of Alabama Press, 1950); Richard M. Scammon, comp., *Southern Primaries '58* (Washington, D.C.: Governmental Affairs Institute, 1959); and Numan V. Bartley and Hugh D. Graham, eds., *Southern Elections: County and Precinct Data, 1950–1972* (Baton Rouge: Louisiana State Univ. Press, 1978). Election statistics for the individual states are available in their manuals and registers and in a variety of special publications, among which are Annie M. Hartsfield and Elston E. Roady, comps., *Florida Votes, 1920–1962* (Tallahassee: Institute of Governmental Research, Florida State Univ., 1963); F. Glenn Abney, ed., *Mississippi Election Statistics, 1900–1967* (University, Miss.: Bureau of Governmental Research, Univ. of Mississippi, 1968); Donald R. Matthews et al., comps., *North Carolina Votes: General Election Returns by County . . . 1868–1960* (Chapel Hill: Univ. of North Carolina Press, 1962); Joe C. Carr and Shirley Hassler, eds., *Fifty Years of Tennessee Elections, 1916–1966* (Nashville: State Government, n.d.); and Ralph Eisenberg, ed., *Virginia Votes, 1924–1968* (Charlottesville: Governmental and Administrative Research Division, Univ. of Virginia, 1971).

General Studies

Students of southern politics since the end of Reconstruction can turn to three preeminent general works as a point of departure: C. Vann Woodward, *Origins of the New South, 1877–1913* (Baton Rouge: Louisiana State Univ. Press, 1951); George Brown Tindall, *The Emergence of the New South, 1913–1945* (Baton Rouge: Louisiana State Univ. Press, 1967); and V.O. Key, Jr., with the assistance of Alexander Heard, *Southern Politics in State and Nation* (New York: Knopf, 1949). The first two volumes chart the course of southern politics within the broad frame of the region's social and cultural development. The third volume provides an illuminating analysis of contemporary southern politics against the backdrop of its historical experience. An ambitious new study by Earl Black and Merle Black, *Politics and Society in the South* (Cambridge: Harvard Univ. Press, 1987), throws light on the South's changing electorate and contrasts the era of classic one-party politics (1920–49) with the emergence of the new southern politics (1950–85). Three stimulating volumes that deal more broadly with the southern experience are W.J. Cash, *The Mind of the South* (New York: Knopf, 1941); Frank E. Vandiver, ed., *The Idea of the South: Pursuit of a Central Theme* (Chicago: Univ. of Chicago Press, 1964); and C. Vann Woodward, *The Burden of Southern History*, rev. ed. (Baton Rouge: Louisiana State Univ. Press, 1968). John B. Boles and Evelyn Thomas Nolen, eds., *Interpreting Southern History: Historiographical Essays in Honor of Sanford W. Higginbotham* (Baton Rouge: Louisiana State Univ. Press, 1987), is a valuable source for all serious students of southern history.

Coverage of the period since Key wrote in 1949 is provided by William C. Havard, ed., *The Changing Politics of the South* (Baton Rouge: Louisiana State Univ. Press, 1972); Numan V. Bartley and Hugh D. Graham, *Southern Politics and the Second Reconstruction* (Baltimore: Johns Hopkins Univ. Press, 1975); Jack Bass and Walter DeVries, *The Transformation of Southern Politics: Social Change and Political Consequence since 1945* (New York: Basic Books, 1976); and Alexander P. Lamis, *The Two-Party South* (New York: Oxford Univ. Press, 1984). Monroe Billington's brief survey, *Southern Politics since the Civil War* (Malabar, Fla.: R.E. Krieger, 1984), is helpful in understanding the broad sweep of the region's political affairs in the late nineteenth and the twentieth centuries.

Several short interpretive works deal broadly with southern politics since the late nineteenth century. These include Jasper Berry Shannon, *Toward a New Politics in the South* (Knoxville: Univ. of Tennessee Press, 1949); T. Harry Williams, *Romance and Realism in Southern Politics* (Athens: University of Georgia Press, 1961); Dewey W. Grantham, *The Democratic South* (Athens: Univ. of Georgia Press, 1963); and George Brown Tindall, *The Disruption of the Solid South* (Athens: Univ. of Georgia Press, 1972). Numan V. Bartley's essay, "The South and Sectionalism in American Politics," *Journal of Politics* 38 (Aug. 1976): 239–57, offers a valuable overview. An important and often neglected aspect of regional politics is examined in Tod A. Baker, Robert P. Steed, and Laurence W. Moreland, eds., *Religion and Politics in the South: Mass and Elite Perspectives* (New York: Praeger, 1983). In this connection see also Samuel S. Hill, Jr., ed., *Religion and the Solid South* (Nashville: Abington, 1972).

For the South's involvement in the evolution of national party systems, consult William Nisbet Chambers and Walter Dean Burnham, eds., *The American Party Systems: Stages of Political Development* (New York: Oxford Univ. Press, 1967); Walter Dean Burnham, *Critical Elections and the Mainsprings of American Politics* (New York: Norton, 1970); Everett Carll Ladd, Jr., with Charles D. Hadley, *Transformations of the American Party System: Political Coalitions from the New Deal to the 1970s*, 2d ed. (New York: Norton, 1978); and James L. Sundquist, *Dynamics of the Party System: Alignment and Realignment of Political Parties in the United States*, rev. ed. (Washington, D.C.: Brookings

Institution, 1983). Richard Franklin Bensel, *Sectionalism and American Political Development, 1880–1980* (Madison: Univ. of Wisconsin Press, 1984), the analysis of a political scientist, focuses on policy decisions in the U.S. House of Representatives. Ira Sharkansky's *Regionalism in American Politics* (Indianapolis: Bobbs-Merrill, 1970), is a more general study.

Only a few southern states are the subjects of comprehensive political histories during the period covered by this book. Among the best of these are Allen W. Moger, *Virginia: Bourbonism to Byrd, 1870–1925* (Charlottesville: Univ. Press of Virginia, 1968); Perry H. Howard, *Political Tendencies in Louisiana*, rev. ed. (Baton Rouge: Louisiana State Univ. Press, 1971); James R. Scales and Danney Goble, *Oklahoma Politics: A History* (Norman: Univ. of Oklahoma Press, 1982); Numan V. Bartley, *The Creation of Modern Georgia* (Athens: Univ. of Georgia Press, 1983); and Bennett H. Wall, ed., *Louisiana: A History* (Arlington Heights, Ill.: Forum Press, 1984). Less satisfactory but instructive is William R. Majors, *Change and Continuity: Tennessee Politics since the Civil War* (Macon, Ga.: Mercer Univ. Press, 1986). Two older, unpublished studies remain useful: Herman L. Horn, "The Growth and Development of the Democratic Party in Virginia since 1890" (Ph.D. diss., Duke Univ., 1949), and Boyce A. Drummond, Jr., "Arkansas Politics: A Study of a One-Party System" (Ph.D. diss., Univ. of Chicago, 1957). Reliable information on the modern governors of four southern states is provided by David R. Colburn and Richard K. Scher, *Florida's Gubernatorial Politics in the Twentieth Century* (Tallahassee: Univ. Presses of Florida, 1980); Timothy P. Donovan and Willard B. Gatewood, Jr., eds., *The Governors of Arkansas: Essays in Political Biography* (Fayetteville: Univ. of Arkansas Press, 1981); Edward Younger and James Tice Moore, eds., *The Governors of Virginia, 1860–1978* (Charlottesville: Univ. Press of Virginia, 1982); and Lowell H. Harrison, ed., *Kentucky's Governors, 1792–1985* (Lexington: Univ. Press of Kentucky, 1985). Coleman E. Ransone, Jr., *The Office of Governor in the South* (University, Ala.: Univ. of Alabama Press, 1951), and Fred Gantt, Jr., *The Chief Executive in Texas: A Study in Gubernatorial Leadership* (Austin: Univ. of Texas Press, 1964), are also helpful.

More restricted studies that throw light on state politics or that deal with significant features of southern politics include Paul Casdorph, *A History of the Republican Party in Texas, 1865–1965* (Austin: Pemberton Press, 1965); Peter D. Klingman, *Neither Dies Nor Surrenders: A History of the Republican Party in Florida, 1867–1970* (Gainesville: Univ. Presses of Florida, 1984); Andrew Buni, *The Negro in Virginia Politics, 1902–1965* (Charlottesville: Univ. Press of Virginia, 1967); Idus A. Newby, *Black Carolinians: A History of Blacks in South Carolina from 1895 to 1968* (Columbia: Univ of South Carolina Press, 1973); James R. Soukup, Clifton McCleskey, and Harry Holloway, *Party and Factional Division in Texas* (Austin: Univ. of Texas Press, 1964); Jack D. Fleer, *North Carolina Politics: An Introduction* (Chapel Hill: Univ. of North Carolina Press, 1968); Samuel A. Kirkpatrick, David R. Morgan, and Thomas G. Kielhorn, *The Oklahoma Voter: Politics, Elections and Parties in the Sooner State* (Norman: Univ. of Oklahoma Press, 1977); and James Bolner, ed., *Louisiana Politics: Festival in a Labyrinth* (Baton Rouge: Louisiana State Univ. Press, 1982).

Finally, one additional source of central importance should be mentioned:

the large periodical literature dealing with southern politics in the twentieth century. Scholarly articles and essays on southern political topics have mushroomed during the last quarter-century, appearing in a variety of historical journals, political science quarterlies, and other social science publications. One has only to examine the *Journal of Southern History's* annual bibliography of periodical articles to discover how extensive this scholarship is. Although essays and articles are cited in this book only to provide the source of direct quotations, the author is deeply indebted to the hundreds of contributors responsible for this impressive body of scholarly writings.

Forging the Solid South

Woodward's *Origins of the New South*, previously cited, is indispensable for an understanding of the post-Reconstruction decades in which the Solid South gradually took shape. Richard H. Abbott, *The Republican Party and the South, 1855–1877: The First Southern Strategy* (Chapel Hill: Univ. of North Carolina Press, 1986), and Michael Perman, *The Road to Redemption: Southern Politics, 1869–1879* (Chapel Hill: Univ. of North Carolina Press, 1984), provide useful background on the political situation in the South following Reconstruction. Several state studies are valuable sources for southern politics in the late nineteenth century. The best of these studies are William J. Cooper, *The Conservative Regime: South Carolina, 1877–1890* (Baltimore: Johns Hopkins Univ. Press, 1968); William Ivy Hair, *Bourbonism and Agrarian Protest: Louisiana Politics, 1877–1900* (Baton Rouge: Louisiana State Univ. Press, 1969); Jack P. Maddex, Jr., *The Virginia Conservatives, 1867–1879: A Study in Reconstruction Politics* (Chapel Hill: Univ. of North Carolina Press, 1970); Alwyn Barr, *Reconstruction to Reform: Texas Politics, 1876–1906* (Austin: Univ. of Texas Press, 1971); Roger L. Hart, *Redeemers, Bourbons, & Populists, 1870–1896* (Baton Rouge: Louisiana State Univ. Press, 1975); and Edward C. Williamson, *Florida Politics in the Gilded Age, 1877–1893* (Gainesville: Univ. Presses of Florida, 1976). Moger's *Virginia*, Bartley's *The Creation of Modern Georgia*, and Wall's *Louisiana*, all mentioned above, are also important in this connection. Political affairs in a major southern city are discussed by Joy J. Jackson, *New Orleans in the Gilded Age: Politics and Urban Progress, 1880–1896* (Baton Rouge: Louisiana State Univ. Press, 1969).

For good illustrations of Bourbon Democracy, see Allen Johnston Going, *Bourbon Democracy in Alabama, 1874–1890* (University, Ala.: Univ. of Alabama Press, 1951), and Judson Clements Ward, Jr., "Georgia under the Bourbon Democracy, 1872–1890" (Ph.D. diss., Univ. of North Carolina, 1947). Joseph H. Parks, *Joseph E. Brown of Georgia* (Baton Rouge: Louisiana State Univ. Press, 1977), is an informative biography of an important Bourbon leader. George Brown Tindall, *The Persistent Tradition in New South Politics* (Baton Rouge: Louisiana State Univ. Press, 1975), includes a thoughtful characterization of the Redeemers. Paul M. Gaston's *The New South Creed: A Study in Mythmaking* (New York: Knopf, 1970) illuminates the social thought of the region's dominant leaders in the 1880s and 1890s. The theme of intersectional reconciliation is sympathetically explored by Paul H. Buck in *The Road to Reunion, 1865–1900* (Boston: Little, Brown, 1937), while the South's fear of "northernization" is considered by Richard N. Current in *Northernizing the South* (Athens: Univ. of Georgia Press, 1983). The mythology of the Lost Cause is treated in Charles Reagan Wilson's fine book, *Baptized in Blood: The Religion of the Lost Cause, 1865–1920* (Athens: Univ. of Georgia Press, 1980). The influence of southern oratory in this period is suggested in Waldo W. Braden, ed., *Oratory in the New South* (Baton Rouge: Louisiana State Univ. Press, 1979). Carl V. Harris, "Right Fork or Left Fork? The Section-Party Alignments of Southern Democrats in Congress, 1873–1897," *Journal of Southern History* 42 (Nov. 1976): 471–506, and Harold D. Woodman, "Sequel to Slavery: The New History Views the Postbellum South," ibid. 43 (Nov. 1977): 523–54, are challenging and important essays.

The shifting Republican approach to the "southern question" following Reconstruction is described by Vincent P. De Santis, *Republicans Face the Southern Question—The New Departure Years, 1877–1897* (Baltimore: Johns Hopkins Univ. Press, 1959), and Stanley P. Hirshson, *Farewell to the Bloody Shirt: Northern Republicans & the Southern Negro, 1877–1893* (Bloomington: Indiana Univ. Press, 1962). The nature of the Republican party within the South is shown in Olive Hall Shadgett, *The Republican Party in Georgia: From Reconstruction through 1900* (Athens: Univ. of Georgia Press, 1964); Gordon B. McKinney, *Southern Mountain Republicans, 1865–1900: Politics and the Appalachian Community* (Chapel Hill: Univ. of North Carolina Press, 1978); and the previously cited studies of Republicanism in Texas by Casdorph and in Florida by Klingman. Lawrence Grossman, *The Democratic Party and the Negro: Northern and National Politics, 1868–92* (Urbana: Univ. of Illinois Press, 1976), is a notable study of the role of the Democratic party in the North in dealing with the race question.

Opposition to the Bourbon Democrats in Virginia is explored by two older studies: Charles Chilton Pearson, *The Readjuster Movement in Virginia* (New Haven: Yale Univ. Press, 1917), and Nelson Morehouse Blake, *William Mahone of Virginia: Soldier and Political Insurgent* (Richmond: Garret and Massie, 1935). The sources of internal dissension—and of the agrarian revolt—in other states are studied by Albert D. Kirwan, *Revolt of the Rednecks: Mississippi Politics, 1876–1925* (Lexington: Univ. of Kentucky Press, 1951); Steven Hahn, *The Roots of Southern Populism: Yeoman Farmers and the Transformation of the Georgia Upcountry, 1850–1890* (New York: Oxford Univ. Press, 1983); Charles L. Flynn, Jr., *White Land, Black Labor: Caste and Class in Late Nineteenth-Century Georgia* (Baton Rouge: Louisiana State Univ. Press, 1983); and Paul D. Escott, *Many Excellent People: Power and Privilege in North Carolina, 1850–1900* (Chapel Hill: Univ. of North Carolina Press, 1985). Another side of the postwar agricultural economy is described in Jay R. Mandle, *The Roots of Black Poverty: The Southern Plantation Economy after the Civil War* (Durham: Duke Univ. Press, 1978). Jonathan M. Wiener, in *Social Origins of the New South: Alabama, 1860–1885* (Baton Rouge: Louisiana State Univ. Press, 1978), and Dwight B. Billings, Jr., in *Planters and the Making of a "New South": Class, Politics, and Development in North Carolina, 1865–1900* (Chapel Hill: Univ. of North Carolina Press, 1979), seek to explain the process of modernization and argue that the upper classes headed by the old landed elite imposed an industrial society on Alabama and North Carolina. For a broader perspective, see Gavin Wright, *Old South, New South: Revolutions in the Southern Economy since the Civil War* (New York: Basic Books, 1986).

Populism, a topic discussed by Woodward and several other authors mentioned above, has been investigated with renewed energy in recent years. This scholarly inquiry has produced two significant general studies: Robert C. McMath, Jr., *Populist Vanguard: A History of the Southern Farmers' Alliance* (Chapel Hill: Univ. of North Carolina Press, 1975), and Lawrence Goodwyn, *Democratic Promise: The Populist Moment in America* (New York: Oxford Univ. Press, 1976). The ideas of southern Populists are revealingly analyzed in Bruce Palmer, *"Man Over Money": The Southern Populist Critique of American Capitalism* (Chapel Hill: Univ. of North Carolina Press, 1980). Michael Schwartz, *Radical Protest and Social Structure: The Southern Farmers' Alliance and Cotton Tenancy, 1880–1890* (New York: Academic Press, 1976), is more controversial but is useful in pointing out the class struggle within the Farmers' Alliance. Other studies of farm politics and populism include Sheldon Hackney, *Populism to Progressivism in Alabama* (Princeton: Princeton Univ. Press, 1969); William Warren Rogers, *The One-Gallused Rebellion: Agrarianism in Alabama, 1865–1896* (Baton Rouge: Louisiana State Univ. Press, 1970); Barton C. Shaw, *The Wool-Hat Boys: Georgia's Populist Party* (Baton Rouge: Louisiana State Univ. Press, 1984); Donna A. Barnes, *Farmers in Rebellion: The Rise and Fall of the Southern Farmers Alliance and People's Party in Texas* (Austin: Univ. of Texas Press, 1984); Theodore Saloutos, *Farmer Movements in the South, 1865–1933* (Berkeley: Univ. of California Press, 1960); Robert F. Durden, *The Climax of Populism: The Election of 1896* (Lexington: Univ. of Kentucky Press, 1965); and Gerald H. Gaither, *Blacks and the Populist Revolt: Ballots and Bigotry in the "New South"* (University, Ala.: Univ. of Alabama Press, 1977). Carl N. Degler's *The Other South: Southern Dissenters in the Nineteenth Century* (New York: Harper and Row, 1974), provides a useful context for the evaluation of southern political dissent.

Helpful biographical studies include C. Vann Woodward, *Tom Watson: Agrarian Rebel* (New York: Macmillan, 1938); Stuart Noblin, *Leonidas LaFayette Polk: Agrarian Crusader* (Chapel Hill: Univ. of North Carolina Press, 1949); Francis B. Simkins, *Pitchfork Ben Tillman: South Carolinian* (Baton Rouge: Louisiana State Univ. Press, 1944); Robert C. Cotner, *James Stephen Hogg: A Biography* (Austin: Univ. of Texas Press, 1959); Daniel Merritt Robison, *Bob Taylor and the Agrarian Revolt in Tennessee* (Chapel Hill: Univ. of North Carolina Press, 1935); and Sam Hanna Acheson, *Joe Bailey: The Last Democrat* (New York: Macmillan, 1932).

One aspect of the political upheaval of the 1890s was the fusion of Populists and Republicans in North Carolina. The trials and tribulations of that turbulent movement are described in Helen G. Edmonds, *The Negro and Fusion Politics in North Carolina, 1894–1901* (Chapel Hill: Univ. of North Carolina Press, 1951); Jeffrey J. Crow and Robert F. Durden, *Maverick Republican in the Old North State: A Political Biography of Daniel L. Russell* (Baton Rouge: Louisiana State Univ. Press, 1977); Frederick A. Bode, *Protestantism and the New South:*

North Carolina Baptists and Methodists in Political Crisis, 1894–1903 (Charlottesville: Univ. Press of Virginia, 1975); and H. Leon Prather, Sr., We Have Taken
a City: Wilmington Racial Massacre and Coup of 1898 (Rutherford, N.J.: Farleigh
Dickinson Univ. Press, 1984). Broader aspects of race and politics are considered in Vernon L. Wharton, The Negro in Mississippi, 1865–1890 (Chapel Hill:
Univ. of North Carolina Press, 1947); George B. Tindall, South Carolina Negroes,
1877–1900 (Columbia: Univ. of South Carolina Press, 1952); Charles E. Wynes,
Race Relations in Virginia, 1870–1902 (Charlottesville: Univ. of Virginia Press,
1961); Lawrence D. Rice, The Negro in Texas, 1874–1900 (Baton Rouge: Louisiana State Univ. Press, 1971); and Joseph H. Cartwright, The Triumph of Jim
Crow: Tennessee Race Relations in the 1880's (Knoxville: Univ. of Tennessee Press,
1976). Eric Anderson, Race and Politics in North Carolina, 1872–1901: The Black
Second (Baton Rouge: Louisiana State Univ. Press, 1981), focuses on a center
of black political strength in the post-Reconstruction period.

Negro disfranchisement is analyzed by J. Morgan Kousser in The Shaping
of Southern Politics: Suffrage Restriction and the Establishment of the One-Party
South, 1880–1910 (New Haven: Yale Univ. Press, 1974), a comprehensive and
critical reevaluation of antisuffrage campaigns and legislation. Several older
works remain useful: Ralph Clipman McDanel, The Virginia Constitutional Convention of 1901–1902 (Baltimore: Johns Hopkins Press, 1928); Paul Lewinson,
Race, Class, & Party: A History of Negro Suffrage and White Politics in the South
(New York: Russell and Russell, 1932); William Alexander Mabry, Studies in
the Disfranchisement of the Negro in the South (Durham: Duke Univ. Press, 1938);
and Malcolm Cook McMillan, Constitutional Development in Alabama, 1798–
1901: A Study in Politics, the Negro, and Sectionalism (Chapel Hill: Univ. of North
Carolina Press, 1955). For a "reform" movement that often restricted the
suffrage, in the South and in other regions, see L.E. Fredman, The Australian
Ballot: The Story of an American Reform (East Lansing: Michigan State Univ.
Press, 1968), which contains a detailed treatment of Louisiana.

The political and social milieu in which disfranchisement and racial proscription were carried out is recreated in several illuminating volumes: Ray-
ford W. Logan, The Negro in American Life and Thought: The Nadir, 1877–1901
(New York: Dial Press, 1954); August Meier, Negro Thought in America, 1880–
1915: Racial Ideologies in the Age of Booker T. Washington (Ann Arbor: Univ. of
Michigan Press, 1963); Joel Williamson, The Crucible of Race: Black-White Relations in the American South since Emancipation (New York: Oxford Univ. Press,
1984); George M. Fredrickson, The Black Image in the White Mind: The Debate
on Afro-American Character and Destiny, 1817–1914 (New York: Harper and
Row, 1971); John W. Cell, The Highest Stage of White Supremacy: The Origins of
Segregation in South Africa and the American South (Cambridge: Cambridge Univ.
Press, 1982); C. Vann Woodward, The Strange Career of Jim Crow, 3d rev. ed.
(New York: Oxford Univ. Press, 1974); Howard W. Rabinowitz, Race Relations
in the Urban South, 1865–1890 (New York: Oxford Univ. Press, 1978); Idus A.
Newby, Jim Crow's Defense: Anti-Negro Thought in America, 1900–1930 (Baton
Rouge: Louisiana State Univ. Press, 1965); and James M. McPherson, The
Abolitionist Legacy: From Reconstruction to the NAACP (Princeton: Princeton
Univ. Press, 1975).

The One-Party System

The best general accounts of southern politics in the early years of the twentieth century, when the one-party system became firmly established, are Woodward's *Origins of the New South* and Tindall's *The Emergence of the New South*. Jack Temple Kirby's lively volume, *Darkness at the Dawning: Race and Reform in the Progressive South* (Philadelphia: Lippincott, 1972), concentrates on the interaction of the race issue with reform in the region. For two other general studies, see Hugh C. Bailey, *Liberalism in the New South: Southern Social Reformers and the Progressive Movement* (Coral Gables, Fla.: Univ. of Miami Press, 1969), and Dewey W. Grantham, *Southern Progressivism: The Reconciliation of Progress and Tradition* (Knoxville: Univ. of Tennessee Press, 1983). James R. Green, *Grass-Roots Socialism: Radical Movements in the Southwest, 1895–1943* (Baton Rouge: Louisiana State Univ. Press, 1978), offers a revealing perspective for an examination of progressivism in Texas, Oklahoma, Louisiana, and Arkansas. For a penetrating treatment of social reform ideas in the South at the turn of the century, see Bruce Clayton, *The Savage Ideal: Intolerance and Intellectual Leadership in the South, 1890–1914* (Baltimore: Johns Hopkins Press, 1972). One of the region's social critics and reformers is treated in a model biography by John Milton Cooper, Jr., *Walter Hines Page: The Southerner as American, 1855–1918* (Chapel Hill: Univ. of North Carolina Press, 1977).

Among the most impressive state studies of reform politics in the early twentieth-century South are Kirwan, *Revolt of the Rednecks*, and Hackney, *Populism to Progressivism in Alabama*, both cited earlier; Raymond H. Pulley, *Old Virginia Restored: An Interpretation of the Progressive Impulse, 1870–1930* (Charlottesville: Univ. Press of Virginia, 1968); and Danney Goble, *Progressive Oklahoma: The Making of a New Kind of State* (Norman: Univ. of Oklahoma Press, 1980). Seth Shepard McKay, *Texas Politics, 1906–1944, With Special Reference to the German Counties* (Lubbock: Texas Tech Press, 1952), is also useful. Lewis L. Gould's *Progressives and Prohibitionists: Texas Democrats in the Wilson Era* (Austin: Univ. of Texas Press, 1973) provides a comprehensive treatment of reform politics in that state during the latter part of the progressive era. An informative unpublished study of another state is Joseph Flake Steelman's "The Progressive Era in North Carolina, 1884–1917" (Ph.D. diss., Univ. of North Carolina, 1955). The conditions and activities of blacks in an era of racial segregation and political demagoguery are examined in John Dittmer, *Black Georgia in the Progressive Era, 1900–1920* (Urbana: Univ. of Illinois Press, 1977); Lester C. Lamon, *Black Tennesseans, 1900–1930* (Knoxville: Univ. of Tennessee Press, 1977); and the previously cited books by Buni and Newby.

The best introduction to the party mechanisms and procedures that became characteristic of the Solid South are Key's *Southern Politics in State and Nation* and Kousser's *The Shaping of Southern Politics*, both referred to above. More specialized studies include Cortez A.M. Ewing, *Primary Elections in the South: A Study in Uniparty Politics* (Norman: Univ. of Oklahoma Press, 1953); Frederic D. Ogden, *The Poll Tax in the South* (University, Ala.: Univ. of Alabama Press, 1958); L.M. Holland, *The Direct Primary in Georgia* (Urbana: Univ. of Illinois Press, 1949); Darlene Clark Hine, *Black Victory: The Rise and Fall of the*

White Primary in Texas (Millwood, N.Y.: KTO Press, 1979); Larry Sabato, *The Democratic Party Primary in Virginia: Tantamount to Election No Longer* (Charlottesville: Univ. Press of Virginia, 1977); and Allen W. Jones, "A History of the Direct Primary in Alabama, 1840–1903" (Ph.D. diss., University of Alabama, 1964).

Important political issues in the early twentieth-century South are analyzed in James F. Doster, *Railroads in Alabama Politics, 1875–1914* (University, Ala.: Univ. of Alabama Press, 1957); Paul E. Isaac, *Prohibition and Politics: Turbulent Decades in Tennessee, 1885–1920* (Knoxville: Univ. of Tennessee Press, 1965); C.C. Pearson and J. Edwin Hendricks, *Liquor and Anti-Liquor in Virginia, 1619–1919* (Durham: Duke Univ. Press, 1967); Jimmie Lewis Franklin, *Born Sober: Prohibition in Oklahoma, 1907–1959* (Norman: Univ. of Oklahoma Press, 1971); James H. Timberlake, *Prohibition and the Progressive Movement, 1900–1920* (Cambridge: Harvard Univ. Press, 1963); Mark T. Carleton, *Politics and Punishment: A History of the Louisiana State Penal System* (Baton Rouge: Louisiana State Univ. Press, 1971); Pete Daniel, *The Shadow of Slavery: Peonage in the South, 1901–1969* (Urbana: Univ. of Illinois Press, 1972); Elizabeth H. Davidson, *Child Labor Legislation in the Southern Textile States* (Chapel Hill: Univ. of North Carolina Press, 1939); Louis R. Harlan, *Separate and Unequal: Public School Campaigns and Racism in the Southern Seaboard States, 1901–1915* (Chapel Hill: Univ. of North Carolina Press, 1958); and Leonard Dinnerstein, *The Leo Frank Case* (New York: Columbia Univ. Press, 1968). Woman suffrage campaigns in the South have been studied intensively by A. Elizabeth Taylor. She is the author of *The Woman Suffrage Movement in Tennessee* (New York: Bookman Associates, 1957), and a series of valuable articles on other southern states. In this connection, see also Aileen S. Kraditor, *The Ideas of the Woman Suffrage Movement, 1890–1920* (New York: Columbia Univ. Press, 1965), and Paul E. Fuller, *Laura Clay and the Woman's Rights Movement* (Lexington: Univ. Press of Kentucky, 1975).

A good brief survey of the urban political scene in the early twentieth-century South is contained in Blaine A. Brownell and David R. Goldfield, eds., *The City in Southern History: The Growth of Urban Civilization in the South* (Port Washington, N.Y.: Kennikat Press, 1977). Bradley Robert Rice, *Progressive Cities: The Commission Government Movement in America, 1901–1920* (Austin: Univ. of Texas Press, 1977), is a key study of structural reform in municipal government in the South and other parts of the country. Carl V. Harris's *Political Power in Birmingham, 1871–1921* (Knoxville: Univ. of Tennessee Press, 1977) is a pioneering analysis of the influence wielded by economic and social interest groups. Urban politics and reform are considered in George M. Reynolds, *Machine Politics in New Orleans, 1897–1926* (London: P.S. King and Son, 1936); William D. Miller, *Memphis during the Progressive Era, 1900–1917* (Memphis: Memphis State Univ. Press, 1957), and idem, *Mr. Crump of Memphis* (Baton Rouge: Louisiana State Univ. Press, 1964); James R. McGovern, *The Emergence of a City in the Modern South: Pensacola, 1900–1945* (Pensacola: n.p., 1976); Evan Anders, *Boss Rule in South Texas: The Progressive Era* (Austin: Univ. of Texas Press, 1982); Don H. Doyle, *Nashville in the New South, 1880–1930* (Knoxville: Univ. of Tennessee Press, 1985), and idem, *Nashville since the 1920s*

(Knoxville: Univ. of Tennessee Press, 1985); and Christopher Silver, *Twentieth-Century Richmond: Planning, Politics, and Race* (Knoxville: Univ. of Tennessee Press, 1984).

Scholarly studies of political leadership in the southern states during this period constitute an indispensable source for the historian of the region's politics. See, for example, William E. Larsen, *Montague of Virginia: The Making of a Southern Progressive* (Baton Rouge: Louisiana State Univ. Press, 1965); Jack Temple Kirby, *Westmoreland Davis: Virginia Planter-Politician, 1859–1942* (Charlottesville: Univ. Press of Virginia, 1968); Henry C. Ferrell, Jr., *Claude A. Swanson of Virginia: A Political Biography* (Lexington: Univ. Press of Kentucky, 1985); Oliver H. Orr, Jr., *Charles Brantley Aycock* (Chapel Hill: Univ. of North Carolina Press, 1961); Joseph L. Morrison, *Josephus Daniels Says . . . : An Editor's Political Odyssey from Byran to Wilson and F.D.R., 1894–1913* (Chapel Hill: Univ. of North Carolina Press, 1962); Robert Milton Burts, *Richard Irvine Manning and the Progressive Movement in South Carolina* (Columbia: Univ. of South Carolina Press, 1974); Lewis Pinckney Jones, *Stormy Petrel: N.G. Gonzales and His State* (Columbia: Univ. of South Carolina Press, 1973); Dewey W. Grantham, *Hoke Smith and the Politics of the New South* (Baton Rouge: Louisiana State Univ. Press, 1958); Samuel Proctor, *Napoleon Bonaparte Broward: Florida's Fighting Democrat* (Gainesville: Univ. of Florida Press, 1950); Wayne Flynt, *Duncan Upshaw Fletcher: Dixie's Reluctant Progressive* (Tallahassee: Florida State Univ. Press, 1971), and idem, *Cracker Messiah: Governor Sidney J. Catts of Florida* (Baton Rouge: Louisiana State Univ. Press, 1977); William F. Holmes, *The White Chief: James Kimble Vardaman* (Baton Rouge: Louisiana State Univ. Press, 1970); Raymond Arsenault, *The Wild Ass of the Ozarks: Jeff Davis and the Social Bases of Southern Politics* (Philadelphia: Temple Univ. Press, 1984); Rupert N. Richardson, *Colonel Edward M. House: The Texas Years, 1858–1912* (Abilene, Tex.: Hardin-Simmons Univ. Press, 1964); Edward Everett Dale and James D. Morrison, *Pioneer Judge: The Life of Robert Lee Williams* (Cedar Rapids, Iowa: Torch Press, 1958); and Keith L. Bryant, Jr., *Alfalfa Bill Murray* (Norman: Univ. of Oklahoma Press, 1968).

In the National Arena

Although there is as yet no good book on the South's participation and influence in early twentieth-century national politics, some light is thrown on the subject by Willard B. Gatewood, Jr., *Theodore Roosevelt and the Art of Controversy: Episodes of the White House Years* (Baton Rouge: Louisiana State Univ. Press, 1970); John Milton Cooper, Jr., *The Warrior and the Priest: Woodrow Wilson and Theodore Roosevelt* (Cambridge: Harvard Univ. Press, 1983); and Anne Firor Scott, "A Progressive Wind from the South, 1906–1913," *Journal of Southern History* 29 (Feb. 1963): 53–70. C. Vann Woodward, *American Counterpoint: Slavery and Race in the North-South Dialogue* (Boston: Little, Brown, 1971), provides some essential background. The movement in the South to nominate and elect Woodrow Wilson as president has been described in impressive detail by Arthur S. Link in *Wilson: The Road to the White House* (Princeton: Princeton Univ. Press, 1947), and idem, *The Higher Realism of Woodrow*

Wilson and Other Essays (Nashville: Vanderbilt Univ. Press, 1971). Also see Paul D. Casdorph, *Republicans, Negroes, and Progressives in the South, 1912–1916* (University, Ala.: Univ. of Alabama Press, 1981). Tindall's *The Emergence of the New South* contains an authoritative treatment of the interrelationship between the South and the Wilson administration. That relationship is also clarified in Link's multivolume biography of Wilson, which carries the story to American entrance into the war in 1917. Aspects of the South's role in Wilson's New Freedom are described in John M. Blum, *Joe Tumulty and the Wilson Era* (Boston: Houghton Mifflin, 1951), and John J. Broesamle, *William Gibbs McAdoo: A Passion for Change, 1863–1917* (Port Washington, N.Y.: Kennikat Press, 1973). Saloutos, *Farmer Movements in the South*, cited earlier, includes two valuable chapters on the New Freedom and southern agriculture.

The role of the southern congressional delegations during the Wilson years is given some attention in the works by Link and Tindall. A number of biographies explore this topic in greater detail, including George Coleman Osborn, *John Sharp Williams: Planter-Statesman of the Deep South* (Baton Rouge: Louisiana State Univ. Press, 1943); Francis B. Simkins, *Pitchfork Ben Tillman: South Carolinian* (Baton Rouge: Louisiana State Univ. Press, 1944); Monroe Billington, *Thomas P. Gore: The Blind Senator from Oklahoma* (Lawrence: Univ. of Kansas Press, 1967); Evans C. Johnson, *Oscar W. Underwood: A Political Biography* (Baton Rouge: Louisiana State Univ. Press, 1980); and the studies of Duncan U. Fletcher, Hoke Smith, Claude A. Swanson, and James K. Vardaman mentioned above. The contributions of southern congressmen to the demands of the war are analyzed in two impressive articles by Richard L. Watson, Jr.: "A Testing Time for Southern Congressional Leadership: The War Crisis of 1917–1918," *Journal of Southern History* 44 (Feb. 1978): 3–40, and "Principle, Party, and Constituency: The North Carolina Congressional Delegation, 1917–1919," *North Carolina Historical Review* 56 (July 1979): 298–323. The broader congressional context is provided by Seward W. Livermore, *Politics Is Adjourned: Woodrow Wilson and the War Congress, 1916–1918* (Middletown: Wesleyan Univ. Press, 1966). Southern involvement in the struggle over one important national issue is revealed in David Morgan, *Suffragists and Democrats: The Politics of Woman Suffrage in America* (East Lansing: Michigan State Univ. Press, 1972). The reaction of a North Carolina congressional leader to the difficult problems of American neutrality is examined in Alex Mathews Arnett, *Claude Kitchin and the Wilson War Policies* (Boston: Little, Brown, 1937). The nature of the South's powerful influence in Congress in this period and afterward is made clear by David M. Potter in *The South and the Concurrent Majority* (Baton Rouge: Louisiana State Univ. Press, 1972). See also Cortez A.M. Ewing, *Congressional Elections, 1896–1944: The Sectional Basis of Political Democracy in the House of Representatives* (Norman: Univ. of Oklahoma Press, 1947).

Southern involvement in national politics during the 1920s is considered in David Burner's excellent study, *The Politics of Provincialism: The Democratic Party in Transition, 1918–1932* (New York: Knopf, 1968), and in Tindall's *The Emergence of the New South*. For the role of several major issues in national politics during the decade, see Arnold Rice, *The Ku Klux Klan in American Politics* (Washington, D.C.: Public Affairs Press, 1962); Lawrence W. Levine,

Defender of the Faith, William Jennings Bryan: The Last Decade, 1915–1925 (New York: Oxford Univ. Press, 1965); Peter H. Odegard, *Pressure Politics: The Story of the Anti-Saloon League* (New York: Columbia Univ. Press, 1928); Andrew Sinclair, *Era of Excess: A Social History of the Prohibition Movement* (New York: Harper and Row, 1964); and David E. Kyvig, *Repealing National Prohibition* (Chicago: Univ. of Chicago Press, 1979). Outside criticism of southern institutions in the 1920s is revealed in Frank Tannenbaum, *Darker Phases of the South* (New York: G.P. Putnam's Sons, 1924), and Fred C. Hobson, *Serpent in Eden: H.L. Mencken and the South* (Chapel Hill: Univ. of North Carolina Press, 1974). Robert K. Murray's *The 103rd Ballot: Democrats and the Disaster in Madison Square Garden* (New York: Harper and Row, 1976) is worth reading.

The most authoritative analysis of sectionalism as a factor in the election of 1928 is that of Allan J. Lichtman in *Prejudice and the Old Politics: The Presidential Election of 1928* (Chapel Hill: Univ. of North Carolina Press, 1979). But also see Edmund A. Moore, *A Catholic Runs for President: The Campaign of 1928* (New York: Ronald Press, 1956). Virginius Dabney, *Dry Messiah: The Life of Bishop Cannon* (New York: Knopf, 1949), and Kenneth K. Bailey, *Southern White Protestantism in the Twentieth Century* (New York: Harper and Row, 1964), are also useful in this connection. For the Republican party and the South in this period, consult Richard B. Sherman, *The Republican Party and Black America: From McKinley to Hoover, 1896–1933* (Charlottesville: Univ. Press of Virginia, 1973), and Donald J. Lisio, *Hoover, Blacks & Lily-Whites: A Study of Southern Strategies* (Chapel Hill: Univ. of North Carolina Press, 1985).

The Classic Period of Southern Politics

Key's *Southern Politics in State and Nation* brilliantly illuminates the South's political assumptions and practices during this period. Two other general works are also helpful: Tindall, *The Emergence of the New South*, and Taylor Cole and John H. Hallowell, eds., *The Southern Political Scene, 1938–1948* (Gainesville: Univ. of Florida Press, 1948). A number of more specialized books deal with the politics of individual states during this period, including Allan P. Sindler, *Huey Long's Louisiana: State Politics, 1920–1952* (Baltimore: Johns Hopkins Univ. Press, 1956); David D. Lee, *Tennessee in Turmoil: Politics in the Volunteer State, 1920–1932* (Memphis: Memphis State Univ. Press, 1979); Norman D. Brown, *Hood, Bonnet, and Little Brown Jug: Texas Politics, 1921–1928* (College Station: Texas A&M Univ. Press, 1984); Elmer L. Puryear, *Democratic Party Dissension in North Carolina, 1928–1936* (Chapel Hill: Univ. of North Carolina Press, 1962); Joseph L. Bernd, *Grass Roots Politics in Georgia: The County Unit System and the Importance of the Individual Voting Community in Bifactional Elections, 1942–1954* (Atlanta: Emory Univ. Research Committee, 1960); Malcolm E. Jewell and Everett W. Cunningham, *Kentucky Politics* (Lexington: Univ. of Kentucky Press, 1968); and William D. Barnard, *Dixiecrats and Democrats: Alabama Politics, 1942–1950* (University, Ala.: Univ. of Alabama Press, 1974). Two state studies mentioned earlier are also important: Scales and Goble, *Oklahoma Politics*, and Bartley, *The Creation of Modern Georgia*. For one state's wartime experience, see Francis Howard Heller, *Virginia's State Government during the Second World War: Its Constitutional, Legislative, and Administrative Adaptations, 1942–1945* (Richmond: Virginia State Library, 1949).

Various aspects of state politics in the 1920s are considered by Norman F. Furniss, *The Fundamentalist Controversy, 1918–1931* (New Haven: Yale Univ. Press, 1954); Willard B. Gatewood, Jr., *Preachers, Pedagogues, & Politicians: The Evolution Controversy in North Carolina, 1920–1927* (Chapel Hill: Univ. of North Carolina Press, 1966); George M. Marsden, *Fundamentalism and American Culture: The Shaping of Twentieth-Century Evangelicalism: 1870–1925* (New York: Oxford Univ. Press, 1980); Charles C. Alexander, *The Ku Klux Klan in the Southwest* (Lexington: Univ. of Kentucky Press, 1965); David Mark Chalmers, *Hooded Americanism: The First Century of the Ku Klux Klan, 1865–1965* (Garden City: Doubleday, 1965); and Kenneth T. Jackson, *The Ku Klux Klan in the City, 1915–1930* (New York: Oxford Univ. Press, 1967). Blaine A. Brownell's *The Urban Ethos in the South, 1920–1930* (Baton Rouge: Louisiana State Univ. Press, 1975) is a significant study of urban boosterism and business progressivism. Jacquelyn Dowd Hall's *Revolt against Chivalry: Jessie Daniel Ames and the Women's Campaign against Lynching* (New York: Columbia Univ. Press, 1979) examines a reform movement that was spearheaded by southern women.

Among the more notable biographical studies of southern politicians in this period are Joseph L. Morrison, *Governor O. Max Gardner: A Power in North Carolina and New Deal Washington* (Chapel Hill: Univ. of North Carolina Press, 1971); T. Harry Williams, *Huey Long* (New York: Knopf, 1969); Virginia Van der Veer Hamilton, *Hugo Black: The Alabama Years* (Baton Rouge: Louisiana State Univ. Press, 1972); William Anderson, *The Wild Man from Sugar Creek: The Political Career of Eugene Talmadge* (Baton Rouge: Louisiana State Univ. Press, 1975); William R. Majors, *The End of Arcadia: Gordon Browning and Tennessee Politics* (Memphis: Memphis State Univ. Press, 1982); William Bryan Crawley, Jr., *Bill Tuck: A Political Life in Harry Byrd's Virginia* (Charlottesville: Univ. Press of Virginia, 1978); Seth Shepard McKay, *W. Lee O'Daniel and Texas Politics, 1938–1942* (Lubbock: Texas Technological College Research Funds, 1944); Carl Grafton and Anne Permaloff, *Big Mules & Branchheads: James E. Folsom and Political Power in Alabama* (Athens: Univ. of Georgia Press, 1985); and George E. Sims, *The Little Man's Big Friend: James E. Folsom in Alabama Politics, 1946–1958* (University, Ala.: Univ. of Alabama Press, 1985). Also useful are Miller, *Mr. Crump of Memphis*, mentioned before; Stan Opotowsky, *The Longs of Louisiana* (New York: Dutton, 1960); and A.J. Liebling, *The Earl of Louisiana* (New York: Simon and Schuster, 1961). For two enlightening personal accounts, see Ellis G. Arnall, *The Shore Dimly Seen* (Philadelphia: Lippincott, 1946), and Francis Pickens Miller, *The Man from the Valley: Memoirs of a 20th-Century Virginian* (Chapel Hill: Univ. of North Carolina Press, 1971). Several southern "men of the people" are considered in Alan A. Michie and Frank Ryhlick, *Dixie Demagogues* (New York: Vanguard Press, 1939), a journalistic work; Reinhard H. Luthin, *American Demagogues: Twentieth Century* (Boston: Beacon Press, 1954); and Cal M. Logue and Howard Dorgan, eds., *The Oratory of Southern Demagogues* (Baton Rouge: Louisiana State Univ. Press, 1981).

The South and the New Deal

Tindall's *The Emergence of the New South* provides an informative and reliable treatment of the South in the 1930s and the years of World War II. For the effects of the Great Depression on the region, see Robert E. Snyder, *Cotton Crisis* (Chapel Hill: Univ. of North Carolina Press, 1984); Donald W. Whisenhunt, *The Depression in Texas: The Hoover Years* (New York: Garland, 1983); Nan Elizabeth Woodruff, *As Rare as Rain: Federal Relief in the Great Drought of 1930–31* (Urbana: Univ. of Illinois Press, 1985); John W. Hevener, *Which Side Are You On? The Harlem County Miners, 1931–39* (Urbana: Univ. of Illinois Press, 1978); John L. Robinson, ed., *Living Hard: Southern Americans in the Great Depression* (Lanham, Md.: Univ. Press of America, 1981); Tom E. Terrill and Jerrold Hirsch, eds., *Such As Us: Southern Voices of the Thirties* (Chapel Hill: Univ. of North Carolina Press, 1978); and Kenneth D. Hendrickson, Jr., ed., *Hard Times in Oklahoma: The Depression Years* (Oklahoma City: Oklahoma Historical Society, 1983). For a notorious incident that focused national attention on the South in the early 1930s, see Dan T. Carter, *Scottsboro: A Tragedy of the American South* (Baton Rouge: Louisiana State Univ. Press, 1969).

New Deal policies and the South's ambivalent reaction to them are touched upon by Frank Freidel, *F.D.R. and the South* (Baton Rouge: Louisiana State Univ. Press, 1965); James C. Cobb and Michael V. Namorato, eds., *The New Deal and the South* (Jackson: Univ. Press of Mississippi, 1984); and V.O. Key, *Southern Politics in State and Nation*. Useful state studies include Ronald L. Heinemann, *Depression and New Deal in Virginia: The Enduring Dominion* (Charlottesville: Univ. Press of Virginia, 1983); Michael S. Holmes, *The New Deal in Georgia: An Administrative History* (Westport, Conn.: Greenwood Press, 1975); John Dean Minton, *The New Deal in Tennessee, 1932–1938* (New York: Garland, 1979); Anthony J. Badger, *North Carolina and the New Deal* (Raleigh: North Carolina Department of Cultural Resources, 1981); George T. Blakey, *Hard Times and New Deal in Kentucky, 1929–1939* (Lexington: Univ. Press of Kentucky, 1986); Lionel V. Patenaude, *Texans, Politics and the New Deal* (New York: Garland, 1983); and John Braeman, Robert H. Bremner, and David Brody, eds., *The New Deal: The State and Local Levels* (Columbus: Ohio State Univ. Press, 1975), which includes chapters on Virginia, Louisiana, and Oklahoma. Roger Biles's *Memphis in the Great Depression* (Knoxville: Univ. of Tennessee Press, 1986) is a workmanlike monograph. Robert C. Cotner et al., *Texas Cities and the Great Depression* (Austin: Univ. of Texas Press, 1973), is also useful.

The New Deal and the States: Federalism in Transition (Princeton: Princeton Univ. Press, 1969), by James T. Patterson, provides valuable perspective on the federal-state relationship in the 1930s. The South's involvement in and reaction to specific New Deal programs are shown in David Eugene Conrad, *The Forgotten Farmers: The Story of Sharecroppers in the New Deal* (Urbana: Univ. of Illinois Press, 1965); Donald H. Grubbs, *Cry from the Cotton: The Southern Tenant Farmers' Union and the New Deal* (Chapel Hill: Univ. of North Carolina Press, 1971); Sidney Baldwin, *Poverty and Politics: The Rise and Decline of the Farm Security Administration* (Chapel Hill: Univ. of North Carolina Press, 1968);

Donald Holley, *Uncle Sam's Farmers: The New Deal Communities in the Lower Mississippi Valley* (Urbana: Univ. of Illinois Press, 1975); Paul E. Mertz, *New Deal Policy and Southern Rural Poverty* (Baton Rouge: Louisiana State Univ. Press, 1978); Thomas K. McCraw, *TVA and the Power Fight, 1933–1939* (Philadelphia: Lippincott, 1971); Erwin C. Hargrove and Paul K. Conkin, eds., *TVA: Fifty Years of Grass-Roots Bureaucracy* (Urbana: Univ. of Illinois Press, 1983); Michael J. McDonald and John Muldowny, *TVA and the Dispossessed: The Resettlement of Population in the Norris Dam Area* (Knoxville: Univ. of Tennessee Press, 1982); Anthony J. Badger, *Prosperity Road: The New Deal, Tobacco, and North Carolina* (Chapel Hill: Univ. of North Carolina Press, 1980); Theodore Saloutos, *The American Farmer and the New Deal* (Ames: Iowa State Univ. Press, 1982); Pete Daniel, *Breaking the Land: The Transformation of Cotton, Tobacco, and Rice Cultures since 1880* (Urbana: Univ. of Illinois Press, 1985); and James A. Hodges, *New Deal Labor Policy and the Southern Cotton Textile Industry, 1933–1941* (Knoxville: Univ. of Tennessee Press, 1986). An important southern movement is examined by Robert A. Lively, *The South in Action: A Sectional Crusade against Freight Discrimination* (Chapel Hill: Univ. of North Carolina Press, 1949), and William H. Joubert, *Southern Freight Rates in Transition* (Gainesville: Univ. of Florida Press, 1949).

Southern political leaders and the New Deal are considered by John Robert Moore, *Senator Josiah William Bailey of North Carolina: A Political Biography* (Durham: Duke Univ. Press, 1968); Williams, *Huey Long*, previously mentioned; Richard B. Henderson, *Maury Maverick: A Political Biography* (Austin: Univ. of Texas Press, 1970); Martha H. Swain, *Pat Harrison: The New Deal Years* (Jackson: Univ. Press of Mississippi, 1978); Irvin M. May, Jr., *Marvin Jones: The Public Life of an Agrarian Advocate* (College Station: Texas A&M Univ. Press, 1980); Robert A. Caro, *The Years of Lyndon Johnson: The Path to Power* (New York: Knopf, 1982); Ronnie Dugger, *The Politician: The Life and Times of Lyndon Johnson, the Drive for Power from the Frontier to Master of the Senate* (New York: Norton, 1982); Anthony Champagne, *Congressman Sam Rayburn* (New Brunswick, N.J.: Rutgers Univ. Press, 1984); John A. Salmond, *A Southern Rebel: The Life and Times of Aubrey Willis Williams, 1890–1965* (Chapel Hill: Univ. of North Carolina Press, 1983); and Chester M. Morgan, *Redneck Liberal: Theodore G. Bilbo and the New Deal* (Baton Rouge: Louisiana State Univ. Press, 1985).

Southern liberal responses to the New Deal are described in Thomas A. Krueger, *And Promises to Keep: The Southern Conference for Human Welfare, 1938–1948* (Nashville: Vanderbilt Univ. Press, 1967); Morton Sosna, *In Search of the Silent South: Southern Liberals and the Race Issue* (New York: Columbia Univ. Press, 1977); John T. Kneebone, *Southern Liberal Journalists and the Issue of Race, 1920–1944* (Chapel Hill: Univ. of North Carolina Press, 1985); and Anthony P. Dunbar, *Against the Grain: Southern Radicals and Prophets, 1929–1959* (Charlottesville: Univ. Press of Virginia, 1981). Southern conservative opposition to Franklin D. Roosevelt and the New Deal is illuminated by James T. Patterson's *Congressional Conservatism and the New Deal: The Growth of a Conservative Coalition in Congress, 1933–1939* (Lexington: Univ. of Kentucky Press, 1967). See also George L. Grassmuck, *Sectional Biases in Congress on Foreign Policy* (Baltimore: Johns Hopkins Press, 1951); Julius Turner, *Party and Constituency: Pressures on Congress* (Baltimore: Johns Hopkins Press, 1951); George E.

Mowry, *Another Look at the Twentieth-Century South* (Baton Rouge: Louisiana State Univ. Press, 1973); and John D. Stark, *Damned Upcountryman: William Watts Ball, A Study in American Conservatism* (Durham: Duke Univ. Press, 1973).

Blacks and racial politics in the 1930s are analyzed by John B. Kirby, *Black Americans in the Roosevelt Era: Liberalism and Race* (Knoxville: Univ. of Tennessee Press, 1980); Harvard Sitkoff, *A New Deal for Blacks: The Emergence of Civil Rights as a National Issue* (New York: Oxford Univ. Press, 1978); Nancy J. Weiss, *Farewell to the Party of Lincoln: Black Politics in the Age of FDR* (Princeton: Princeton Univ. Press, 1983); and Raymond Wolters, *Negroes and the Great Depression: The Problem of Economic Recovery* (Westport, Conn.: Greenwood, 1970). One racial and sectional issue is effectively treated by Robert L. Zangrando in *The NAACP Crusade against Lynching, 1909–1950* (Philadelphia: Temple Univ. Press, 1980). The stirrings of Republicanism in the South during the 1940s are revealed in Alexander Heard, *A Two-Party South?* (Chapel Hill: Univ. of North Carolina Press, 1952). The road to the Dixiecrat revolt of 1948 is charted by Robert A. Garson, *The Democratic Party and the Politics of Sectionalism, 1941–1948* (Baton Rouge: Louisiana State Univ. Press, 1974); Emile B. Ader, *The Dixiecrat Movement: Its Role in Third Party Politics* (Washington, D.C.: Public Affairs Press, 1955); and Samuel Lubell, *The Future of American Politics* (New York: Harper, 1952).

The Politics of Massive Resistance

Three scholarly works are indispensable for an understanding of massive resistance: Numan V. Bartley, *The Rise of Massive Resistance: Race and Politics in the South during the 1950's* (Baton Rouge: Louisiana State Univ. Press, 1969); Neil R. McMillen, *The Citizens' Council: Organized Resistance to the Second Reconstruction, 1954–64* (Urbana: Univ. of Illinois Press, 1971); and Earl Black, *Southern Governors and Civil Rights: Racial Segregation as a Campaign Issue in the Second Reconstruction* (Cambridge: Harvard Univ. Press, 1976). The best overall treatments of southern politics in this period are Numan V. Bartley and Hugh D. Graham, *Southern Politics and the Second Reconstruction* (Baltimore: Johns Hopkins Univ. Press, 1975), and Havard, ed., *The Changing Politics of the South*, mentioned earlier in this essay. Two wide-ranging state studies are also valuable in this connection: J. Harvie Wilkinson III, *Harry Byrd and the Changing Shape of Virginia Politics, 1945–1966* (Charlottesville: Univ. Press of Virginia 1968), and Numan V. Bartley, *From Thurmond to Wallace: Political Tendencies in Georgia, 1948–1968* (Baltimore: Johns Hopkins Press, 1970). John Ed Pearce, *Divide and Dissent: Kentucky Politics, 1930–1963* (Lexington: Univ. Press of Kentucky, 1987), is a helpful survey of gubernatorial politics in another state. For developments in one southern city during this period, see David M. Tucker, *Memphis since Crump: Bossism, Blacks, and Civic Reformers, 1948–1968* (Knoxville: Univ. of Tennessee Press, 1980). For the broader context, see George Brown Tindall, *The Disruption of the Solid South* (Athens: Univ. of Georgia Press, 1972); Charles P. Roland, *The Improbable Era: The South since World War II*, rev. ed. (Lexington: Univ. Press of Kentucky, 1976); and Garson, *The Democratic Party and the Politics of Sectionalism*, cited above. Richard Kluger's *Simple Justice, The*

History of Brown v. Board of Education: Black America's Struggle for Equality (New York: Knopf, 1976) is a superb account.

A number of specialized studies supplement Bartley's *The Rise of Massive Resistance*. Virginia's leading role in the movement is examined by Benjamin Muse, *Virginia's Massive Resistance* (Bloomington: Indiana Univ. Press, 1961); Robbins L. Gates, *The Making of Massive Resistance: Virginia's Politics of Public School Desegregation, 1954–1956* (Chapel Hill: Univ. of North Carolina Press, 1964); Robert Collins Smith, *They Closed Their Schools: Prince Edward County, Virginia, 1951–1964* (Chapel Hill: Univ. of North Carolina Press, 1965); and James W. Ely, Jr., *The Crisis of Conservative Virginia: The Byrd Organization and the Politics of Massive Resistance* (Knoxville: Univ. of Tennessee Press, 1976). The struggle over desegregation is described in two useful general works: Benjamin Muse, *Ten Years of Prelude: The Story of Integration since the Supreme Court's 1954 Decision* (New York: Viking, 1964), and Reed Sarratt, *The Ordeal of Desegregation: The First Decade* (New York: Harper and Row, 1966). More restricted but important are Tony Freyer, *The Little Rock Crisis: A Constitutional Interpretation* (Westport, Conn.: Greenwood Press, 1984); Hugh Davis Graham, *Crisis in Print: Desegregation and the Press in Tennessee* (Nashville: Vanderbilt Univ. Press, 1967); Morton Inger, *Politics and Reality in an American City: The New Orleans School Crisis of 1960* (New York: Center for Urban Education, 1969); and Jack W. Peltason, *Fifty-Eight Lonely Men: Southern Federal Judges and School Desegregation*, rev. ed. (Urbana: Univ. of Illinois Press, 1971). The attitudes and policies of Dwight D. Eisenhower are described by Robert Fredrick Burk, *The Eisenhower Administration and Black Civil Rights* (Knoxville: Univ. of Tennessee Press, 1984). Southern white attitudes are revealed in James Graham Cook, *The Segregationists* (New York: Appleton-Century-Crofts, 1962), and I.A. Newby, *Challenge to the Court: Social Scientists and the Defense of Segregation, 1954–1966* (Baton Rouge: Louisiana State Univ. Press, 1969).

Various aspects of state politics in the South during the 1950s are considered in Hugh D. Price, *The Negro and Southern Politics: A Chapter of Florida History* (New York: New York Univ. Press, 1957); William C. Havard and Loren P. Beth, *The Politics of Mis-Representation: Rural-Urban Conflict in the Florida Legislature* (Baton Rouge: Louisiana State Univ. Press, 1962); Soukup, McCleskey, and Holloway, *Party and Factional Division in Texas*, cited earlier; George Norris Green, *The Establishment in Texas Politics: The Primitive Years, 1938–1957* (Westport, Conn.: Greenwood Press, 1979); and Don E. Carleton, *Red Scare! Right-Wing Hysteria, Fifties Fanaticism, and Their Legacy in Texas* (Austin: Texas Monthly Press, 1985). James Reichley, *States in Crisis: Politics in Ten American States, 1950–1962* (Chapel Hill: Univ. of North Carolina Press, 1964), contains chapters on Virginia and Texas. For more information on legislative malapportionment in the South, see Gordon Baker, *Rural versus Urban Political Power: The Nature and Consequences of Unbalanced Representation* (Garden City, N.Y.: Doubleday, 1955); Paul T. David and Ralph Eisenberg, *Devaluation of the Urban and Suburban Vote: A Statistical Investigation of Long-Term Trends in State Legislative Representation* (Charlottesville: Bureau of Public Administration, Univ. of Virginia, 1961); and Malcolm E. Jewell, ed., *The Politics of Reapportionment* (New York: Atherton Press, 1962).

While they vary in quality, biographies of southern politicians constitute a major source for the political historian of the 1950s. Among such studies are W.D. Workman, Jr., *The Bishop from Barnwell: The Political Life and Times of Senator Edgar A. Brown* (Columbia, S.C.: R.L. Bryan Co., 1963); A.G. Ivey, *Luther Hodges, Businessman in the Statehouse: Six Years as Governor of North Carolina* (Chapel Hill: Univ. of North Carolina Press, 1962); Floyd Martin Clay, *Coozan Dudley LeBlanc: From Huey Long to Hadacol* (Gretna, La.: Pelican Publishing Co., 1973); Edward F. Haas, *DeLesseps S. Morrison and the Image of Reform: New Orleans Politics, 1946–1961* (Baton Rouge: Louisiana State Univ. Press, 1974); Jim Lester, *A Man for Arkansas: Sid McMath and the Southern Reform Tradition* (Little Rock: Rose Publishing Co., 1976); Glen Jeansonne, *Leander Perez: Boss of the Delta* (Baton Rouge: Louisiana State Univ. Press, 1977); Lee Seifert Greene, *Lead Me On: Frank Goad Clement and Tennessee Politics* (Knoxville: Univ. of Tennessee Press, 1982); and Tom R. Wagy, *Governor LeRoy Collins of Florida: Spokesman of the New South* (University, Ala.: Univ. of Alabama Press, 1985). See also the two books on James E. Folsom by Carl Grafton and Anne Permaloff, *Big Mules and Branchheads*, and George E. Sims, *The Little Man's Big Friend*, cited earlier.

Southern congressional leaders during this period are treated by John E. Huss, *Senator for the South: A Biography of Olin D. Johnston* (Garden City, N.Y.: Doubleday, 1961); Frank E. Smith, *Congressman from Mississippi* (New York: Pantheon Books, 1964); Joseph Bruce Gorman, *Kefauver: A Political Biography* (New York: Oxford Univ. Press, 1971); Anne Hodges Morgan, *Robert S. Kerr: The Senate Years* (Norman: Univ. of Oklahoma Press, 1977); Elmer L. Puryear, *Graham A. Barden: Conservative Carolina Congressman* (Buie's Creek, N.C.: Campbell Univ. Press, 1979); Warren Ashby, *Frank Porter Graham: A Southern Liberal* (Winston-Salem: John F. Blair, 1981); Bruce J. Dierenfield, *Keeper of the Rules: Congressman Howard W. Smith of Virginia* (Charlottesville: Univ. Press of Virginia, 1986); Alberta Lachicotte, *Rebel Senator: Strom Thurmond of South Carolina* (New York: Devin-Adair, 1966); and Ronnie Dugger, *The Politician: The Life and Times of Lyndon Johnson*, mentioned earlier. The collective behavior of southern members of Congress is illustrated in Hubert R. Fowler, *The Unsolid South: Voting Behavior of Southern Senators, 1947–1960* (University, Ala.: Univ. of Alabama Press, 1968); H. Wayne Shannon, *Party, Constituency and Congressional Voting: A Study of Legislative Behavior in the United States House of Representatives* (Baton Rouge: Louisiana State Univ. Press, 1968); David R. Mayhew, *Party Loyalty among Congressmen: The Difference between Democrats and Republicans, 1947–1962* (Cambridge: Harvard Univ. Press, 1966); and Barbara Hinckley, *The Seniority System in Congress* (Bloomington: Indiana Univ. Press, 1971). The waning of southern internationalism and the implications of that development for the region's politics are explored by Malcolm E. Jewell, *Senatorial Politics and Foreign Policy* (Lexington: Univ. of Kentucky Press, 1962); Charles O. Lerche, Jr., *The Uncertain South: Its Changing Patterns in Foreign Policy* (Chicago: Quadrangle Books, 1964); and Alfred O. Hero, Jr., *The Southerner and World Affairs* (Baton Rouge: Louisiana State Univ. Press, 1965).

Light on the presidential elections of the 1950s is provided by Samuel Lubell, *The Revolt of the Moderates* (New York: Harper's, 1956); Angus Campbell et al., *The American Voter* (New York: Wiley, 1960); and V.O. Key, Jr., *The Responsible Electorate: Rationality in Presidential Voting, 1936–1960* (Cambridge:

Harvard Univ. Press, 1966). Paul T. David, Malcolm Moos, and Ralph M. Goldman, *Presidential Nominating Politics in 1952* (Baltimore: Johns Hopkins Press, 1954), a valuable multivolume work, devotes one volume to the South. For other examples of presidential politics in various southern states, see L. Vaughn Howard and David R. Deener, *Presidential Politics in Louisiana, 1952* (New Orleans: Tulane Univ., 1954); O. Douglas Weeks, *Texas Presidential Politics in 1952* (Austin: Institute of Public Affairs, Univ. of Texas, 1953), and idem, *Texas One-Party Politics in 1956* (Austin: Institute of Public Affairs, Univ. of Texas, 1957); and Donald L. Fowler, *Presidential Voting in South Carolina, 1948–1964* (Columbia: Bureau of Governmental Research and Service, Univ. of South Carolina, 1966).

The Second Reconstruction

Among the best general accounts of the civil rights movement are Anthony Lewis, *Portrait of a Decade: The Second American Revolution* (New York: Random House, 1964); Benjamin Muse, *The American Negro Revolution: From Nonviolence to Black Power, 1963–1967* (Bloomington: Indiana Univ. Press, 1968); Harvard Sitkoff, *The Struggle for Black Equality, 1954–1980* (New York: Hill and Wang, 1981); Rhoda Lois Blumberg, *Civil Rights: The 1960s Freedom Struggle* (Boston: Twayne, 1984); Aldon D. Morris, *The Origins of the Civil Rights Movement: Black Communities Organizing for Change* (New York: Free Press, 1984); Michael V. Namorato, ed., *Have We Overcome? Race Relations since "Brown"* (Jackson: Univ. Press of Mississippi, 1979); and Charles W. Eagles, ed., *The Civil Rights Movement in America* (Jackson: Univ. Press of Mississippi, 1986). For the movement's outstanding leader, see David Levering Lewis, *King: A Biography*, 2d ed. (Urbana: Univ. of Illinois Press, 1978); David J. Garrow, *Bearing the Cross: Martin Luther King, Jr., and the Southern Christian Leadership Conference* (New York: Morrow, 1987); and Adam Fairclough, *To Redeem the Soul of America: The Southern Christian Leadership Conference and Martin Luther King, Jr.* (Athens: Univ. of Georgia Press, 1987).

Particular episodes and groups are dealt with by Bernard Taper, *Gomillion versus Lightfoot: The Tuskegee Gerrymander Case* (New York: McGraw-Hill, 1962); Charles Fager, *Selma, 1965* (New York: Scribner's 1974); David J. Garrow, *Protest at Selma: Martin Luther King, Jr., and the Voting Rights Act of 1965* (New Haven: Yale Univ. Press, 1978); John R. Salter, Jr., *Jackson, Mississippi: An American Chronicle of Struggle and Schism* (Hicksville N.Y.: Exposition Press, 1979); Clayborne Carson, *In Struggle: SNCC and the Black Awakening of the 1960s* (Cambridge: Harvard Univ. Press, 1981); Robert J. Norrell, *Reaping the Whirlwind: The Civil Rights Movement in Tuskegee* (New York: Knopf, 1985); and David R. Colburn, *Racial Change and Community Crisis: St. Augustine, Florida, 1877–1980* (New York: Columbia Univ. Press, 1985). See also Florence Mars, *Witness in Philadelphia* (Baton Rouge: Louisiana State Univ. Press, 1977), and Clarice T. Campbell and Oscar Allan Rogers, Jr., *Mississippi: The View from Tougaloo* (Jackson: Univ. Press of Mississippi, 1979).

The Kennedy administration's handling of civil rights issues is examined in a good book by Carl M. Brauer, *John F. Kennedy and the Second Reconstruction*

(New York: Columbia Univ. Press, 1977). Robert F. Kennedy's role is treated in Victor S. Navasky, *Kennedy Justice* (New York: Atheneum, 1971), and Arthur M. Schlesinger, Jr., *Robert Kennedy and His Times* (Boston: Houghton Mifflin, 1978). Although the Johnson administration has not yet received similar treatment, its racial policies are discussed by James L. Sundquist, *Politics and Policy: The Eisenhower, Kennedy, and Johnson Years* (Washington, D.C.: Brookings Institution, 1968); Jim F. Heath, *Decade of Disillusionment: The Kennedy-Johnson Years* (Bloomington: Indiana Univ. Press, 1975); Allen J. Matusow, *The Unraveling of America: A History of Liberalism in the 1960s* (New York: Harper and Row, 1984); and Paul K. Conkin, *Big Daddy from the Pedernailes: Lyndon Baines Johnson* (Boston: Twayne, 1986). Michael Foley, *The New Senate: Liberal Influence on a Conservative Institution, 1959–1972* (New Haven: Yale Univ. Press, 1980), helps illuminate the Washington scene. Foster Rhea Dulles, *The Civil Rights Commission, 1957–1965* (East Lansing: Michigan State Univ. Press, 1968), and U.S. Commission on Civil Rights, *The Voting Rights Act: After Ten Years* (Washington, D.C., 1975), are useful for conditions in the South. For the continuing federal involvement, see Gary Orfield, *The Reconstruction of Southern Education: The Schools and the 1964 Civil Rights Act* (New York: Wiley-Interscience, 1969); Donald S. Strong, *Negroes, Ballots, and Judges: National Voting Rights Legislation in the Federal Courts* (University, Ala.: Univ. of Alabama Press, 1968); Charles V. Hamilton, *The Bench and the Ballot: Southern Federal Judges and Black Voters* (New York: Oxford Univ. Press, 1973); Tinsley E. Yarbrough, *Judge Frank Johnson and Human Rights in Alabama* (University, Ala.: Univ. of Alabama Press, 1981); and J. Harvie Wilkinson III, *From "Brown" to "Bakke": The Supreme Court and School Integration, 1954–1978* (New York: Oxford Univ. Press, 1979).

Avery Leiserson, ed., *The American South in the 1960's* (New York: Praeger, 1964), provides a wide-ranging introduction to southern politics in the 1960s. Robert Sherrill, *Gothic Politics in the Deep South: Stars of the New Confederacy* (New York: Grossman Publishers, 1968), and Ira Sharkansky, *Regionalism in American Politics* (Indianapolis: Bobbs-Merrill, 1970), are also helpful. Richard C. Cortner, *The Apportionment Cases* (Knoxville: Univ. of Tennessee Press, 1970), throws light on the "apportionment revolution." Political developments in different southern states are described by James R. Spence, *The Making of a Governor: The Moore-Preyer-Lake Primaries of 1964* (Winston-Salem, N.C.: J.F. Blair, 1968), about North Carolina; Jim Ranchino, *Faubus to Bumpers: Arkansas Votes, 1960–1970* (Arkadelphia, Ark.: Action Research, 1972); David M. Landry and Joseph B. Parker, eds., *Mississippi Government and Politics in Transition* (Dubuque, Iowa: Kendall/Hunt, 1976); Larry Sabato, *The Democratic Party Primary in Virginia: Tantamount to Election No Longer* (Charlottesville: Univ. Press of Virginia, 1977); and James Bolner, ed., *Louisiana Politics: Festival in a Labyrinth* (Baton Rouge: Louisiana State Univ. Press, 1982).

A disparate collection of southern politicians is portrayed in Charles L. Weltner, *Southerner* (Philadelphia: Lippincott, 1966); Bruce Galphin, *The Riddle of Lester Maddox* (Atlanta: Camelot Publishing Co., 1968); M. Carl Andrews, *No Higher Honor: The Story of Mills E. Godwin, Jr.* (Richmond: Dietz Press, 1970); Jerry D. Conn, *Preston Smith: The Making of a Texas Governor* (Austin: Jenkins Publishing Co., 1972); John L. Ward, *The Arkansas Rockefeller* (Baton Rouge: Louisiana State Univ. Press, 1978); Marshall Frady, *Wallace*, enlarged and updated (New York: New American Library, 1976); and Jody Carlson, *George C. Wallace and the Politics of Powerlessness: The Wallace Campaigns for the Presidency, 1964–1976* (New Brunswick, N.J.: Transaction Books, 1981). Internal pressures to resolve the desegregation crisis are revealed in Robert L. Crain, *The Politics of School Desegregation: Comparative Case Studies of Community Structure and Policy-Making* (Chicago: Aldine Publishing Co., 1968), and Elizabeth Jacoway and David R. Colburn, eds., *Southern Businessmen and Desegregation* (Baton Rouge: Louisiana State Univ. Press, 1982). For two Mississippi reactions, see the classic account by James W. Silver, *Mississippi: The Closed Society*, rev. ed. (New York: Harcourt, Brace and World, 1966), and Frederick M. Wirt, *Politics of Southern Equality: Law and Social Change in a Mississippi County* (Chicago: Aldine Publishing Co., 1970). The possibilities for a more enlightened coalition politics are suggested by Chandler Davidson, *Biracial Politics: Conflict and Coalition in the Metropolitan South* (Baton Rouge: Louisiana State Univ. Press, 1972).

The best place to begin a consideration of the long-delayed reentry of blacks into southern politics are two excellent complementary volumes: Donald R. Matthews and James W. Prothro, *Negroes and the New Southern Politics* (New York: Harcourt, Brace and World, 1966), and Steven F. Lawson, *Black Ballots: Voting Rights in the South, 1944–1969* (New York: Columbia Univ. Press, 1976). Pat Watters and Reese Cleghorn, *Climbing Jacob's Ladder: The Arrival of Negroes in Southern Politics* (New York: Harcourt, Brace and World, 1967), is especially useful for its account of the Southern Regional Council's Voter Education Project. Darlene Clark Hine's *Black Victory: The Rise and Fall of the White Primary in Texas* (Millwood, N.Y.: KTO Press, 1979) is an important state study. A number of general works should be mentioned here, including Harry A. Bailey, Jr., ed., *Negro Politics in America* (Columbus, Ohio: C.E. Merrill Books, 1967); William R. Keech, *The Impact of Negro Voting: The Role of the Vote in the Quest for Equality* (Chicago: Rand McNally, 1968); Harry Holloway, *The Politics of the Southern Negro: From Exclusion to Big City Organization* (New York: Random House, 1969); and Hanes Walton, Jr., *Black Political Parties: An Historical and Political Analysis* (New York: Free Press, 1972). Emerging black leaders are discussed by Daniel C. Thompson, *The Negro Leadership Class* (Englewood Cliffs, N.J.: Prentice Hall, 1963); Everett Carll Ladd, Jr., *Negro Political Leadership in the South* (Ithaca: Cornell Univ. Press, 1966); and Julian Bond, *Black Candidates: Southern Campaign Experiences* (Atlanta: Southern Regional Council, 1969). See also Chuck Stone, *Black Political Power in America*, rev. ed. (New York: Dell Publishing Co., 1970); John Rozier, *Black Boss: Political Revolution in a Georgia County* (Athens: Univ. of Georgia Press, 1982); and two books mentioned before: Buni, *The Negro in Virginia Politics*, and Newby, *Black Carolinians*.

In considering national politics, one should not overlook the vivid journalistic accounts of presidential campaigns in the 1960s and 1970s written by Theodore H. White. The first of these was *The Making of the President, 1960* (New York: Atheneum, 1961). For other studies of the election of 1960, see Paul T. David, Ralph M. Goldman, and Richard C. Bain, *The Politics of National Party Conventions* (Washington, D.C.: Brookings Institution, 1960); Lucy S. Dawidowicz and Leon J. Goldstein, *Politics in a Pluralistic Democracy: Studies*

of Voting in the 1960 Election (New York: Institute of Human Relations, 1963);
Paul T. David, ed., *The Presidential Election and Transition, 1960–1961* (Wash-
ington, D.C.: Brookings Institution, 1961); O. Douglas Weeks, *Texas in the
1960 Presidential Election* (Austin: Institute of Public Affairs, Univ. of Texas,
1961); and William C. Havard et al., *The Louisiana Elections of 1960* (Baton
Rouge: Louisiana State Univ. Press, 1963). The Goldwater movement in the
South is perceptively analyzed in Bernard Cosman, *Five States for Goldwater:
Continuity and Change in Southern Presidential Voting Patterns* (University, Ala.:
Univ. of Alabama Press, 1966). Other aspects of the election of 1964 are con-
sidered by Bernard Cosman and Robert Huckshorn, eds., *Republican Politics:
The 1964 Campaign and Its Aftermath for the Party* (New York: Praeger, 1968);
Angus Campbell et al., *Elections and the Political Order* (New York: Wiley, 1966);
and O. Douglas Weeks, *Texas in 1964: A One-Party State Again?* (Austin: In-
stitute of Public Affairs, Univ. of Texas, 1965).

The election of 1968 is described in great detail by Lewis Chester, Godfrey
Hodgson, and Bruce Page, *An American Melodrama: The Presidential Campaign
of 1968* (London: Deutsch, 1969). Several contemporary publications throw
light on the policies and expectations of the Nixon administrations. These
include Kevin P. Phillips, *The Emerging Republican Majority* (New Rochelle,
N.Y.: Arlington House, 1969); Richard M. Scammon and Ben J. Wattenberg,
The Real Majority (New York: Coward-McCann, 1970); and Reg Murphy and
Hal Gulliver, *The Southern Strategy* (New York: Scribner's, 1971). For other
works on national politics, see Stephen Hess and David S. Broder, *The Republican Establishment: The Present and Future of the G.O.P.* (New York: Harper
and Row, 1967); Frederick G. Dutton, *Changing Sources of Power: American
Politics in the 1970s* (New York: McGraw-Hill, 1971); Louis M. Seagull, *Southern
Republicanism* (Cambridge, Mass.: Schon Kman Publishing Co., 1975); and
James Reichley, *Conservatives in an Age of Change: The Nixon and Ford Administrations* (Washington, D.C.: Brookings Institution, 1981).

Toward a Two-Party South

Alexander P. Lamis's *The Two-Party South* (New York: Oxford Univ. Press,
1984) is an intelligent and persuasive interpretation of southern politics from
the late 1960s into the 1980s. Earl Black and Merle Black, *Politics and Society
in the South,* cited earlier in this essay, is illuminating and suggestive. Other
recent works of note include Merle Black and John Shelton Reed, eds., *Perspectives on the American South,* vol. 1 (New York: Gordon and Breach, 1981),
and vol. 2 (New York: Gordon and Breach, 1982); James C. Cobb and Charles
R. Wilson, eds., *Perspectives on the American South,* vol. 3 (New York: Gordon
and Breach, 1985); and Robert P. Steed, Laurence W. Moreland, and Tod A.
Baker, eds., *Contemporary Southern Political Attitudes and Behavior: Studies and
Essays* (New York: Praeger, 1982). See also the informative general volumes
by Neal R. Peirce: *The Deep South States of America: People, Politics, and Power
in the Seven Deep South States* (New York: Norton, 1974), and *The Border South
States: People, Politics, and Power in the Five Border South States* (New York:
Norton, 1975).

The Democratic resurgence of the early 1970s in the South is described by Bass and DeVries in *The Transformation of Southern Politics*, cited earlier. One source of the Democratic revival is examined in Steven F. Lawson's *In Pursuit of Power: Southern Blacks & Electoral Politics, 1965–1982* (New York: Columbia Univ. Press, 1985), a worthy sequel to the same author's *Black Ballots*. Other pertinent studies deal with the transition of black leaders from protest to politics, with black-white political coalitions, and with the emergence of a more issue-oriented politics. Among such works are Chandler Davidson, *Biracial Politics: Conflict and Coalition in the Metropolitan South* (Baton Rouge: Louisiana State Univ. Press, 1972); Harold H. Martin, *William Berry Hartsfield: Mayor of Atlanta* (Athens: Univ. of Georgia Press, 1978); Barbara Jordan and Shelby Hearon, *Barbara Jordan: A Self-Portrait* (Garden City, N.Y.: Doubleday, 1979); William Madsen, *Mexican-Americans of South Texas*, 2d ed. (New York: Holt, Rinehart and Winston, 1973); David R. Johnson et al., *The Politics of San Antonio: Community, Progress, & Power* (Lincoln: Univ. of Nebraska Press, 1983); Malcolm E. Jewell, *Legislative Representation in the Contemporary South* (Durham: Duke Univ. Press, 1967); Thad Beyle and Merle Black, eds., *Politics and Policy in North Carolina* (New York: MSS Information Corp., 1975); and Donald S. Strong, *Issue Voting and Party Realignment* (University, Ala.: Univ. of Alabama Press, 1977). Continuing obstacles to the realization of still greater minority political influence are examined in Howard Ball, Dale Krane, and Thomas P. Larth, *Compromised Compliance: Implementation of the 1965 Voting Rights Act* (Westport, Conn.: Greenwood Press, 1982), and Chandler Davidson, ed., *Minority Vote Dilution* (Washington, D.C.: Howard Univ. Press, 1984). Busing and other desegregation issues are analyzed in Richard A. Pride and J. David Woodard, *The Burden of Busing: The Politics of Desegregation in Nashville, Tennessee* (Knoxville: Univ. of Tennessee Press, 1985), and Raymond Wolters, *The Burden of Brown: Thirty Years of School Desegregation* (Knoxville: Univ. of Tennessee Press, 1984).

Among the reform governors in the post–civil rights era was James Earl Carter, Jr., whose background and gubernatorial administration are discussed in Numan V. Bartley, *Jimmy Carter and the Politics of the New South* (St. Louis: Forum Press, 1979), and Gary M. Fink, *Prelude to the Presidency: The Political Character and Legislative Leadership Style of Governor Jimmy Carter* (Westport, Conn.: Greenwood Press, 1980). The Carter "phenomenon"—and his election and presidency—has not yet received much scholarly attention. The following books are useful: Martin Schram, *Running for President, 1976: The Carter Campaign* (New York: Stein and Day, 1977); William Lee Miller, *Yankee from Georgia: The Emergence of Jimmy Carter* (New York: Time Books, 1978); Betty Glad, *Jimmy Carter: In Search of the Great White House* (New York: Norton, 1980); and Laurence H. Shoup, *The Carter Presidency, and Beyond: Power and Politics in the 1980s* (Palo Alto, Calif.: Ramparts Press, 1980). For the election of 1980, see Thomas Ferguson and Joel Rogers, eds., *The Hidden Election: Politics and Economics in the 1980 Presidential Campaign* (New York: Pantheon Books, 1981).

Contemporary southern Republicanism has received little scholarly analysis thus far. But see, in addition to Lamis, *The Two-Party South*, John C. Topping, Jr., et al., *Southern Republicanism and the New South* (Cambridge, Mass.: Republicans for Progress and the Ripon Society, 1966), and the state studies cited above by Olien, *From Token to Triumph: Texas Republicans since 1920*, and Klingman, *Neither Dies Nor Surrenders: A History of the Republican Party in Florida*. One well-publicized Republican victory is described by William D. Snider, *Helms and Hunt: The North Carolina Senate Race, 1984* (Chapel Hill: Univ. of North Carolina Press, 1985). David W. Reinhard, *The Republican Right since 1945* (Lexington: Univ. Press of Kentucky, 1983), is of some value, especially for the early postwar years. Robert P. Steed, Laurence W. Moreland, and Tod A. Baker, eds., *The 1984 Presidential Election in the South: Patterns of Southern Party Politics* (New York: Praeger, 1986), includes a state-by-state analysis. Various aspects of national politics in recent years are discussed by Roger H. Davidson et al., *Congress in Crisis: Politics and Congressional Reform* (Belmont, Calif.: Wadsworth Publishing Co., 1966); Robert G. Dixon, Jr., *Democratic Representation: Reapportionment in Law and Politics* (New York: Oxford Univ. Press, 1968); George Goodwin, Jr., *The Little Legislatures: Committees of Congress* (Amherst: Univ. of Massachusetts Press, 1970); David L. Porter, *Congress and the Waning of the New Deal* (Port Washington, N.Y.: Kennikat Press, 1980); John R. Petrocik, *Party Coalitions: Realignments and the Decline of the New Deal Party System* (Chicago: Univ. of Chicago Press, 1981); Walter Dean Burnham, *The Current Crisis in American Politics* (New York: Oxford Univ. Press, 1982); and John E. Chubb and Paul E. Peterson, eds., *The New Direction in American Politics* (Washington, D.C.: Brookings Institution, 1985).

Economic and social changes since World War II have had a profound effect on political attitudes and behavior in the South. Some of the dimensions of the region's economic and social metamorphosis are discussed by Calvin B. Hoover and Benjamin U. Ratchford, *Economic Resources and Policies of the South* (New York: Macmillan, 1951); John M. Maclachlan and Joe S. Floyd, Jr., *This Changing South* (Gainesville: Univ. of Florida Press, 1956); William H. Nicholls, *Southern Tradition and Regional Progress* (Chapel Hill: Univ. of North Carolina Press, 1960); Allan P. Sindler, ed., *Change in the Contemporary South* (Durham: Duke Univ. Press, 1963); M.L. Greenhut and W. Tate Whitman, eds., *Essays in Southern Economic Development* (Chapel Hill: Univ. of North Carolina Press, 1964); Robert B. Highsaw, ed., *The Deep South in Transformation: A Symposium* (University, Ala.: Univ. of Alabama Press, 1964); John C. McKinney and Edgar T. Thompson, eds., *The South in Continuity and Change* (Durham: Duke Univ. Press, 1965); James G. Maddox, *Advancing South: Manpower Prospects and Problems* (New York: Twentieth Century Fund, 1967); Thomas D. Clark, *The Emerging South*, 2d ed. (New York: Oxford Univ. Press, 1968); J. Oliver Emmerich, *Two Faces of Janus: The Saga of Deep South Change* (Jackson: Univ. Press of Mississippi, 1973); Thomas H. Naylor and James Clotfelter, *Strategies for Change in the South* (Chapel Hill: Univ. of North Carolina Press, 1975); E. Blaine Liner and Lawrence K. Lynch, eds., *The Economics of Southern Growth* (Durham: Southern Growth Policies Board, 1977); and James C. Cobb, *The Selling of the South: The Southern Crusade for Industrial Development, 1936–1980* (Baton Rouge: Louisiana State Univ. Press, 1984).

For the South and the Sunbelt phenomenon, see Bernard L. Weinstein and Robert E. Firestine, *Regional Growth and Decline in the United States: The Rise of the Sunbelt and the Decline of the Northeast*, 2d ed. (New York: Praeger, 1985); Kirkpatrick Sale, *Power Shift: The Rise of the Southern Rim and Its Challenge to the Eastern Establishment* (New York: Random House, 1975); David C. Perry and Alfred J. Watkins, eds., *The Rise of the Sunbelt Cities* (Beverly Hills, Calif.: Sage Publications, 1977); Carl Abbott, *The New Urban America: Growth and Politics in Sunbelt Cities* (Chapel Hill: Univ. of North Carolina Press, 1981); Robert Jay Dilger, *The Sunbelt/Snowbelt Controversy: The War over Federal Funds* (New York: New York Univ. Press, 1982); and Richard M. Bernard and Bradley R. Rice, eds., *Sunbelt Cities: Politics and Growth since World War II* (Austin: Univ. of Texas Press, 1983).

Other aspects of the South's transformation are analyzed in Dudley L. Poston, Jr., and Robert H. Weller, eds., *The Population of the South: Structure and Change in Social Demographic Context* (Austin: Univ. of Texas Press, 1981); Gilbert Courtland Fite, *Cotton Fields No More: Southern Agriculture, 1865–1980* (Lexington: Univ. Press of Kentucky, 1984); David R. Goldfield, *Cotton Fields and Skyscrapers: Southern City and Region, 1607–1980* (Baton Rouge: Louisiana State Univ. Press, 1982), and idem, *Promised Land: The South since 1945* (Arlington Heights, Ill.: Harlan Davidson, 1987); James C. Cobb, *Industrialization and Southern Society, 1877–1984* (Lexington: Univ. Press of Kentucky, 1984); and H. Brandt Ayers and Thomas H. Naylor, eds., *You Can't Eat Magnolias* (New York: McGraw-Hill, 1972). Organized labor in the South is discussed in F. Ray Marshall, *Labor in the South* (Cambridge: Harvard Univ. Press, 1967), and Merl E. Reed et al., eds., *Southern Workers and Their Unions, 1880–1975: Selected Papers, The Second Southern Labor History Conference, 1978* (Westport, Conn.: Greenwood Press, 1981). Albert E. Cowdrey's *This Land, This South: An Environmental History* (Lexington: Univ. Press of Kentucky, 1983) is a splendid historical study of the human response to the southern environment.

Southern values, regional consciousness, and cultural distinctiveness are thoughtfully considered in several notable books by John Shelton Reed: *The Enduring South: Subcultural Persistence in Mass Society* (Lexington, Mass.: Heath, 1972); *One South: An Ethnic Approach to Regional Culture* (Baton Rouge: Louisiana State Univ. Press, 1982); and *Southerners: The Social Psychology of Sectionalism* (Chapel Hill: Univ. of North Carolina Press, 1983). See also, in this connection, John Egerton, *The Americanization of Dixie: The Southernization of America* (New York: Harper's Magazine Press, 1974), and Merle Black et al., *Political Attitudes in the Nation and States* (Chapel Hill: Institute for Research in Social Science, 1974). Robert E. Botsch's *We Shall Not Overcome* (Chapel Hill: Univ. of North Carolina Press, 1980) is a revealing study of working-class southerners. For religious ideas and values, see Baker, Steed, and Moreland, eds., *Religion and Politics in the South*, mentioned above; David Edwin Harrell, Jr., *White Sects and Black Men in the Recent South* (Nashville: Vanderbilt Univ. Press, 1971); and John R. Earle, Dean D. Knudsen, and Donald W. Shriver, *Spindles and Spires: A Re-Study of Religion and Social Change in Gastonia* (Atlanta: John Knox Press, 1976). The changing role of women in southern life is suggested in Joanne V. Hawks and Sheila L. Skemp, eds., *Sex, Race, and the Role of Women in the South* (Jackson: Univ. Press of Mississippi, 1983).

Index